RIVERSIDE COMMUNITY COLLEGE
1916

D0953212

Clothing Concepts

Clothing

A SOCIAL-PSYCHOLOGICAL APPROACH

The Macmillan Company, New York

Concepts

by Mary Lou Rosencranz

University of Connecticut

Collier-Macmillan Limited, London

Printed in the United States of America

The Macmillan Company
866 Third Avenue, New York, New York 10022

Collier-Macmillan Canada, Ltd., Toronto, Ontario

Library of Congress catalog card number: 72–152817

First Printing

To the memory of my
father and to my mother,
who designed and made my clothes for the
first fifteen years of my life

Preface

Earliest man left evidence that he was aware of himself and his appearance even before he was a toolmaker. Remains of ornamental shells and teeth tell the story of the first human creature who thought and acted as we do; indeed, copper, iron, and glass were used as ornaments before they became important for technology. "As with language and ritual, body decoration was an effort to establish a human identity." [1]

Awareness of clothing and appearance is a matter of individual sensitivity and is affected by one's personal environment, both past and present. Awareness is usually a visual experience and, ideally, an aesthetic one. However, an awareness of other sensual qualities is important. The psychological "feel" of clothing ranges from an extension of the body in space and time to its functions of protection and support. Clothes are also a psychological means of belonging to, or of merging with, the environment, or of being unique and individual. Awareness may be directed toward others or focused on the self; yet a person with high clothing awareness in an objective sense still may not use his sensitivity in his own manipulation of clothing. Although many of the dimensions of awareness are difficult to measure, some progress is being made that will eventually provide important clues to an understanding of clothing behavior.

Clothing *symbols* are used daily as a kind of silent lan-

[1] Lewis Mumford, *The Myth of the Machine* (New York: Harcourt Brace Jovanovich, Inc., 1966), p. 111.

guage at both the conscious and unconscious levels. Although symbolic meanings are acquired within a matrix of social structure and culture, clothing and appearance symbols do not have fixed and absolute values. Meanings change with time and place, and within the social milieu. The possibilities of the use of clothing symbols are wide ranging; symbols can be polar opposites—as different as individuality and conformity, custom and fashion, work and leisure, masculinity and femininity, age and youth, taste and indifference to taste. All of these symbols have values within limits of their social referents. Clothing has value as a social medium just as money has exchange value in the economy. "Conformity to a fashion literally gives currency to a style." [2]

As world communication systems bring us closer together, the symbolic implications of clothing between cultures are numerous. The Oriental idea of presenting oneself in one's best attire runs against the idea of the underplayed, underdressed, casual American. The many cartoons depicting natives in a loincloth and silk hat also illustrate incongruous cultural patterns.

Awareness of clothing symbols and of the self-image mediates the way in which a person performs social acts and social *roles*. Culture and society reciprocate by assigning values to and exerting social pressures on role performance. Thus clothing may reflect one's feeling of esteem, deference, approval, toleration, scorn, or hostility toward roles and role performers. Honor and flattery accompany roles that reflect esteem and approval; shame, embarrassment, and social isolation may be the end result of a hostile role performance. The title of best-dressed woman of the year is bestowed as an honor; the expelling of long-haired hippies from job or school is an example of social isolation. Indeed, the complex field of role behavior can be examined on a single theme—the instrumental use of clothing and appearance symbols during the social act. Appearance attributes are evident in role preparation and are at times the only props used for switching among multiple roles and in stimulating patterns of conduct in response to expectations of significant others.

M. L. R.

[2] Marshall McLuhan, *Understanding Media* (New York: Signet Books, 1964), p. 127.

Contents

Part One

CLOTHING AWARENESS

Clothing awareness takes many forms. Indeed, it varies in both shades of meaning and in degree for all of us. We probably know some people who seem to be oblivious to clothing and some who are extremely aware of clothing among our immediate friends or acquaintances.

Berelson and Steiner, in their book entitled *Human Behavior*, make the following observation:

> The observer plays a part in determining what will be allowed to stimulate receptors: we look *at* some things, ignore others, look away from still others.[1]

This, of course, reminds us of the clothes-conscious person, the man who never notices his wife's new clothes or new hat, and the woman with a closet full of clothes who claims she has nothing to wear.

An interesting example of clothes-consciousness is illustrated in a journal kept by a young girl who first lived in Virginia, then traveled west to Texas and Missouri during the 1840's. As she recorded events during the day, she often included the clothes she wore or the clothes she was making. "For the last week we finished our dresses. . . . We made a blue jeans coat and brown jeans pantaloons." ". . . I began my flax stockings. Last Monday we worked on Amanda's white dress; I spun wool the rest of the time." While she was traveling in horse and wagon she made comments such as these: "I now have on my red cotton dress." "Mr. McClure bought me a checked shawl." She also commented on the clothing of others, "The most fashionable men here wear pleated pants and no gallouses, long narrow vests, long towed boots, coats very long and full in the skirts." [2]

Obviously, people who work with clothing as an occupation or profession are going to be more aware of clothing, even in situations where clothing will be very far from the consciousness of the ordinary person. The following illustration is an excellent case in point:

[1] Bernard Berelson and Gary Steiner, *Human Behavior: An Inventory of Scientific Findings* (New York: Harcourt, Brace and World, Inc., 1964), p. 100.

[2] Edward D. Jervey and James E. Moss, editors, "The Journal of Elizabeth Ann Cooley," *Missouri Historical Review*, Vol. LX, No. 2 (January, 1966), pp. 162–206.

The specialist is by nature environmental. He is committed to what McLuhan calls a fragmented function within a given process linkage. If his environment changes he will not necessarily become extra-environmental. It is more likely that he will carry his tendency to specialism with him the way a snail does his shell. A born specialist will tend to interpret all experience in the light of his own expertise. Illustrative story: One time a cloak and suit manufacturer went to Rome and while he was there managed to get an audience with His Holiness. Upon his return a friend asked him, "What did the Pope look like?" The tailor answered, "A 41 Regular." [3]

[3] Howard Luck Gossage, "You can see why the mighty would be curious," in *McLuhan: Hot and Cool,* edited by Gerald E. Stearn (New York: The Dial Press, Inc., 1967), p. 12.

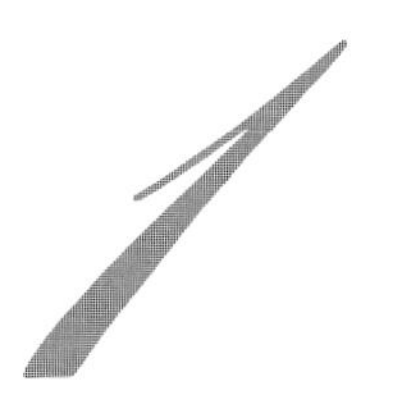

Clothing Memories

Perhaps the best measure of past clothing awareness is found in clothing memories or incidents recalled that have clothing as a focal point of the remembrance. Some of us have excellent clothing memories in that we remember specific clothes of our own and of others from the time we were very small children. Nancy Hale wrote a delightful essay for *Harper's Bazaar* some years ago that illustrated an extraordinary clothing memory:

> Clothes had early taken on one sort of significance for me. As a little girl I went to a school in the country, where my classmates, children of commuting bankers, brokers, and businessmen, were dressed in striped chambray or checked gingham, the belts worn low around the hips. For dancing school on late, snow-muffled winter afternoons, they wore white embroidered muslin with pink or blue taffeta sashes.
>
> I, alas, was not dressed similarly. My mother, a painter, had what I now realize was a more sophisticated taste in children's clothes. For school I wore little, short linen dresses in gray or tan, with their corded waists up under my armpits. They must have been charming, but I wanted to die; my clothes were wrong. What I wore for dancing school conformed even less to local fashion: black velveteen, very straight and short, with a gold moiré sash run through slots at a high waistline; or the same dress in brown

velveteen with a Roman stripe sash. With these, I wore black patent leather ankle-tie slippers with the straps coming from behind the ankle to button in front; even this was wrong, for the others wore slippers whose straps came from one side to cross the instep to the other side. For a number of years I experienced the full horror of being the black sheep in a white pack.[1]

Clothing Memories from Early Childhood

On the experimental level at the University of Missouri, several groups of people were asked to describe their earliest clothing memories; the pattern seemed to be that college students majoring in home economics could remember their own clothes at an average age of four years. Very often the color or texture remained vivid in one's memory—

> When I was about four, I had a pink and grey taffeta checked dress with pink velvet on the bodice front. I liked the dress very much because it rustled when I moved.

Sometimes dresses for occasions were particularly important—

> My Sunday dress was red dotted swiss with matching panties, white ruffles on the sleeves and collar. The yoke was smocked with white.

Or a costume—

> I remember a Red, Red Robin costume I wore in the first grade. It had a red construction paper hat with a yellow beak, red blouse and red shorts with a small red tail.

[1] Nancy Hale, "The Dresses You Never Forgot," *Harper's Bazaar* (March, 1957).

Or something that belonged to someone else—

> I wore an army suit in the first and second grade that was a hand-me-down from my brother. It was army green in color with brass buttons, and an over shoulder belt. I also wore the hat and long pants. I was a Tom Boy.[2]

In general, the details of one's own clothing are much clearer than other people's clothing. Color is almost always mentioned, with red and blue and pink being predominant. Ruffles, bows, and buttons are often remembered in addition to unusual textures—taffeta, organdy, velvet, eyelet embroidery, and dotted swiss.

Memories of Own Clothes and Clothes of Others

Student informants stated that they became conscious of others' clothes at about age five or six. The person remembered most often is one's mother or friend. Accessories, such as shoes and hats, are remembered more often than dresses. Textures such as fur, felt, leather, and shiny buttons are mentioned repeatedly.

The earliest memories of a group of middle-aged women differ from those of the college girls in two respects: their memories do not go back quite so far, with averages of six years for their own memories and seven years for the clothing of others; they more often remembered embarrassing situations or had more feelings of clothing deprivation than the college students. Examples of embarrassing situations described by middle-aged women are as follows:

> I remember a silk dress (rose, black, and beige print) mother attempted to make over for me (unsuccessfully). She cried.

[2] This and the three preceding quotes are memories of college age students.

> When I was four I had my first two colored dresses —for train travel. I was so proud of them I went up and down the train showing off my colored dress. Mother felt that little girls should dress in white and be ladies. I was such a disappointment, I was no lady.[3]

Deprivation is expressed in these descriptions:

> I was in junior high school when I first noticed a difference between my clothes and the girl I went to school with. I had just come from the farm and having discarded the long underwear, had to put on a knit slip, cotton undies, and long hose to walk two miles to school. My girl friend had silk undies and I noticed and *felt* the difference.
>
> Two older neighbor girls who were in high school had formals that impressed me and had few clothes made at home—ninety per cent of mine were "home-made."[4]

Male responses to early clothing memories show that the average age of recall for their own clothing is about seven or eight years. Many of their memories appear to be unpleasant ones. For example:

> When I was in the first grade I was haled before the class as the bad example in clothing worn by students. I particularly remember a blue cotton work shirt, terribly wrinkled, soiled, no doubt, and several sizes large. The teacher was merciless in pointing out what a sloppy dresser I was.
>
> Being forced to put on fresh, cleaned, scratchy long underwear on Sunday morning.
>
> Sunsuit. Always matched exactly that of my sister. I disliked very much being dressed like a twin in what seemed like *girl's* clothing.[5]

Men in general remember the clothes of a variety of other people—grandparents, parents, peers—rather than an overwhelming preponderance of their mothers' clothes, as was the case for the women and girls.

[3] Memories of middle-aged women.
[4] Memories of middle-aged women showing deprivation.
[5] Three responses from middle-aged men.

Clothes for Special Occasions

9
Clothing Memories

Some especially interesting descriptions of other people by the men are:

> World War I uniforms, either relatives or members of the community. The wrap leggings were striking particularly; perhaps the trimness and closeness of fit was in sharp contrast to the loose, floppy clothes that working class and farm people in the area were wearing.
>
> I remember once I was very ill (somewhere between six and ten years of age) and I asked my mother to put on her white full dress (a brocade) and dance for me.
>
> I recall the aprons and housedresses of my grandmothers. They were simple, clean, and indicated what I would more describe as a devotion to domesticity. I also recall the work clothes of my grandfather, who worked on the railroad—blue denim overalls and cap in the summertime, always soaked with perspiration when he arrived home—and much the same outfit, but with felt boots, often covered with ice and snow, when he arrived home in the wintertime.[6]

Mignon McLaughlin, former editor of *Glamour*, has said that a woman can remember exactly what she was wearing on every important occasion of her life. Although this statement at first seems a little exaggerated, almost all women can remember what they were wearing on several occasions. A class of clothing-and-textiles majors at the University of Missouri came up with an impressive list of occasions—many of them remembering twenty or more incidents. The composite list was made up of some seventy types of occasions ranging from holidays, special trips, job interviews, and being lavaliered,[7] pinned, or engaged, to picnics, weddings, and funerals.

[6] Three responses from adult males.

[7] It is a custom in some southern college fraternities to give a lavalier to a girl before giving her a fraternity pin.

2 Awareness of Physical Attributes

Awareness of General Appearance

Because clothing awareness is being used in its broadest connotation we will begin with appearance factors, including the body upon which clothes are worn. Indeed, historically speaking, the body is visible through clothing or only partially draped with clothing from time to time. In these eras the use of clothing incorporates the displayed or partially veiled body as a part of the costume.

Man has always used general appearance and body build as an important gauge in assessing other human beings. Whether illogically or judiciously, most of us are aware of the physical appearance of both ourselves and others.

> The pump-priming capacity of both beauty and ugliness is well known in human relations, in spite of the fact that all historical periods have their own notions of aesthetics. Whether beauty is inherent in the object or merely a function of the perceiver, it is sufficient to point out here that any morphology carrying the stamp of popular or expert appreciation forces the perceiver to take a stand; to acknowledge,

> refute, or ignore. For example, a beautiful woman asking a favor is likely to receive more spontaneous and speedy service than an unattractive one; people hire, fire, marry and divorce, attract and "reject" others on the basis of a compound assessment of both appearance and performance.[1]

We are living in an age when much stress is placed on physical appearance. This trend in contemporary times has developed since 1850, when nice women used only skin lotions for curing blemishes; 1865, when face powders no longer oxidized and turned dark from fumes of candle or gas light; 1870, when vegetable rouge was secretly used by many women; 1895, when cold cream became popular with other than theatrical people; 1910, when deodorants and depilatories appeared; 1915, manicuring made its debut; and 1930, when eye makeup was used by housewives and stenographers to achieve eyebrows like Greta Garbo's and cheek shadows like those of Marlene Dietrich.[2]

Currently, it is difficult to find a single page of a newspaper or magazine that does not have a beautiful woman or handsome male depicted on it. Soaps, cosmetics, perfumes, all claim to enhance the physical attractiveness of both males and females. This constant bombardment on the part of the mass media has been labeled the Beatification of Beauty by Albert Ellis, who goes on to describe the modern woman's plight:

> But the modern woman's feelings of physical inadequacy also stem from culture-centered and socially propagated influences which make it virtually impossible for any contemporary female, no matter how psychologically secure she may be, not to have a wide-ranging and deep-ranging horror of several of her own physical attributes.[3]

Female beauty seems not only to be the desired prerequisite for sex, love, and marriage, but also a means for women to use to impress other women:

[1] Jurgen Ruesch and Weldon Kees, *Nonverbal Communication* (Los Angeles: University of California Press, 1956), p. 40.

[2] "Women Look Their Best," *American Druggist* (October, 1933), p. 64.

[3] Albert Ellis, *The American Sexual Tragedy* (New York: Grove Press, 1962), p. 16.

> Indeed, although the implication behind the modern emphasis on feminine loveliness is that it is largely for the attraction and distraction of males, beauty in its own right, beauty for the sake of female appraisal and approval, has become as much the rule as the exception today. Witness, for example, styles in women's hats, toenail polish, and hairdos, which seem to be considerably more important to the modern misses and matrons than to their lords and masters.[4]

Although Erving Goffman [5] cites many convincing episodes showing that when a person presents himself to an audience, he is much more aware of his appearance than when he is behind the scenes, recent advertising by the cosmetics industry is aimed at exactly this market. We now have bedtime perfume, bedtime eye make-up, and bedtime lipstick.

To enhance our daytime appearance, Albert Ellis [6] documents 926 advertisements from fifty women's magazines under the general headings of body odor, breasts, eyes, face, hair, hands, hips and body, menstrual functions, mouth, posture, skin, weight-reducing, and general beauty aids. Skin, hair, and breasts are the categories with the most numerous entries.

A clothing and textiles survey at the University of Missouri relating to the use of make-up brought out a few differences between male and female awareness. Women stated that they wore make-up to achieve a natural look and to bring out good features; men thought women wore make-up to look more attractive. Women said they chose make-up according to hair, eye, and complexion coloring, while men felt that women chose make-up according to their personalities. Women said they spent between ten and twenty dollars a year on make-up, while men were sure that women spent over fifty dollars a year.

It is a well-known fact that teenagers use a high proportion of their spending money on cosmetic aids. Though they comprise only 11 per cent of the female population, teenage girls account for 23 per cent of all cosmetic and toilet goods sales (or $450 million worth each year).[7]

[4] Ibid., p 17.

[5] Erving Goffman, *The Presentation of Self in Everyday Life* (New York: Anchor Books, 1959).

[6] Ellis, op. cit., pp. 25–27.

[7] "The Teenage Tide," *Time* (October 9, 1964), p. 96.

Men do not escape the dilemma of desired appearance versus reality. They, too, are the subject and the vehicle of much advertising in the various media. A recent article on family relations makes this observation:

> Today, a young husband is constantly being compared, because of our mass communications, to the best athlete's manliness and the finest gentleman's manners. It goes without saying that relatively few men in our society can stand such a comparison.[8]

Ads for male beauty aids are ever increasing. In the early 1960's, approximately 71 such advertisements appeared in 35 men's magazines in a single month. By 1965, 60 ads appeared in 16 magazines. The greatest jump was taken in face lotions and colognes, which leaped from 5 to 40 ads in the same type of magazine. Body building, important in the first half century, seemed to be played down in 1965; perhaps the brainy man is more important now than the athlete but he too has to "smell nice." [9]

An interesting article in *Vogue* called "Men and Their Looks," [10] goes into great detail about men's skin and hair problems. Concern for hair and baldness is labeled the "Samson mystique," which seems to affect men of all ages. However, the article offers the encouraging fact that men change very little between forty and sixty and are still considered as romantic figures, even for movie leads. In today's advertising it is possible to couple young girls with men ten, fifteen, and sometimes twenty years their seniors.

> Today male idols are not necessarily the best-looking. A handsome face is no longer synonymous with the classic profile; men with broken noses, wrinkled foreheads, crooked mouths, eye patches, and even bald heads are considered attractive. . . . Women tend to confuse prettiness in men with softness.[11]

[8] Richard H. Klemer, "The Empathetic Approach to Teaching Family Relations," *Journal of Home Economics*, Vol. 57 (1965), p. 622.

[9] 1960 data are taken from *The American Sexual Tragedy*, op. cit., by Ellis; 1965 data are taken from a student survey at the University of Missouri.

[10] "Men and Their Looks, Tape-Talk from a Famous Doctor," *Vogue* (November 15, 1965), pp. 118–121.

[11] Stephen Baker, *Visual Persuasion* (New York: McGraw-Hill, Inc., 1961).

Of course, in other times and other places men have tried to be beautiful with the use of cosmetics, perfumes, and other beauty aids. One outstanding example is documented among the Jivaros of the Eastern Andes who, by the way, are also head hunters and head shrinkers.

> If you should meet a Jivaro on the trail, he will be wearing a short skirt of brown material with maroon vertical stripes. Above this wrap-around his body will be bare except for painted designs and various ornaments. If "fully dressed," he will also have on a fur and feather crown. He likes delicately applied face paint in geometrical designs and never travels without a "vanity case," a little square bag containing feathers, face paint, and other toiletries. He adorns himself with necklaces and other ornaments and is hypersensitive about his lustrous black hair. He cuts it straight across the forehead and lets it grow to about waist length in the back. He can be identified by his three pigtails—a long one behind, and a short one at each ear. He believes that hair possesses a sort of soul power and the belt of human hair he wears is of more than ornamental or practical value to him.[12]

Children, too, are aware of their appearance. Young girls may have haircuts, shampoos, sets, and manicures in a beauty salon. Two of the most costly skin specialists (Erno Laszlo and Venner Kelsen) do a big business in treating adolescent skins.[13] In addition youngsters may have their teeth straightened and capped before they reach high school.

> Eddie, like other high-priced hairstylists, is now giving $7 haircuts and $12 hair-straightening jobs to prep-school boys before they go off to Andover or Groton, and his clients for hairpieces today include several Ivy League college boys. At an early age, the children of the rich are learning the importance of staying young, healthy, and attractive.[14]

Awareness of general appearance has many facets. Do

[12] Edward Weyer, Jr., *Primitive Peoples Today* (New York: Doubleday and Company, Inc., 1959), p. 91.

[13] Stephen Birmingham, "How the Rich Stay Young and Beautiful," *McCall's* (April, 1968), p. 106.

[14] Ibid.

Jivaro Tribesman

we really know how we appear to others? Here is an example from the other side of the social spectrum.

Recently an imaginative school principal in a slum area provided each student in school with a photograph of himself. The classrooms of the school were abundantly supplied with large mirrors. The result was an astounding increase in the learning rate. The slum child has ordinarily very little visual orientation. He does not see himself as becoming something. He is deeply involved in his own world from day to day and can establish no beachhead in the highly specialized sense life of visual man.[15]

The mirrors and the photograph made the slum children aware of what they were—and of what they could become.

Physical Type

People in all ages have seemingly been aware of body types and have aspired to certain physical proportions. The proportions are not universal but change with peoples, places, and times. Several historical examples showing the varieties of the body beautiful might include the Cretan woman with her tiny waist, splendid bosom, and long curly hair. Later, the Greeks valued natural figures, firm and well-developed—"Their waists, unlike their Minoan forebears, were not constricted; their breasts set high and far apart; their legs and arms were long with finely turned wrists and ankles." [16] In contrast the medieval maiden is illustrated with a protruding stomach, low-slung buttocks, and small breasts placed high on her elongated torso. The Renaissance fancied an angular line of youth, spurning the ripeness of maturity. During the eighteenth century the preferred female was petite, pouting, and corseted. About 1900, Wagnerian ideals of "amply displayed bosoms counter-balanced by a backward movement of hips and buttocks in an S-shape, joined by a waist so small that but for its steel girder of corset one feels it would snap. Necks were referred to as columns and looked like them." [17] Later the twenties evolved a flat-chested, skinny ideal.

[15] Marshall McLuhan, *Understanding Media* (New York: Signet Books, 1966), p. 120.

[16] Madge Garland, "The Changing Face of Beauty," *Harper's Bazaar* (October, 1957), p. 151.

[17] Ibid., p. 231.

Beauty Ideals

W. H. Sheldon, one of the most noted researchers on classification of physical type, out of three hundred forty-three theoretical possibilities lists three extreme types and nineteen combinations. The three extreme types include the endomorph (relative predominance of soft roundness throughout various regions of the body), the mesomorph (a predominance of muscle, bone, and connective tissue), and the ectomorph (relative linearity and fragility). The nineteen combinations are as follows:

1. Extreme endomorph
2. Strong endomorph
3. Moderate endomorph
4. Mesomorphic-endomorph
5. Mesomorph-endomorph
6. Ectomorphic-endomorph
7. Ectomorph-endomorph
8. Extreme mesomorph
9. Strong mesomorph
10. Moderate mesomorph
11. Endomorphic-mesomorph
12. Ectomorphic-mesomorph
13. Ectomorph-mesomorph
14. Extreme ectomorph
15. Strong ectomorph
16. Moderate ectomorph
17. Endomorphic-ectomorph
18. Mesomorphic-ectomorph
19. Balance—all three [18]

Although most of us are aware of two categories, "fat" people and "thin" people, Sheldon and his associates relate certain types of clothing to the three extreme types.

> The extreme ectomorph appears to need a high stiff collar which protects and supports his ectomorphic neck. The endomorph and the mesomorph apparently need no collar at all. The individual with a highly developed torso has an understandable urge to display his body. Exhibitionism, the ectomorphic moralist calls it. But it is probably as natural as the frequent desire to write and publish a poem. Magnificent mesomorphic bodies are things of beauty and they deserve, perhaps, to be exhibited.

[18] W. H. Sheldon, S. S. Stevens, and W. B. Tucker, *The Varieties of Human Physique* (New York: Harper & Row, Publishers, 1940), p. 65.

> During the past twenty years in the styles of both street and beach, there has been a sharp swing away from dress adapted to ectomorphic dominance and toward styles suited to endomorphic-meso dominance. The stiff collar has almost disappeared. The bathing suit has dropped away piece by piece. The severe lines of the coat men used to wear, with its straight four-button front and high lapel, have given way to the rounded, short-fronted model which is ideally cut for the 451 but next to impossible for the 145.[19] The earlier high-waisted "ectomorphic" pants have been replaced by low-waisted, wide-bottomed ones. High shoes can hardly be purchased any more. Even the garter is strongly threatened and the umbrella has all but disappeared from the American scene. All this amounts to a kind of revolution.[20]

Twentieth-century Russian women have had a reputation for being heavy and muscular. A retired school teacher has explained that thirty or forty years ago, thin women were not valued because there was so much heavy work to be done and one felt bad asking a thin, sickly woman to do work. "Today," she adds, "things are different, work is not so hard, fashion has changed and even I think the heavier women look like cows rather than women."[21] The average height and weight of Russian fashion models are, in fact, 5 feet 6 inches and 125 pounds. However, at least one portly model is kept in every fashion show to appeal to the majority of women over thirty years old.[22]

In like manner, many European women have aspired to a well-padded figure, but for them the extra weight was a sign of prosperity. Certain African tribes practice excessive fattening of young girls before marriage. At the time of puberty the child is placed in a special fattening house and fed a special diet. The time of fattening is in direct proportion to the economic status of the parents and in some cases may last as long as two years.[23]

[19] 451 is a mesomorph type; 145 is an ectomorph.

[20] Sheldon et al., op cit., p. 251.

[21] Tamara Gilmore, "Rise of Russian Women," *Science Digest* (September, 1963), p. 10.

[22] Ibid., p. 13.

[23] See descriptions and pictures in Bernard Rudofsky, *Are Clothes Modern?* (Chicago: Paul Theobald, 1947), p. 60.

Stevie Smith, an English poet, was responsible for this couplet—

The English woman is so refined,
She has no bosom and no behind.

Although this seemed to be true twenty-five years ago, Colin MacInnes argues that the English girl today not only dresses better, "but even her actual figure seems to have become more seductive. . . . Why? Vitamins, yes—better food, too. My own belief is this: how girls want to look does affect their bodies." [24]

Our present cultural ideal seems to be the very thin female. However, this type actually appears more frequently in the middle and upper classes than in the lower classes.[25] It would seem that those who are financially well off are more likely to take the trouble to retain a slender figure in our age of abundance. A report from the medical field documents this fact:

> A striking relationship between socioeconomic status and obesity was discovered. Some 30% of the women in the lowest socioeconomic category were obese . . . in the highest socioeconomic status category, only 4% were obese. For men, the same tendency existed, although to a lesser extent.[26]

But we don't all attain the ideal regardless of social class; Marya Mannes has written an amusing article about the plight of the person who is size 16 and over.

> My trouble is that through genetic circumstances beyond my control I belong to a minority discriminated against by the ninth-largest industry in the United States, the garment trade, and known as women. It must be here explained that the word *women* in the dress business does not mean females, as distinguished from males, but sizes 18, 20 and on-

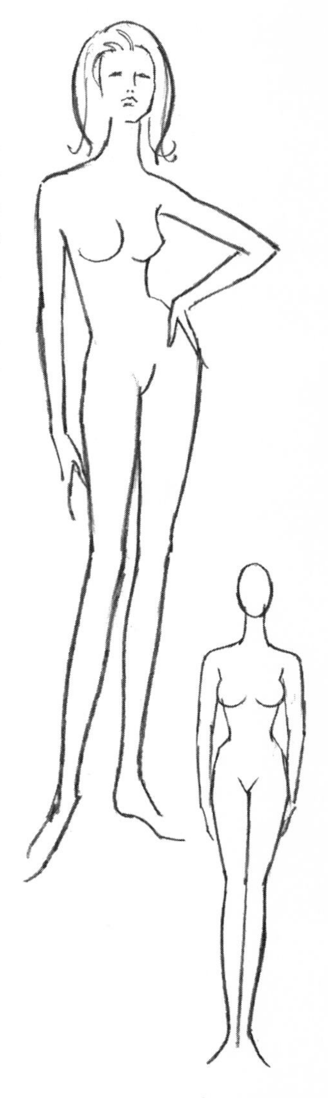

Fashion Figure

[24] Colin MacInnes, "Mothers and Daughters, Jane: Plain; Emma: Independent, Rational, Sexy," *Mademoiselle* (March, 1966), p. 186.

[25] See William H. Whyte, *The Organization Man* (Garden City, N. Y.: Doubleday Anchor Book Co., 1957), p. 350.

[26] Mary E. Moore, Albert Stunkerd, and Leo Strole, "Obesity, Social Class, and Mental Illness," *Journal of American Medical Association*, Vol. 181 (September 15, 1962), p. 964.

> wards as distinguished from sizes 5 through 16 known as juniors or misses.
>
> If you cannot get into misses, you've had it. For the corporate fashion thinking has long since established that the woman who needs a size 18 or 20 has lost hope. The best they can do for the menopause market (they assume that all big women are not only stout but elderly) is to provide some modest shrouds in sleazy fabrics to cover the unmentionable form and announce at the same time, as discreetly as possible, that the wearer has resigned from such temporal pleasures as sex and beauty and is merely sitting out the twilight period before final interment. In some good department stores, the women's section is given a cover name like "Westchester" or "Beekman Place" and is tucked away in some distant corner to save the client's embarrassment at openly acknowledging the deformity that brings her there.[27]

Jean Kerr, noted essayist and playwright, also humorously laments her figure problems:

> I have read that Mrs. Michelene Lerner keeps life-sized foam-rubber models of her figure in various fashion houses in Rome, Paris, London and New York. Then, if she sees a picture of a dress she admires, she doesn't even have to go in for a fitting. She can just call London or Paris and order it. I think this is a marvelous plan. And the reason I haven't had a dozen foam-rubber models made of my figure is not just that there isn't enough foam rubber in the world. The real reason I'm hesitant is that I don't think a life-sized foam-rubber model of me could be stashed away in a closet someplace, between fittings. It would absolutely require a proper setting. It would have to be placed like Michelangelo's David—in a rotunda, with perhaps a skylight. Now, I have never been in a fashion house, but I doubt if they have rotundas. Also, I have the feeling that it would be rather depressing to have yourself duplicated all over the place. Imagine trying to eat some *crême brulée* and realizing that you were getting fat in four different cities.[28]

[27] Marya Mannes, "Juno in Limbo: The Trauma of Size 16," *Harper's Magazine* (July, 1964), p. 37.

[28] Jean Kerr, "I Just Stepped Out of Vogue," *Ladies' Home Journal* (May, 1966), p. 164.

Extension Through Clothes —Queen Elizabeth I

J. C. Flugel stresses awareness of clothes as an extension of the body. Full, swirling skirts, draped shawls, top hats, walking sticks all enable us to fill more space and give us an "increased sense of power, a sense of extension of our bodily self." [29] William James observed that clothing was as much a part of the self as the body—a part of what he

[29] J. C. Flugel, *The Psychology of Clothes* (London: Hogarth Press, 1930), p. 34.

called the "material me."[30] Norma Compton, while studying female mental patients, found that those with weak body-image boundaries preferred types of clothing that tended to define body limits (such as saturated colors and strong figure ground contrasts).[31]

Genevieve Dariaux remarks that the simplest form of the female figure is either an I or an O. The O she divides into 8 (heavier on top than on the bottom) and the 8 (heavier on the bottom).[32] Her general advice in relation to the figure and clothes is that you should realize exactly what your physical type is, resist styles that are not for you, and limit yourself to what is most becoming.

The fact that cultural ideals of beauty and of body proportions do change with time is re-emphasized by the exploratory research on body measurements being planned by the Agricultural Research Service. This exploratory research will determine whether or not a change in body proportions in the past thirty-five years warrants a complete new study of body measurements.[33]

There seem to be some general physical differences between racial groups in addition to the color of their skins. Orientals, for example, are generally shorter and have fewer "curves." Even male Orientals are aware of their lack of buttocks in comparison to Occidentals when they try to fit into ready-made clothing in the United States.

The black male physique, according to Jason Benning, president of the New Breed, a Harlem-based organization, is different from that of the white male:

> Our measurements are different from the white man's. The black male is thinner in the waist, a little heavier through the chest and has a slightly protruding backside. To fit this physique, the six-month-old firm features jackets with pinched waists, wider lapels

[30] William James, *Psychology* (New York: Holt, Rinehart and Winston, 1892), p. 177.

[31] Norma Compton, "Body-image Boundaries in Relation to Clothing Fabric and Design Preferences of a Group of Hospitalized Psychotic Women," *Journal of Home Economics*, Vol. 56 (1964), p. 44.

[32] Genevieve Dariaux, *Elegance* (Garden City, N. Y.: Doubleday & Company, Inc., 1964), p. 83.

[33] From *Report and Recommendations of the Human Nutrition and Consumer Use Advisory Committee*, December 13–16, 1965, Lincoln, Nebraska.

> and "peacock flares" in the back (high center vents which flare slightly over the seat).[34]

The human body has been changed by many peoples. Some cultures value elongated heads, others value an elongated torso. Mutilation and scarification have been practiced since the beginning of time. Eicher suggests that we must carefully consider our point of view when judging so-called body mutilations:

> ethnocentric definitions of body "mutilation" need to be reassessed. Frequent African examples of "mutilation" include scarring, piercing, tooth chipping and ornamenting with lip plugs. I propose the term body modification which more objectively describes human beings' acts of body alteration on themselves or others for decorative or symbolic purposes. Face lifting involving surgery and "mutilation" may be socially acceptable in one society while body scarification, also involving surgery and "mutilation," may be socially acceptable in another.[35]

Skin Color

In respect to skin color, Occidentals no longer desire the white camellia look that was the ideal when Dolly Madison was a girl. The future President's wife wore to school "a white linen mask to keep every ray of sunshine from her complexion, a sunbonnet sewed on her head every morning, and long white gloves covering the hand and arms."[36]

For the past several decades, a sun-tanned look seemed to be the most desired, in fact, the darker the skin the better. Only during the last few years have beauty experts

[34] "Selling Soul Style," *Newsweek* (July 1, 1968), p. 84.

[35] Joanne Bubolz Eicher, *African Dress: A Select and Annotated Bibliography of Subsaharan Countries* (East Lansing, Mich.: African Studies Center, Michigan State University, 1970), p. vii.

[36] Florence E. Young, *Clothing the Child* (New York: McGraw-Hill, Inc., 1938), p. 35.

suggested a light tan or a creamy beige, no doubt as a result of publicity concerning a possible relationship of skin cancer and exposure to the sun.

Among the Negro groups, lighter shades of skin color have been more desirable than the dark hues. An interesting picture of Jamaican beauty queens showing ten variations of color has the girls arranged in order of hue, with these categories—Miss Ebony, Miss Mahogany, Miss Satinwood, Miss Allspice, Miss Sandalwood, Miss Golden Apple, Miss Jasmine, Miss Pomegranate, Miss Lotus, and Miss Appleblossom.[37]

Since 1968 a growing identity movement within the black community has promoted the importance of being

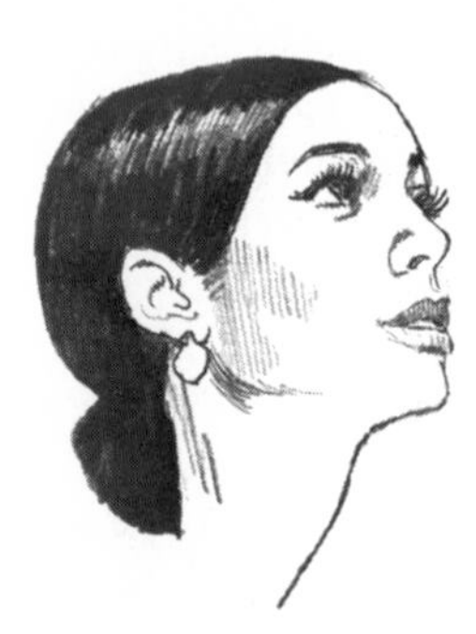

Black Is Beautiful

black. The slogan adopted has been, "Black is Beautiful and it's so Beautiful to be Black." [38]

Stephen Baker says that, increasingly, both blondes and brunettes are developing an image of themselves. Blondes are associated with two well-defined prototypes. There is the "dumb blonde," beautiful, baby-faced, bedecked with jewelry and a fur coat. Her speciality is sex. Then there is

[37] "Speaking of Pictures," *Life* (February 20, 1956), pp. 12–13.

[38] Accompanying the pride in black skin has been the popularization of natural "Afro" hair styling for both male and female Negroes.

the wholesome freckle-faced blonde who typifies "the girl next door." She is the marrying type. Almost always she is an "outdoor girl." Dark-haired girls have a more subtle kind of sex appeal based on their alleged seductiveness. This type is often found indoors. Brunettes—in the minds of the public—are apt to be taller, talk more slowly, and have less need of protection than blondes. The brunette is more apt to be associated with "class." Pictures of brunettes get more attention from women than those of blondes.[39]

The preoccupation with hair for both men and women reached high levels during the decade of the 1960's. The hairdresser became a national celebrity—in Paris, Alexandre; in New York, Kenneth; in London, Vidal Sassoon. Average women made weekly trips to the hairdresser and "not so average women like Babe Paley sometimes see a hairdresser as often as three times a day—before lunch, after lunch and again in the evening." [40]

Most people credit the Beatles for the popularity of long hair with men. After Jackie Kennedy spread the message of bouffant hair for women, "Brigitte Bardot got everyone to let their hair down and Baby Jane Holzer uncaged the lion's mane. . . . Then everyone gave up hats. . . . Then came the fall, hairpiece, and wig. . . . Just about the time everyone invested in a fall or hairpiece, Mia Farrow in a fit of temper cut off her long blond hair." [41]

In respect to both form and color, at no time in history has the human body been left as it naturally was. Man (and woman) has changed or corrected it from the era of the cave man to the most recent times.

> Natural, natural, natural, . . . they're always telling you to be the most natural girl in the world and you want to cooperate but . . . well, they just ought to see you in your natural state! Pale . . . lashless . . . lusterless . . . bustless and occasionally, after a grinding day at the typewriter, almost fingernailless! Darling, not another word . . . you wouldn't believe some of the things the very loveliest girls are doing to look "naturally" beautiful these days. . . .

[39] Baker, op. cit.
[40] *Women's Wear Daily* (January 7, 1969), pp. 4–5.
[41] Ibid., p. 5.

> All of them completely, utterly phony . . . would you believe it?! [42]

The article from which this extract is taken is called "The Beautiful Phony" and pictures a girl wearing the following accouterments—wig, false eyelashes, tinted contact lenses, beauty spot, false toenails and fingernails, new nose, padded bra, false derrière, and fake jewelry.

[42] "The Beautiful Phony," *Cosmopolitan* (March, 1966), pp. 104–105.

3 Some of the Specifics

Specific Articles of Clothing

Both in fashion magazines and on college campuses during the middle and late sixties there was an emphasized awareness of legs with their coverings (shoes, boots, socks, and stockings). Courrèges was the first to glamorize boots, while many designers, including Oleg Cassini, promoted textured, figured, flowered, ribbed, and flocked stockings. The written copy accompanying photographs of such stockings claimed they had an aura of everything from the innocent little-girl look to that of the naughty entertainers of the nineties. Smaller heels on shoes made them less obvious than the spike heels or platform soles of earlier eras. From the spring of 1966 onward, the increasing use of color gave more stress to shoes; the trend was followed by heavier looking heels and broader toes in 1968 and 1969.

Hats and purses have had their periods of importance. We were certainly aware of the typical shoulder bag of the forties, the huge suitcase type of the fifties, and the clutch bag of the early sixties. Perhaps we are less aware of purses now because they are unobtrusive. As for

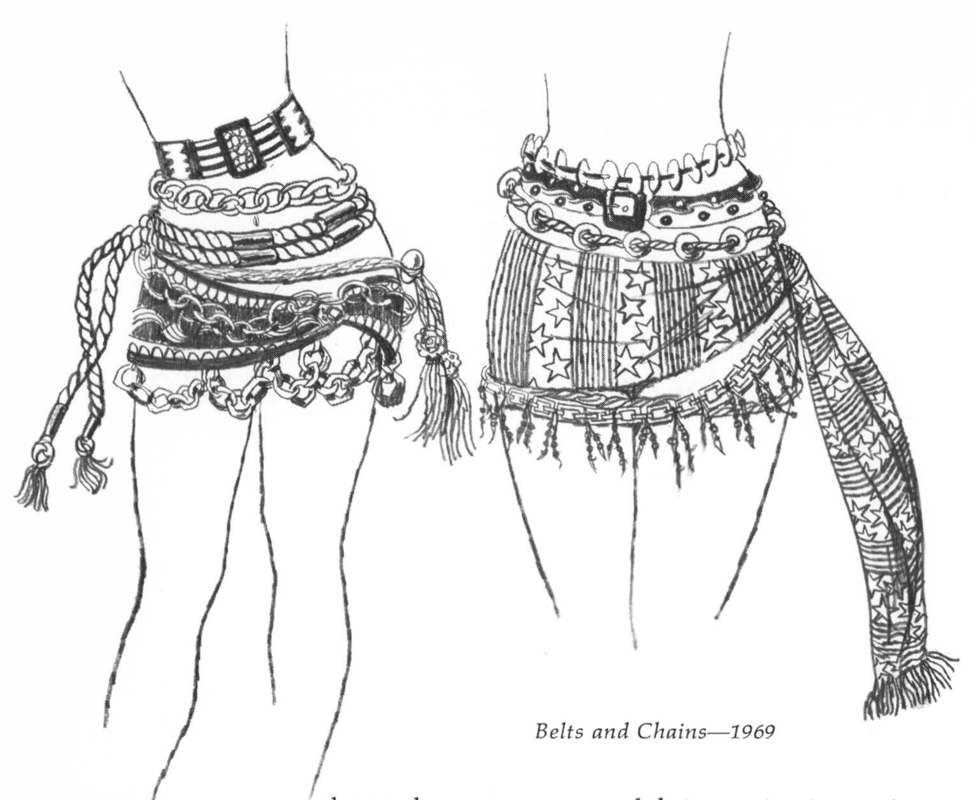

Belts and Chains—1969

hats today, we are aware of their scarcity, in certain parts of the country. The last style of hat that was adopted to any noticeable degree was an adaptation of Jackie Kennedy's famous pillbox. When asked what type of hats are in fashion or are being worn today, people give a variety of answers (ranging from a turban or toque to a wide brim) or just stare at you as if to say, "What is a hat?"

Chambers and Moulton remind us that various dress silhouettes are usually accompanied by certain hat silhouettes: high waistlines (Empire silhouette) seem to go with hats higher in the crown; full, bulky silhouettes with small hats; high collars with small hats. For men, "when the natural drape in men's suits is fashionable, hat brims have become narrower. Whenever the full drape and the padded shoulder are popular in suits, the brim of the hat is considerably wider." [1]

The return of the belt in the late 1960's marked a new era—women again had waistlines. Belts were narrow and wide, made of fabric, leather, or metal with dangling

[1] Helen G. Chambers and Verna Moulton, *Clothing Selection* (Philadelphia: J. B. Lippincott Company, 1969), p. 304.

purses, watches, and chains. Vests for women in 1969 could indeed be thought of as an extension of the belt when made of fur or metal links, or fashioned from strings of beads.

Genevieve Dariaux says that "the accessories worn with an outfit—gloves, hat, shoes, and handbag—are among the most important elements of an elegant appearance. A modest dress or suit can triple its face value when it is worn with an elegant hat, bag, gloves, and shoes, while a designer's original can lose much of its prestige if its accessories have been carelessly selected." [2]

In general, women seem to be more aware of accessories than men. In the Clothing TAT (see page 69) women made more comments about purses, hats, shoes, and jewelry than did the men. Women's comments on accessories also cover a variety of topics (style, color, relation to age) while men are notorious for their awareness of condition, i.e., shine on the shoes, holes in soles, or run-down heels.

Color

Color is one of the most important elements of design, whether one is considering clothing, personal coloring, or any of the visual arts. Chambers and Moulton declare that "color is the design factor to which many people react first and most strongly." [3] Color is a valuable tool in advertising because of its attention-getting power; in order to entice the prospective buyer many retail establishments display merchandise packaged in bright primary colors. In the theater, attention may be drawn to a particular actor by the use of brilliant hues. "An actor can also be brought into the spotlight by the use of strong contrasts. The main character might be dressed in a light color and the other actors and the background might be kept in a darker color, in which case the other actors would also serve as back-

[2] Genevieve Dariaux, *Elegance* (Garden City, N.Y.: Doubleday & Company, Inc., 1964), p. 1.
[3] Chambers and Moulton, op. cit., p. 54.

ground and by comparison emphasize the main character."[4]

There are many cultural variations in the awareness and use of color terminology. Roger Brown describes lexical mappings of the color spectrum in three languages: English, Bassa (language used in Liberia), and Shona (a language of Rhodesia). From Figure 8, it can be noted that

Bassa

ziza	hui

Shona

cips$^{\omega}$uka	cicena	citena	cips$^{\omega}$uka

English

red	orange	yel-low	green	blue	purple

Color Spectrum in Three Languages

Bassa has two main color terms: *hui* for the entire blue-green end of the spectrum and *ziza* for the red-orange end. The Shona language puts the reds and purples together, uses one word for blues and blue-greens, and another for yellows and greens. Many other languages have single words for the entire range of blue-greens. "In languages that have a single word for blue and green that word is often also the name for the sea."[5]

A look at color usage in particular cultures shows a wide range of differing patterns. For example, early Navajo color choices followed the natural colors of wool—white, black, brown, and gray. Later, contact with the Mexicans introduced indigo to the Navajo color palette; still later, red and yellow were borrowed from the colorful uniforms of Spanish soldiers.[6]

In certain regions of India special color combinations and color intensities are often identified with a geographic area. In the north, elegant fabrics bearing minute and complex

[4] Ibid.

[5] Roger Brown, *Social Psychology* (New York: The Free Press, 1965), p. 316.

[6] Marilyn J. Horn, *The Second Skin* (Boston: Houghton Mifflin Company, 1968), p. 44.

designs are generally found in two harmonizing colors. Colors are generally chosen from the warm yellow, orange, and red ranges. In western India, faded, dull designs of lemon yellow, green, and brick red are common, due in part to the resist method of dyeing. The printed fabrics of southern India are bolder and more brightly colored than in any other part of the country.[7]

Color reactions within a culture may vary from one individual to another. A color that is pleasing to one person may be depressing to another. Most people have definite color preferences for the clothes they wear. Males as well as females can be intensely aware of their color preferences. Designer Hardy Amies confesses:

> Two years ago, I decided I liked all the blue suits in my wardrobe best, so I went over completely to blue (said Amies, an azure vision in a sapphire-blue suit with a gold and black silk kerchief stuffed in its breast pocket, a robin's egg blue shirt and a nearly navy blue knit tie).
>
> I always wear bright navy blue now. . . . When I go on a trip, I pack a couple dozen shirts. I know they are going to be blue. A dozen ties. I know they will be blue. My dinner jackets are dark blue.[8]

Some people are probably more aware than others of color in clothing—if one uses color coordination as a means of judging this phenomenon. Even excluding those that are color blind, there are people who wear only browns together or blues together, without much color mixing. Others seem to pick colors at random in assembling an outfit. Some women, aware of color to an extreme degree, try to match clothing and accessories exactly. Genevieve Dariaux deplores this practice: "The woman who spends hours running from one shop to another trying to match a shoe or a glove is spending an immense amount of time and effort in vain, for she will only succeed in giving the impression that everything she owns has been dipped into the same vat of dye." [9]

The psychological method of using Rorschach's ink blots as a clinical diagnostic tool has also produced ex-

[7] Informants were women graduate students from India attending the University of Missouri and the University of Connecticut.

[8] Reported in Marylin Bender, *The Beautiful People* (New York: Coward-McCann, Inc., 1967), p. 294.

[9] Dariaux, op. cit., p. 2.

perimental data related to "color shock." One such finding states that "not only is the color responsible for the shock, but an objective difference in the affective reactions to color between stable and unstable persons has been demonstrated." [10]

Other less dramatic psychological reactions to color have been noted by color theorists. Faber Birren states that wavelength is a fundamental factor in determining color preference. He points out that warm colors are generally preferred by extroverts, who respond more directly to objects and objective events of the external environment. Those preferring warm colors usually accept outside influences and "submerge themselves readily in a social environment." [11] In addition, these people like outdoor activities and enjoy entertaining frequently in their homes." [12]

Introverts are found to prefer colors on the cool side of the spectrum—the blues, greens, and purples. These individuals have a detached attitude toward the outside world, do not adapt readily to new circumstances and often find it difficult to express themselves freely. According to Birren those with cool color preferences are often highly educated, widely read, yet emotionally reserved.[13]

Results from more than fifty tests have shown that color preferences shift with maturity levels. Babies are more aware of brighter colors, as judged by eye fixation, and the young child prefers red, blue, green, violet, orange, and yellow in that order.[14] As children advance in age and grade there is a rise in preference for blue, green, and violet and a corresponding decline in values for red, orange, and yellow.[15]

[10] Albert I. Robin, "Validating and Experimental Studies with Rorschach Method," in Harold H. Anderson and Gladys L. Anderson, editors, *Introduction to Projective Techniques* (Englewood Cliffs, N. J.: Prentice-Hall, Inc., 1951), p. 139.

[11] Faber Birren, *New Horizons in Color* (New York: Reinhold Publishing Corporation, 1955), p. 110.

[12] Jacquelyn H. McInnis and Jane L. Shearer, "Relationship Between Color Choices and Selected Preferences of the Individual," *Journal of Home Economics*, Vol. 56 (March, 1964), pp. 181–187.

[13] Birren, op. cit., p. 110.

[14] Faber Birren, *Selling Color to People* (New York: University Books, 1956), p. 173.

[15] S. E. Katz and F. S. Breed, "The Color Preferences of Children," *Journal of Applied Psychology*, Vol. 6 (September, 1922), pp. 255–266.

Color is seemingly very important to the adolescent. In ranking twenty-eight possible criteria for a winter skirt, ninth-grade girls in the North Central states placed color second only to the fit of the garment.[16] These girls also stated that they noticed color on others. In answer to the question "Susie is wearing a new skirt today. What did you notice first about Susie's skirt?" 72 per cent mentioned color, the highest response for any attribute of the skirt.[17]

Color is always an important component of fashion and fashion change. Color terminology used by fashion writers rivals the lyric poet. *Harper's Bazaar,* in its September, 1970 issue, reports:

> *Colors* in Paris: A whole vineyard of shades we call tastevin wines; purples and wild violets still holding their own; a gamut of greens including eucalyptus, a new neutral; a bounty of taupey browns and a ravishing return of black.[18]

Clothing selection authorities have developed time-tested guides for the use of color to achieve the most pleasing aesthetic effects. Most of the following suggestions are still worthy of consideration even in this era of "do your own thing":

1. To achieve color unity let one hue predominate in each ensemble.
2. Aim for variety of hue, value and strength (intensity).
3. Use soft related colors for multicolored harmonies.
4. When using a vivid color by itself, stabilize it with darker, self values or neutrals.
5. Arrange colors naturally with the darkest value at the base working up to the lighter, brighter tones at the top.[19]

Relating color of costume to personal coloring is indeed an art requiring experimentation to produce the desired effect.

[16] "Adolescent Girls' Skirts, Part I: Mothers' and Daughters' Opinions of School Skirts," North Central Regional Research Publication, No. 478, Agricultural Experiment Station, University of Minnesota (1965), p. 11.

[17] Ibid., p. 14.

[18] *Harper's Bazaar* (September 1970), p. 148.

[19] Marion S. Hillhouse, *Dress Selection and Design* (New York: The Macmillan Company, 1963), p. 180.

The general rule is to allow costume color to "play up" personal coloring. Awareness of personal coloring was detailed by Brandau in this way:

> To be becoming a color must emphasize the desirable and subdue the undesirable color; it must emphasize the glow rather than the sallowness in the skin; it must make the eyes darker and more colorful; and it must make light hair lighter and dark hair darker or add the blue note to dark hair and the copper note to light hair.[20]

Noting that no two people have the same skin coloring, Chambers and Moulton caution that experimentation with color is a necessity and that "color principles" are only guidelines for such experiments. They stress the importance of the relationship between colors of hair, eyes, and skin. "It is not always possible to flatter all three—skin, eyes and hair. When there is conflict, the skin must be considered first."[21]

COLOR THROUGH COSMETICS

The use of make-up can produce a desired color tone for skin, can camouflage the size and shape of the face or nose, and can bring out the sparkle and hue of one's eyes. In Europe and America Caucasians of the last century wanted skin to appear magnolia white; during the early part of this century a pink tone was favored; in the forties and fifties, the sun-tanned look gained in popularity. By the sixties and seventies, no such simple solution seemed satisfactory. Colorful make-up appeared on the scene, which could be as eye-catching and breath-taking as Indian war paint, or the masklike make-up of a Japanese Geisha girl, or the facial stripes of a Jivaro head hunter. In 1970 *Vogue's* advice was to use color as a rainbow and to drench oneself in another world of fantasy and mystery. An article in the October issue outlines how to go about it. A "new mood for mauve" leads to the lilac-shaded face, using the "palest of lavenders to the most passionate of peonies."

[20] Edna P. Brandau, "An Experiment in Color Analysis," *Journal of Home Economics*, Vol. 34 (December, 1942), p. 716.
[21] Chambers and Moulton, op. cit., p. 57.

Eyes are completely surrounded with a half an inch of Lumina Lilac over Smoking Lilac eye shadow, cheeks blush with Pink Lilac Soufflé Cheek Color, and lips are frosted with Electra-Lilac Lipstick. The rainbow face created by Gil of Max Factor is literally painted—pale green just on the hairline, yellow on the forehead and on the top of the nose, pale orange eyebrows, pink on the cheeks turning to mauve and blue-purple on the chin, neck, and ear lobes. One eye is covered with a green contact lens, the other with purple. According to the copy, "this fabulous face could have surfaced in a Fellini film." [22]

Since the "black is beautiful" ideal for Negroes has become popular, cosmetics are now designed specifically for black skins. Ordinary make-up for the white woman turns black skin ashen and makes eyes recede. Black skin with its great variety of shades may have undertones of browns, oranges, red-golds—even purples—but never pink as in white skins. Lips pose a special problem. "Many black women find it necessary to use two shades of lipstick to equalize skin color, because their bottom lips are often more pink than their top lips." [23]

Whether facial make-up is used to portray a *Vogue*-like fantasy or to identify with an American Indian or the Afro look, it is really being used as a part of a costume. Color in both clothing and make-up is an integral part of the awareness of aesthetic communication.

Awareness of Cost

Thorstein Veblen made millions of readers in several generations aware of the role clothing costs have played in conspicuous leisure, conspicuous waste, and as an expression of the pecuniary culture.[24]

A typical seventeenth-century accounting of clothing costs clearly displays an attempt to economize where pos-

[22] *Vogue* (October 1, 1970), pp. 118–119.

[23] "Black Cosmetics," *Time*, June 29, 1970, p. 47.

[24] See especially Chapter VII in Thorstein Veblen, *The Theory of the Leisure Class* (New York: Modern Library, 1934).

sible. The clothes themselves were less expensive than the trimmings and appurtenances then necessary to complete a gentleman's costume. This particular bill, from the household accounts of the first Duke of Bedford, includes:

		£	s.	d.
April 1663.	For a knotted fringe belt, black.	5	0	0
	For 4 white tabby belts stitched.	4	0	0
	For a girdle and frogged.		8	0
	For a mourning belt.	1	5	0
	For a coloured belt ribboned.		16	0
	For a coloured fringe belt with buttons.	2	5	0
	For a silver buckled belt stitched.	4	10	0
	For a draw girdle and frogged.		16	0
	For a silver embroidered belt.	5	10	0
	For a silver embroidered belt with tufted fringe.	7	10	0
	For a plain Cordivant belt coloured.		10	0[25]

All bills did not, happily for the finances, come to as much as this one. Gold and silver lace was used again and again, as were buttons made of the same precious metals. Nor was it necessary to have so much embroidery every year as in 1663. Fashions changed to simpler styles.

Agnes Rogers reports that at one of the Vanderbilt balls $155,730 was spent on costumes. One lady wore a costume that was described as having white cat tails ornamenting a full skirt, a blue ribbon with a golden bell and the name "Puss" on it around her neck, a headdress consisting of a stiffened white cat's skin with the head perched over the forehead and the tail pendent behind. Several other guests with the help of elaborate costumes twinkled as fixed stars, soared as butterflies, or posed as mountain sheep.[26]

[25] Gladys Scott Thomson, *Life in a Noble Household 1641–1700* (Ann Arbor, Michigan: University of Michigan, Ann Arbor Paperbacks, 1959), p. 338.

[26] Agnes Rogers, *Women Are Here to Stay* (New York: Harper & Row, 1949), p. 10.

Extravagant Costumes—1883

Diamond Jim Brady had a collection of personal jewelry that was worth more than $2 million. A partial listing of his personal evening jewelry included:

Diamond Set	$87,315.00
Pearl Set	79,553.75
Ruby Set	31,570.00
Emerald Set	52,330.00
Cat's-Eye Set	30,840.00
Sapphire Set	36,700.00
Marquise Diamond Set	38,257.50
Racing Set	10,737.50
Transportation Set (Jim had paid $105,000 for this)	13,557.50
Trefoil Set	16,422.50
Star Sapphire Set	21,815.00
Black Opal Set	14,362.50

Opal Set	9,664.00
Turquoise Set	6,716.50
Napoleon Set	8,815.00
Initial "B" Set	6,737.50
Colored Sapphire Set	5,312.50
Garnet Set	5,210.00
Sporting Set	6,080.00
Topaz Set	3,173.25
Abalone Pearl Set	3,834.00
Amethyst Set	4,933.00
Moonstone Set	1,886.00
Coral Set	440.00
U.S. Coin Set (Representing merely face value of coins—not their numismatic value)	809.60
Sardonyx Set	1,095.00
Amatrice Set	2,155.00
Imperial Jade Set	1,157.00
Thomsonite Set	757.00
Plain White Set	290.00[27]

Estimating the cost of being on the "best-dressed" list for women, Eugenia Sheppard suggests $20,000 annually to be an absolute minimum; the really clothes-conscious aspirant will spend $100,000 a year on dresses alone, not counting furs and jewelry.[28]

Recently, however, there has been a de-emphasis on conspicuous display by some members of the higher strata. This has been interpreted as "counter-snobbery," the studied awareness of a lack of ostentation.[29]

Experiments made in consumer classes show that it is extremely difficult to judge the exact prices of garments, whether one is considering high-priced garments or those in the moderately priced range. The great variety of clothes available in our mass market makes it possible to find good-looking clothes in almost any price range. An article in *Life* entitled "Price Puzzle Proves a Point" [30] graphically shows how difficult it is to gauge the price of clothes that

[27] Lucius Beebe, *The Big Spenders* (New York: Pocket Books, 1967), p. 84.

[28] Ibid., p. 289.

[29] See Robert Steiner and Joseph Weiss, "Veblen Revised in the Light of Counter-Snobbery," *Journal of Aesthetics and Art Criticism*, Vol. LX (1951), pp. 263–268.

[30] *Life* (December 24, 1956), pp. 55–59.

Classic Patterns Don't Show Cost

range from $10.95 to $1,020.00. All garments shown are in black, white, or red, which partially eliminates color as a variable. The article contains some sound advice when it states:

> Classic patterns like checks, dots and stripes are a sounder buy than overambitious prints which tend to give away their price. Costly fripperies like embroidery, fussy shaping and ornate trimmings are to be avoided. Black and combinations of black and white are traditionally good fashion while the peculiarly American color, red, is clear and bright even in inexpensive fabrics.[31]

[31] Ibid.

Genevieve Dariaux makes this further suggestion:

> The manner in which a hem is sewn sometimes proclaims more loudly than a label the price you have paid for a garment, and it is often worthwhile to undo the machine-stitched hem of a ready-made dress and to sew it properly before you wear it for the first time.[32]

One of our changing cultural patterns is related to the age of youth and their responsibility in buying personal items including clothing. More young people are buying their own clothes then in any other historical period. According to a study carried on at Hickman High School, in Columbia, Missouri, during 1963–64, the 1,365 students enrolled spent $11,550 or an everage of $8.46 per month each for clothes. This survey also revealed that 70 per cent of the students bought their own clothes.[33]

The relatively slow acceptance of inexpensive paper clothing was for the most part related to "quality." In a study of consumer attitudes toward disposable clothing in the early sixties, these quality-related attributes were described as objectionable: appearance, lack of drape, feel, limited texture varieties, and thinness. Other objections centered upon the texture—plastic-like feel, flimsy, too much like paper—and the look—cheap-looking fabrics. In fact, 70 per cent of the respondents did not consider the samples available at that time to be suitable for dresses.[34] Only by overcoming most of these objections did paper clothes gain some popularity in the mid-sixties. In many cases, the price of the garment also increased to from $8 to $12 for dresses and from $6 to $8 for "at home" wear.

[32] Dariaux, op. cit., p. 123.

[33] Donald R. Roberts, "Does It Pay to Advertise in the P & G?" unpublished study done at Hickman High School, Columbia, Missouri, 1964.

[34] Texanita Randle, "Women's Attitudes Toward Disposable Clothing and Household Items," unpublished Master's thesis, University of Missouri, August, 1962, p. 39.

The Total Picture

Fashion Awareness

Probably most people are aware of the gross features of women's fashion, such as skirt length, general fit, and the presence or absence of ornamentation. Awareness of high fashion, however, is no doubt restricted to the relatively young and affluent. Even these groups spend less time (if not money) following fashion than used to be the case. Bettina Ballard underlines this point by her comments:

> When I first went to Paris for *Vogue,* women had this passion, dreaming of personal fashion triumphs, or individual fashion conceptions. Now daughters of these women would rather go skiing in the winter, sail around Greek isles in the summer, work at some sort of job, become beatniks, go to Russia, or a myriad of alternatives to spending their days at the dressmaker, the bootmaker, the hairdresser. The feeling about time and what to do with it has changed. What has become of those long hours when we brushed out hair, fooled with our nails, tried for the most effective

place for a beauty spot? Fashion is one of the great sacrifices of the jet age—there just isn't time to play at it.[1]

As for designers, the two names known most widely are Dior and Chanel. American designer Rudi Gernreich is also known by reputation (the topless bathing suit syndrome), if not by name.

Designers themselves are aware of what others think of them. Now that fashion is big business, even in France, the designer is particularly aware of the power of the press. Geoffrey Beene says, "The press can make or break a designer; more often make than break." Marc Bohan, mindful of poor notices, remarks:

> Some journalists know fashion, but very few do . . . journalists are always looking for sensational things . . . they go too far . . . we have to accept *critique*—it's the rules of the game . . . but if someone doesn't like it they must know how to explain why they don't like it . . . people who *know* are able to say *why*.[2]

The awareness of fashion change is probably the most discernible characteristic of the total fashion picture. For the general public this is frequently tied to the factor of economic waste, but to the clothing manufacturer it is directly concerned with productivity. Napoleon was farsighted enough to foster the French clothing industry by encouraging fashion change. During his reign it became the custom to change clothing three times a day, with jewelry being especially designed for each outfit. When he saw women dressed in the same clothes more than once Napoleon would say, "Madam, is that the only dress you possess?" [3]

Some critics have deplored the fact that clothing manufacturers have capitalized on the built-in obsolescence created by fashion changes. This characteristic is at present typical of women's clothing, but a similar situation may

[1] Bettina Ballard, *In My Fashion* (New York: David McKay Company, Inc., 1960), p. 309.
[2] *Women's Wear Daily* (September 15, 1964).
[3] As reported in Karlyne Anspach, *The Why of Fashion* (Ames, Iowa: Iowa State University Press, 1968), p. 42.

be in the offing for men's wear. John Morgan, writing in the English weekly, *The New Statesman,* describes the wardrobe of a fashion-conscious young man as follows:

> A smart Mod would need some 18 shirts, eight pairs of trousers, the turnover being necessarily swift since Stephen (John Stephen, who designs and sells Mod Clothes) changes the fashion often.[4]

Marylin Bender notes the masculine fashion revolution in London (especially Carnaby Street where young cocks of the walk find their plumage), but she also describes the new dandies in Paris as dancing to the tune of Pierre Cardin. She emphasizes that Mod never became as sacred in America, in part because the American boy did not have to prove a point of social injustice by buying outrageous clothes and overspending in the manner of English lower-class youth.[5]

The fashion industry tries to make the public aware of its products by using a group of willing exhibitionists as fashion celebrities. Bender describes these people as super-consumers whose publicity demands first claim on the American public's attention. The women who wear the dresses and the men who design them all become leaders in the new "pop" society.[6]

Using a series of pictures of high fashions about which informants were asked to make comments, Judy Eddy found that women were more likely to comment about "fashion" than were men. Men were more apt to comment on overall appearance or pose of the wearer.[7]

A fashion awareness test designed to examine the accuracy of pinpointing fashions to specific years [8] seems to indicate that younger informants are more aware of exact dates for fashions than are older informants, and that college students are the most aware.

[4] John Morgan, "Mods and Rockers," *The New Statesman* (April 10, 1964), pp. 555–556.

[5] Marylin Bender, *The Beautiful People* (New York: Coward McCann, Inc., 1967), p. 287.

[6] Ibid., p. 35.

[7] Judy Wells Eddy, "An Investigation of Attitudes Toward Fashions," unpublished Master's thesis, University of Missouri, 1965, p. 59.

[8] Described on page 84 of this book.

Masculinity Versus Femininity

Woman in Pants

For several centuries the chief distinction between men's and women's clothing in Western societies has been the fact that women wore skirts and that men wore trousers. However, Rudofsky takes issue with this sexual association of garments, asserting that during the course of history more men have worn skirts and more women have worn trousers.[9] (How one would be able to prove this statement would be open to question.)

The adoption of trousers and shorts by women and the wearing of long hair by men has made the confusion of the sexes more of a possibility since the late 1950's. Karlyne Anspach relates this phenomenon in part to increasing casualness.[10] Yet an increased use of or need for ornamentation by men and boys further complicates the situation. Male jewelry—including necklaces and earrings, trimmings, ruffles, patterns, prints, and colors—is as much in evidence these days as the plumage of the male bird. Ernest Dichter uses the term "Peacock Revolution" to describe today's fashionable male.

Current news media are filled with cases of mistaken identity between young boys and girls. There are criticisms that boys not only look like girls but behave in a more feminine way than the girls. A friend cited a recent example of a young couple entering a movie theater with a baby. In the lobby, the young husband handed the baby to his wife (who had very short hair), went over to a mirror and spent several minutes combing and arranging his long tresses and preening his eyebrows. The wife did not attempt to enhance her appearance.

Obviously, the changes in attitudes and awareness of what is male and what is female have both symbolic and role implications. These will be discussed further in Parts II and III which are devoted to symbol and role.

[9] Bernard Rudofsky, *Are Clothes Modern?* (Chicago: Paul Theobald, 1947), p. 129.

[10] Karlyne Anspach, "The American in Casual Dress," *Journal of Home Economics*, Vol. 55, No. 4 (April, 1963), p. 255.

One's Way of Wearing Clothes

It is often not just the clothes themselves, but the way they are worn that catches our attention. Teenagers are well known for their extremes—wearing skirts or pants just a little tighter, skirts just a little shorter, hair a little longer (or shorter, as the case may be).

Books on clothing design and selection suggest various means by which a person can gain individuality. We are all aware of people who have "a way with clothes," as contrasted to others whose clothes look thrown together. Perhaps this is what we mean when we call people "well-dressed"—that they have a way with clothes and that one notices it. A prominent woman lawyer has been given credit for the statement, "A well-dressed woman is never overlooked." [11]

However, one's way of wearing clothes or one's style sense isn't necessarily always associated with being well-dressed. It can mean simply one's awareness of being a particular type of person. Russell Lynes has described several types under the heading of Dress Snobs, who feel that they have a certain sartorial superiority:

a. The Underdressed Snob, who wouldn't be caught dead at a cocktail party in a cocktail dress, and a similar type, the next on our list . . .
b. The Basic Dress Snob, who believes that she has so much personality that she can get away anywhere in a simple black ("basic") dress and one piece of "heirloom" jewelry.
c. The Good Quality Snob, or wearer of tweeds, cut almost exactly the same from year to year, often with a hat of the same material. This type is native to the Boston North Shore, the Chicago North Shore, the North Shore of Long Island, to Westchester County, the Philadelphia Main Line, and the Peninsula area of San Francisco, etc. It rides horses and is rare in Southern California except for Pasadena. In Texas it trades at Neiman-Marcus.

[11] Grace M. Morton, "A Basis for Self-Expression Through Arts of Personal Appearance," *Journal of Home Economics*, Vol. 29 (April, 1937), pp. 232–234.

d. The Band Box Snob, common among professional models and among other young women trying to make their way in the big city. They look as though they had just stepped out of *Vogue* or *Mademoiselle*. They are never ahead of the fashion, but they are screamingly up to date.
e. The Dowdy Snobs, or *Who the hell cares about fashion,* Snobs.
f. The Personal Style Snob, or *I know more about my type than the experts,* Snob. This final type considers her taste to be above the whims of mere fashion. She is so chic that she believes that it is unchic to be merely fashionable.[12]

Lynes also describes a Male Clothes Snob who wants most of all to be conspicuously inconspicuous.[13]

Other ways of expressing a look were yet to appear. The individualized look that emerged in the 1960's by 1970 had become a complete costumed display. In London, boys in old naval uniforms were parading beside girls in "funky" costumes out of granny's trunk. In Rome, girls with American hillbilly patchwork cottons and Swedish Queen Christina velvet and laces were being eyed by boys dressed as Arabian sheiks. In the United States, the city streets were peopled with characters in fringed frontier suede and buckskin, swinging past maidens in East Indian sarongs and Berber princesses. Everyone in the fashion parade seemed to be playing a part. As Eugenia Sheppard commented, it was all a big costume party for "clothes became costumes and costumes became acceptable as clothes." [14]

Condition of Clothes

At least among the middle class, clean neat clothes are considered to be an asset. The very phrase "white collar"

[12] Russell Lynes, *Snobs* (NewYork: Harper & Row, 1950), pp. 44–45.
[13] Ibid., p. 46.
[14] Eugenia Sheppard, "The Big Costume Party," *Harper's Bazaar* (October, 1970), p. 204.

also implies that the white-collar occupations allow their membership to remain clean while on the job.

Awareness of the condition of clothes appears at times to be related to one's general outlook. Elizabeth Cooley entered these revealing statements in her *Journal* in 1846:

> Sun shining . . . in good health and clean clothes, checked cotton frock, McClure in white suit.
>
> They loaded and unloaded till 2 o'clock—sat about out of hope, out of spirits and patience, out of good water . . . right dirty blue cotton dress, cotton cape.[15]

In a regional research project, two important criteria for skirt selection relating to condition of clothes were cited by mothers of ninth grade girls. These were: "It will hold its shape during wear," and "It doesn't wrinkle readily." The girls themselves also included, "It will hold its shape during wear," as among the ten most important to them.[16]

It was also found that neatness or cleanliness of clothes as well as care of clothes was a source of mother-daughter disagreement as reported by the mothers surveyed in the North Central Region.[17]

Even though the condition of clothes is important to the teenager, she does not always help with the washing, ironing, or altering. A study of high school students in Columbia, Missouri, showed that 53 per cent of the girls did not do washing; 24 per cent did not do ironing; 51 per cent did not wash sweaters; 35 per cent did not change or alter hems. However, 64 per cent of these girls had a private closet in which to keep their clothes.[18]

The Japanese are said to assign the idea of cleanliness to a status that would indeed seem strange to us or at least we would place such behavior in the realm of the extremely prim and proper. In describing a Japanese child's impregnation with ideas of cleanliness, Bernard Rudofsky says that he does not "distinguish between what is aes-

[15] Edward D. Jervey and James E. Moss, editors, "The Journal of Elizabeth Ann Cooley," *Missouri Historical Review*, Vol. LX, No. 2 (January, 1966), p. 182.

[16] "Adolescent Girls' Skirts, Part I: Mothers' and Daughters' Opinions of School Skirts," Norton Central Regional Research Publication, No. 478, Agricultural Experiment Station, University of Minnesota (1965), p. 12.

[17] Ibid., p. 15.

[18] Jean B. Griffin, "A Study of Incomes and Clothing Spending Practices of Hickman High School Girls," unpublished study done at University of Missouri, p. 75.

thetically beautiful and hygienically clean. In his language, clean stands for beautiful, and vice versa."[19]

With the rise of the hippie movement during the 1960's, one of the most noticeable features of dress was a total disregard for cleanliness and neatness. Long dirty hair and beards, filthy clothing, and dirty bare feet were part of the male's protest against his middle-class parents' fetish of cleanliness. Females with stringy, dirty hair and equally untidy clothing were also part of the hippie scene. Sometimes adorned in grotesque eyeglasses or draped animal skins, the true hippie was always dirty.

Describing the use of clothes by today's young people, Charles Reich stated that rips, tears, and missing buttons don't really matter because these clothes have to be able to "take it":

> The clothes are earthy and sensual. They express an affinity with nature. . . . The browns, greens, blues are nature's colors, earth's colors, and the materials are tactile. The clothes are like architecture that does not clash with its natural surroundings but blends in. And the clothes have a functional affinity with nature, too; they don't show dirt—they are good for lying on the ground. . . . Work in them, read in them, play touch football, dance, sit on the floor, go on a camping trip, sleep in them.[20]

[19] Bernard Rudofsky, *The Kimono Mind* (Garden City. N. Y.: Doubleday & Company, Inc., 1965), p. 231.

[20] Charles Reich, "The Greening of America," *New Yorker* (September 26, 1970), p. 95.

5 Situational Awareness

Social psychologists have long been cognizant of the great variety of human behavior. A possible explanation of such diversity is that people often adjust their behavior to changing situations. Awareness of situational conditions can be noted by certain visible cues, of which clothing is one of the most important.

> Thus, for example, every change in a significant life situation—birth, entering school, graduation from school, getting a job, marriage, parenthood, and even death—requires a change of wardrobe. Even in the course of daily life, situation after situation requires a change of dress to facilitate and symbolize the situational changes.[1]

Dressing for dinner is an established custom in many areas of the world. Sometimes the practice is continued even when there would seem to be little need for it. A story is told of an English gentleman who was sent to

[1] Gregory P. Stone and William H. Form, "The Local Community Market: A Study of the Social and Social-Psychological Contexts of Shopping," Agricultural Experiment Station, Bulletin No. 262, Michigan State University (1957), p. 8.

serve as governor of an island where the entire population except himself was black.

> He dressed for his solitary dinner every night as carefully as though he were about to take a taxi to the smartest residence in Park Lane. He did so not from habit, but from a knowledge of human nature. "If," he said, "I should drop this convention of civilized society, I should find myself on the level of the class that I govern. Evening clothes are far more important here than they ever were in London." [2]

Another example is that of changing clothes to go shopping. More than 90 per cent of the women in Vansburg, Michigan, reported that they changed their clothing before embarking on a trip to shop for clothes. Several kinds of clothing were mentioned: dress-up clothing, such as a suit, sheer dress, or hat and accessories; semicasual dress, such as a street dress, or a skirt and blouse; and casual dress, which included a house dress, cotton dress, or sweater and slacks.[3]

Many persons change clothes when they come home from work or shopping. This has long been practiced despite such sentiments as those of Thackeray:

> I have always had rather a contempt for a man who, on arriving at home, deliberately takes his best coat from his back and adopts an old and shabby one. It is a mean precaution. Unless very low in the world indeed, one should be above a proceeding so petty.[4]

Of course, one of the differences today is that few men (or women) change into something old and shabby but rather into "leisure" clothes that are apt to add a sizable amount to the clothing budget.

[2] James T. Adams, "The Mucher Pose," from *Essays in Value*, edited by Irving H. White (New York: Appleton-Century-Crofts, 1938), p. 6.

[3] Stone and Form, op. cit., p. 8.

[4] William Makepeace Thackeray, *The Works of William M. Thackeray, XXV* (Miscellaneous Essays) (Philadelphia: J. B. Lippincott Company, 1885), p. 413.

Awareness of Strangers

One's awareness of clothes is perhaps most acute when one is appearing before or presenting himself to a stranger. Many comments have been made concerning the importance of clothes in the formation of first impressions. George Dearborn [5] stated that well-dressed people create first impressions of successful, powerful individuals who are able to make money and in general reflect positive habits of living. Wilhelmina Jacobson [6] noted the high percentage of *unfavorable* responses related to clothing and grooming during her study of first impressions. Form and Stone reported that more than one third of the white-collar workers they surveyed "dressed up" in order to impress the person hiring them.[7]

An observation by Gordon Allport serves to reinforce these statements when he points out further that first judgments are made with astonishing rapidity:

> With briefest visual perception, a complex mental process is aroused, resulting within a very short time, 30 seconds, perhaps, in judgment of the sex, age, size, nationality, profession and social caste of the stranger, together with some estimate of his temperament, his ascendence, friendliness, neatness, and even his trustworthiness and integrity. With no further acquaintance many impressions may be erroneous, but they show the swift totalizing nature of our judgments.[8]

[5] George Van Ness Dearborn, *The Psychology of Clothes* (Princeton, N. J.: Psychological Review Company, 1918).

[6] Wilhelmina Jacobson, "First Impressions of Classmates," *Journal of Applied Psychology*, Vol. 29, No. 2 (1945), pp. 148–155.

[7] William H. Form and Gregory P. Stone, "The Social Significance of Clothing in Occupational Life," Michigan Agricultural Experiment Station Technical Bulletin, No. 247 (1955), p. 4.

[8] Gordon Allport, *Personality—A Psychological Interpretation* (New York: Holt, Rinehart and Winston, 1937), p. 500.

Dressed Exactly Like Others

Most of us are probably unaware of our clothes when we are dressed in similar fashion to those around us. However, women are certainly aware when they are dressed exactly like someone else. Several years ago the news media played up the story of Elizabeth Taylor and Gina Lollobrigida appearing at a film festival in identical designer dresses.

> It was what best-dressed women have nightmares about and why they pay ransoms for Paris originals. But—beyond all belief—it happened when Elizabeth Taylor and Gina Lollobrigida turned up at a Moscow reception in the same white Dior "original." Liz paled, Gina muttered—Dior seemed caught in an ill-fitting slip.[9]

Edward Gross and Gregory Stone report an incident in which two women dressed exactly alike resolved the situation by spending the whole evening on different sides of the ballroom in which the embarrassing confrontation occurred.[10]

Jean Kerr describes an even more agonizing situation:

> Last spring I saw a play . . . I won't tell you the plot. But it was about this young man who was so disturbed that he turned up in the second act wearing a dress. I don't know what he was disturbed about. But I know what I was disturbed about. He was wearing my dress. I mean the one I had on. There it was, the same check, the same little pique collar, the same dreary buttons down the front. Except for the fact that I wear my hair longer and I'm getting quite gray, we could have been twins.
>
> My first instinct was to flee the premises immediately, perhaps on the pretext that I was suffering appendicitis pains. (After all, it is not widely known

[9] "Double by Dior," *Life Magazine* (July 21, 1961), p. 39.

[10] Edward Gross and Gregory P. Stone, "Embarrassment and the Analysis of Role Requirements," *The American Journal of Sociology*, Vol. LXX, No. 1 (July, 1964), p. 4.

> that I have already parted with my appendix.) But it occurred to me that if I dashed up the center aisle looking precisely like the leading man, I might be regarded as part of the entertainment. So I slouched down into my seat and pressed my purse up under my chin in the hope of covering at least the collar of that wretched dress. Thereafter I just waited until the entire audience had dispersed before I crept out under cover of darkness.[11]

Gross and Stone make the point that men, unlike women, would not be embarrassed to be dressed exactly alike. Men actually *want* their clothes to resemble other men's clothes, when they appear in public places. Gross and Stone go on to state that "except for 'the old school tie' [men's] neckties seem to serve as numbers on a uniform marking each man off from every other."[12]

[11] Jean Kerr, "I Just Stepped Out of Vogue," *Ladies' Home Journal* (May, 1966), p. 109.
[12] Gross and Stone, op. cit., p. 4.

6 Awareness of Incongruities

Another occasion on which one is extremely aware of clothes is the situation in which one person is dressed very differently from the other people present. In most cases this is cause for embarrassment, for we do not like to be thought of as ignorant or unfeeling. Many women who find themselves dressed very differently from others at a social function will be so miserable that the whole affair is ruined for them. It may well be that a person is less aware of an incongruity when he is underdressed, rather than overdressed.

One striking incongruity is the dress of foreigners. In our own country, people in diplomatic service representing other countries often wear their national costume in order to differentiate themselves from Americans. Wearing such clothes is also a matter of national pride. Some visitors to this country wear their national costume for special occasions only, while others, notably the Indians and the Thais, habitually wear their national clothes. Sometimes the American climate only serves to underline such incongruities when we see sandals in the snow, or diaphanous saris hanging below heavy coats.

When two cultures are exposed to each other some striking incongruities can occur in the process of acculturation. Typical examples might include African diplomats wearing top hat and black coat, but with a native

Clothing Incongruities—Cartoons 1970 and 1870

skirt instead of trousers. Rudofsky cites an interesting incongruity in modern Japan as he describes a female swimmer:

> [Her bathing suit] is the color of yellow chrysanthemum, reflecting now and then the glint of a sun already low over the neighboring hills. . . . The lone swimmer seems to be done with the day, and with a few vigorous strokes, returns to shore. At the water's edge she looks for the spot where she left her wooden sandals, finds them and slips them on. Then, not without some difficulty—one can easily see she is not used to it—peels off her bathing suit of fashionable but conservative cut. This done, she throws it over her arm, and without a wrap, without a stitch, without a trace of self-consciousness, walks away—a living allegory of modern Japan.[1]

These examples also bring to mind certain fashion incongruities of recent years, which include winter coats with short sleeves and short skirts with knee warmers. Unfashionable incongruities would be fur coats and anklets.

Age incongruities are not as striking as in the past, perhaps because we are gradually erasing age barriers. The granny dress of teenagers is a conspicuous exception. At the other age extreme, one of the most frequent incongruities mentioned on the Clothing TAT[2] was the "young" clothes on the female figure on Card III. Age was also related to clothing on Cards II, IV, and V. In the approach using cartoons (with hidden captions) age incongruities were cited in several of them.

Other striking incongruities of the present time are men wearing women's clothes and vice versa. However, this phenomenon is so related to both symbol and role that we will discuss it more fully in subsequent chapters.

[1] Bernard Rudofsky, *The Kimono Mind* (Garden City, N. Y.: Doubleday & Company, Inc., 1965), p. 151.

[2] See pages 69–80.

7 Measures of Awareness

Because people find it difficult to verbalize their true feelings, indirect measures can be used to relate to certain feelings and attitudes. Three indirect measures of clothing awareness are described below: a study of clothing memories, the Word Association Test, and the Clothing TAT. Each of these techniques gives us measurable results. Degrees of awareness possessed by certain groups or individuals can then be compared with other groups or individuals.

Clothing Memories

Questions used for clothing memories were as follows:

What is the earliest recollection you have of your own clothing? Describe, please.

How old were you?

What is the earliest recollection you have of someone else's clothing? Whose? Describe, please.

How old were you then?

INTERPRETATION

In general, it was assumed that the earlier the informant's age of memory for his own clothes and the clothes of others, the more aware he was. In addition, the number of details such as color, style, fabric, texture, trimmings, and accessories remembered would also provide clues for degree of awareness. Occasion, feelings of deprivation, evaluation, or comparison of clothes could indicate other dimensions also relating to awareness.[1]

Clothing Word Association Test

This is a word association exercise. Put down the idea or object that comes to your mind as you consider each of the items on the list on p. 63. If another image is aroused, also write down the second thought.

FINDINGS

This list of 44 words, each with a double or triple meaning—one of which could be a clothing referent—drew higher clothing responses from women students as opposed to male students. Mean scores for women were 155 compared with 126 for men. Students majoring in arts, humanities, and social science made more clothing associations than those in engineering and physical science. As one would expect, home economics majors scored highest, with an average score of 234 points. Men over sixty-five years of age had the lowest average score (112); women over sixty-five scored approximately the same as younger women.[2]

Women in general responded with twice as many different clothing words as the males did. Older women used

[1] See pages 6–10 for specific types of responses.

[2] Data were collected by Howard and Mary Lou Rosencranz between 1961 and 1965 at the University of Missouri. An adult sample was also selected in central Missouri.

	1st	2nd
alligator		
attractive		
band		
becoming		
Bermuda		
bow		
boxer		
bright		
colorful		
continental		
cool		
drab		
dull		
felt		
fur		
fuzzy		
gray		
ivy		
jersey		
jockey		
lace		
leather		
loose		
muu-muu		
neat		
nylon		
paisley		
pink		
sack		
sash		
scratchy		
sheath		
short		
slip		
soft		
straight		
straw		
stretch		
stripe		
tie		
tight		
tuck		
uneven		
warm		

Scoring method: Ten points for each "clothing" referent in first column. Five points for each in second column: add for total score.

words such as bonnet, double-ring, stylish, homburg, neckpieces, four-in-hand, and baby dress, whereas younger people never used these words. Both older men and women were apt to use expressions relating to clothes that were too tight or too short.

The word *lace* conjured up the most clothing referents (37); other words eliciting fifteen or more referents were: *colorful, gray, jersey, loose, muu-muu, nylon, paisley, pink, sash, scratchy, slip, soft, stretch, stripe, tie,* and *tight.* The words *Bermuda* and *bright* were associated with only two clothing referents.

The list that follows is a composite of clothing associations for each of the test words that received ten or more clothing responses:

Attractive—13	*Band—11*	*Becoming—11*
chic	belt	clothing
clothes	cummerbund	dress
coat	double-ring	dress color
costume	hat	fad
dress	headband	gown
fashion	ring	hat
hair	sleeve	material
hat	waistband	outfit
model	watchband	silk
outfit	wedding	stylish
stylish	uniforms	style
suit		
well-groomed		

Bow—15	*Colorful—15*	*Continental—14*
belt	bathing suit	appearance
blouse	blouse	Beatles' pants
button	clothes	clothes
decoration	coat	dress
dress	corduroy	French design
hair	costume	Italian cut
hat	dress	Ivy League
ribbon	fashionable	men's clothes
sash	hat	sharp
slippers	madras	slacks
shoestring	material	sport coat
tie	print	styles
tux	scarves	stylish
velvet	silk	suit
waist	umbrella	

Felt—13

belt
circle skirt
coat
fur
hat
heel
homburg
material
seam
silk
skirt
velvet
wool

Fur—15

accessories
cape
coat
collar
ermine
fabric
gloves
hat
jacket
lining
mink coat
neckpiece
sable coat
stole
velvet

Fuzzy—13

angora
bag
clothes
coat
collar
dress
hair
hat
mitten
material
mohair
slippers
sweaters

Gray—16

bonnet
coat
dress
fabric
flannel
garment
hat
herringbone
pants
shawl
shoes
silk
skirt
suit
sweater
tailored

Jersey—17

blouse
coat
clingy
dress
garment
jacket
knit
material
silk
shirt
skirt
slacks
socks
stretches
stretch material
suit
sweater

Lace—37

Alençon
baby dress
blouse
Brussels
Chantilly
clothes
collar
decoration
dress
evening gown
frilly
gown
handkerchief
Irish
jacket
lining
mantilla
material
negligee
nightie
nylon
panties
pattern
ribbon
robe
ruffles
satin
scarf
shawl
shoe
silk
slip
tie
trim
underclothes
veil
wedding dress

Leather—13

accessories
belt
boots
buckle
clothes
coat
fabric
gloves
hose
jacket
purse
shoe
trim

Loose—27

baggy trousers
belt
belted with ease
blouse
bloused
clothes
coat
dress
garment
gown
high fashion
jacket
maternity dress
muu-muu
new style
p j's
sack dress
scarf
shift
shirt
shoe
shorts
skirt
sweater
tie
weave
yarn

Muu-Muu—16

bright prints
dress
duster
flannel
garment
gown
house dress
lingerie
loose gown
maternity clothes
nightgown
prints
robe
sacks
shift
shoe

Nylon—22

blends
blouse
cloth
clothes
dacron
dress
drip-dry
fiber
hose
hat
jersey
linens
orlon
pants
sheer
shoes
silk
slip
socks
stockings
underwear
uniform

Paisley—17

blouse
chic
cloth
dress
handkerchief
lace
overall print material
print
print blouse
print fabric
scarf
shawl
shirt
silk
smock
stripes
tie

Pink—18

blouse
dress
Jackie Kennedy suits
material
mohair dress
pajamas
panties
ribbon
satin
shoe
shoelaces
skirt
slip
socks
suit
sweater
tights
umbrella

Sash—18

apron
band
belt
bow
clothes
cummerbund
dress
girdle
Japanese Obi
little girl's dress
ribbon
robe
satin
scarf
silk
sissy
tie
waistband

Scratchy—15

burlap
clothes
dress
flannel
material
mohair
net
nylon
pants
shirt
slip
suit
sweater
underwear
wool

Sheath—10

black dress
chic
dress
muu-muu
no belt
skirt
straight
style
tight dress
umbrella

Short—13

dress
dress too short
garment
hem lines
jacket
kilts
pants
shorts
skirt
sleeve
slip
sportswear
style

Slip—19

Barbizon
bra
chemise
dacron
dress
French
garment
gown
hand-embroidered
lace
lacy
lingerie
nylon
pantaloons
petticoat
silk
too hot for summer
underclothes
white lace

Soft—16

blouse
cashmere
chamois
coat
cotton
felt
flannel
fur
material
mohair
nylon
satin
shoes
silk
sweater
velvet

Stretch—17

belt
clothes
fabric
girdle
gloves
hose
jersey
Lycra
nylon
pants
riding pants
sew
slacks
socks
sweater
tights
worn too tight

Stripe—23

belt
blazer
blouse
clothes
decoration
design
dress
fabric
hat
jacket
material
pants
pin
plaid
polka-dot
robe
shirt
suit
tie
T-shirt
towel
umbrella
wedding

Tie—28

accessory
band
belt
blouse
bow tie
clothing
coat
collar
cravat
dress
dress-up
four-in-hand
hat
madras
necktie
pin
polka-dot
ribbon
scarf
sharp
shirt
shoe
shoestring
silk
skirt
stripes
suit
warp

Tight—19

bathing suit
bad taste in skirt
belt
close fit
clothes
collar
dress
girdle
hat
levis
pants
sheath
shoes
shorts
skirt
slacks
slim jims
stockings
tie

Tuck—16

bib
blouse
clothes
dress
fashion
gather
hem
pleat
sew
sewing
shirt
skirt
slip
trim
trousers
tux

Uneven—10

blue jeans
cuffs
hems
lines
plaid
seams
skirt
slip
trims
unsightly

Warm—10

coat
clothes
dress
fur
hat
long johns
milium-lined
material
sweater
wool [3]

[3] Only those words that elicited ten or more clothing responses are included.

Clothing TAT

The Clothing TAT [4] is a modified Thematic Apperception Test based on the fact that an individual required to interpret an ambiguous social situation is apt to reveal his own personality in the process. Experience has shown that responses are much more meaningful when the subject is asked to tell a dramatic story about each of a series of pictures or drawings. In addition, the TAT avoids some of the misinterpretations that may be inherent in worded questions.

The Clothing TAT consists of seven drawings (see figs.) depicting incongruities between the clothing of the characters in the drawings and other attributes such as age, sex, or build; incongruities between the clothing of two characters; or incongruities between clothing and the background in the drawing. The drawings were designed so that details associated with current fashions were not emphasized. In fact, most of the clothing pictured could have been worn at any time during the past thirty years.

A pretest gauged the effectiveness of the pictures. It also helped to train interviewers, who memorized standardized instructions for presenting the pictures and for probing at certain specific places during the interview. Several pictures were then revised. All interviews were tape-recorded to obtain the complete response and to prevent any interviewer-bias in rewording the responses.

The Clothing TAT was administered to eighty-two married men and women in Vansburg,[5] a small city of

[4] The committee responsible for this project included Gregory P. Stone, William H. Form, Duane L. Gibson, Charles P. Loomis, Charles R. Hoffer, and John Useem of the department of sociology and anthropology; and Hazel B. Strahan and Mary Lou Rosencranz of the department of textiles, clothing, and related arts at Michigan State University. The actual drawings were done by Margaret C. Stone. Credit for the initial idea for the Clothing TAT must be given to Gregory P. Stone. Scoring method and pattern of analysis were developed by Mary Lou Rosencranz in 1959.

[5] Vansburg is a pseudonym used to preserve the anonymity because of the personal nature of many responses.

Card 1

Card II

Card III

Card IV

Card V

Card VI

Card VII

approximately 10,000 population in south-central Michigan. The informants were selected by a stratified-random technique, in that the occupations of all married men in the city were classified and ranked according to a seven-point scale of occupational prestige,[6] then cases were drawn at random from each stratum in proportion to the total number of married men within each occupational stratum.

The revised Clothing TAT took from thirty minutes to an hour and a half to administer. The test was given as the last part of a battery of questionnaires used in a total clothing study. However, the Clothing TAT was given in a separate interview, and the informants were simply told that they were going to be shown a series of pictures—clothing was not mentioned in the interviewer's introductory remarks.

After the informant had responded to all the cards, each card was again presented to the informant, who was then told, "Those were very interesting stories you told me. I am going to show you the cards again briefly one at a time and would like you to tell me what there was about each card that suggested the story to you." If the informant had difficulty in stating the particular element that suggested the story, he or she was then asked, "What did you think was the most outstanding thing about this picture when you looked at it?"

SCORING METHOD

The first concern in the development of a scoring system centered around the design of a clothing awareness score for each protocol. Each TAT response was transposed from the recording tape to typewritten pages. All typewritten lines that were comments about the clothing of the various characters were underlined in colored pencil for easy identification. The clothing awareness score was compiled by a simple addition of the following components:

1. The number of typewritten lines of clothing comments.
2. The number of characters whose clothing was mentioned.

[6] Described in Lloyd Warner, Marchia Meeker, and Kenneth Eels, *Social Class in America* (Chicago: Science Research Associates, 1949).

3. The number of cards about which the informant stated that clothing gave her the idea for her story.

4. The number of clothing incongruities that were mentioned.

5. The number of themes that were expressed in relation to clothing.

The general hypotheses considered were that

1. Social class and its related variables (occupation, income, education, organizational level, and magazine readership) will be positively related to clothing awareness.

2. Age will be negatively related to clothing awareness.

3. Rural/urban background will be positively related to clothing awareness.

4. Verbal intelligence (use of good English; many adjectives and adverbs; complex and compound sentences; good, original stories) will be positively related to clothing awareness.

The average number of lines of clothing comment was twenty-six lines or about one fourth of the total remarks made by the average informant. Fifty per cent of the comments of five women were clothing comments; approximately one third of the comments of the twenty women with highest scores were clothing comments; only one tenth of the comments of the twenty lowest-scoring women were clothing comments. The card evoking the greatest number of clothing comments pictured two women (Card V), whereas the card yielding the fewest lines of clothing comment portrayed two men (Card II). In fact, all cards having more men than women ranked low in amount of clothing comment (for women informants).

In general, the clothing of the woman on Card III evoked more comments than did that of any other character (96 per cent). The apparel of the two girls on Card V was noted by more than 90 per cent of the respondents. The man in a skirt on Card VII was discussed by 80 per cent of the women. More than 70 per cent noted the clothing of each of the women on Card IV and the center girl on Card I.

Men were more likely to notice the boy in the T-shirt in Card I and the male character on Card III than were women. Fifteen per cent of the men identified the sex of the figure on the right of Card II as a female, whereas none of the women respondents were confused by this character.

In analyzing data by social class it was found that upper-class males and females had identical average numbers of lines of clothing comment, while lower-class females had considerably more clothing comment than lower-class males. This difference was statistically significant.

When total clothing awareness scores were tested against selected background variables of the informants, it was found that women with high awareness scores were of the upper social class, belonged to a greater number of organizations, had a higher educational level, had a higher income, subscribed to a greater number of magazines, had higher verbal intelligence, and had husbands in the white-collar occupational group.

Of the nine hypotheses proposed in relation to clothing awareness, seven were substantiated in data analyses. Social class and all of its related indices (occupation, income, education, organizational membership, and magazine readership) were found to have significant relationships to clothing awareness. Verbal intelligence proved to have a significant association with clothing awareness. The two variables *not* significantly related to clothing awareness were age and rural/urban background.

The Clothing TAT produced more clothing responses from women than from men. Although men told longer stories than women (3,335 typewritten pages of comment as compared with 3,250 pages for the same number of women), the latter had 313 more lines of comment about clothing. In six of the seven cards women also stated that clothing gave them their ideas for a story more often than men. The clothing of eleven different characters was noted by 50 per cent or more of the women while the clothing of nine characters was observed by 50 per cent or more of the male informants. However, men did comment on male clothing more often than women.

Social class was related to degree of clothing awareness in that upper-class women had significantly higher awareness scores than lower-class women; upper-class males also had higher scores than lower-class males, although these were not statistically significant.

An adaptation of the original Clothing TAT was made by Carol Sanders Bathke in order to identify clothing responses related to sociocultural differences, specifically in women of Mexican-American and Anglo-American origin. Both groups of women told stories about six pictures with built-in clothing incongruities.

Bathke [7] found that the Mexican-American homemakers were significantly less aware of clothing than were the Anglo-American women. When considering themes, Mexican-Americans were more likely to mention age-related incongruities, while the Anglo-Americans generally mentioned social status differences. Age related to authority for Mexican-Americans, thus clothing inappropriate for age was noted; the Anglo-Americans often felt that people belonged to a particular class because of the clothing. In terms of cultural patterns, Mexican, Negroid, and Oriental influences were mentioned more often by Mexican-Americans than by Anglo-Americans.

Clothing Cartoons

This study was designed to determine individual awareness of clothing pictured in several types of commercial cartoons.

A variety of fourteen cartoons were selected from newspapers and magazines. These cartoons were drawings of children, teenagers, and adults. Some cartoons included both men and women, while others were of women or only of men. The situations illustrated in the cartoons were appropriateness of dress for the times or the occasion, dress for size, and dress for age or status.

The captions to the cartoons were folded under the pictures and then mounted in groups of two or three on different cards. Although several cartoons were in color, all were reduced to black and white when a pretest showed no differences in response to color as compared with black and white.

The cartoons were shown to fifty men and to fifty women of varying ages. Four examples are given below.

[7] Carol Sanders Bathke, "Ethnic Responses to a Modified Clothing TAT," *Journal of Home Economics*, Vol. 60, No. 5 (May, 1968), p. 354.

"I think it gives me a sort of sophisticated look!" (Courtesy of McCall's)

CARTOON I

In this picture of two small children on a beach, 65 per cent of the women and 83 per cent of the men noticed clothing.

Half of the women noticed the type of garment; other women spoke about status. Men, more often than women, referred to age in relation to the type of swimwear.

"It's just a big elastic band to hold my mother together." (Courtesy of McCall's)

CARTOON II

In describing the picture of two little boys (one holding a girdle), some respondents thought of games: "It makes a great big sling shot." Others mentioned that "Mom fights the battle of the bulge with this."

Most people used their imaginations to tell what a little boy would do with an article of this type. The situation directed them away from ideas about the usual purpose of the garment. More men than women talked about the girdle (100 per cent versus 60 per cent of the women).

"Nothing. What's new with you?" (*Courtesy of* McCall's)

CARTOON III

While looking at the picture of two women, one wearing a dress from the twenties, many informants wrote satirical captions indicating social status. An example is "Mr. Cassini designs my clothes." Others tried to rationalize the dress through captions such as "It was sheer impulse."

A few were phrases identified with the style of the dress, such as "23 skidoo."

The high-school girls were actually more analytical in relating comments to the style or age of the garment. Consciousness of style was expressed as "I was looking through my clothes and decided to start a fad." An example indicating age was "I just got to thinking about the good old days." Graduate students seemed to be more concerned about prestige, or lack of it, while high-school students were more verbal in direct relation to the style of the dress and the time.

"I must be getting old. My husband makes it faster than I can spend it." (*Courtesy of Edward Frascino*)

CARTOON IV

In describing the two tired shoppers, the captions were divided almost in half between relationship to money and abstract comments that made no reference to money, clothing, or the specific situation. Women were more apt to mention clothing than were men.

Fashion Awareness Test

A Fashion Awareness Test was given to several hundred men and women ranging in age from twenty to eighty years.[8] Informants were shown a series of twenty-four black and white pictures and were asked to record the date when they believed the picture had originally appeared as fashion news. After a pretest, seventeen pictures were selected as producing the greatest range of discrimination between high- and low-scoring persons. Scores were calculated by subtracting the difference between the year the informant listed and the correct year. The years that the fashions represented ranged from 1926 to 1961.

Scores ranged from 30 points to 412 points. In general, lower scores (which means the most nearly correct dates) were made by young women and the higher scores were typical of older people, particularly men. (One notable exception, however, was a seventy-year-old man who scored 43 points.)

Average scores for people in different categories were:

Students studying the history of costume	68
Females under forty	76
Females over forty	166
Males under forty	154
Males over forty	198

Pictures that were identified correctly most often were a 1926 chemise and a 1958 chemise; the average number of years of mistaken identity were 3.4 and 3.6 respectively. Dates of the more difficult pictures were those of the 1950's, no doubt due to the great variety of fashions worn in that decade.

No illustrations are included for the Fashion Awareness Test, for it is easy to construct such a test with clippings from fashion magazines ranging over several decades. A word of caution—select pictures that show the whole figure, including head and feet. There are periods when skirt length and accessories are the main cues for dating fashions.

[8] This test was given in central Missouri during 1964–1967.

Attitudes Toward Specific Fashions

Twelve photographs of contemporary garments that made fashion "news" during 1964 were shown to both men and women in order to elicit comments and opinions.[9] The subjects were told to look at the photograph of each fashion and were asked: "What do you think of the clothing in this picture?" All subjects were also asked whether or not they would wear the clothes they were shown or, in the case of clothing for the opposite sex, if they would mind being seen with someone dressed in this manner.

The one hundred informants ranged in age from twenty to sixty years, but were all from a middle-income group, living either in Columbia, Missouri, or in Pitman, New Jersey.

Responses were categorized in terms of themes such as modesty, sexual appeal, fashion, status, fit, expense, design and style, comfort, practicality, casualness, femininity or masculinity, and suitability for occasion. Feelings of approval or disapproval were also noted.

FINDINGS

Women were much more concerned about the fashion of the garment and its design and style than the men were. They also were more interested in the ease with which it could be worn ("naturalness and comfort") and the fabric. Women were critical of the model and the setting of the photograph. "Suitability for occasion," "suitability for age of wearer," and "suitability for figure of wearer" were mentioned significantly more times by women than by men. Women also commented on casualness and practicality of the garment more than men did, though men evaluated the photographs as a whole more frequently than women did.

[9] Judy Wells Eddy, "An Investigation of Attitudes and Opinions Toward Selected Clothing Fashions, Utilizing a Projective Technique," unpublished Master's thesis, University of Missouri, 1965.

Men commented significantly more often on "overall appearance and taste," "grooming," and "posture and pose of the wearer" than the women did. These comments seem to be consistent with male tendencies to state nonspecific general themes. In addition, men commented on the sexual appeal inherent in the garment and whether the design appeared to be masculine or feminine to them.

Descriptions of five selected pictures and the themes associated with them are as follows.

London Schoolboys (Terence Spencer, LIFE *Magazine* © *Time Inc.*)

PICTURE 1

Two young men are standing on either side of a lamppost. Both have long, bowl-cut hair styles. The boy on the left is wearing a collarless jacket with a paisley shirt and tie. His shoes are highly polished with pointed toes. The boy on the right is wearing a jacket which has a collar, but no lapels. He is wearing a dark shirt with white polka dots. His trousers are slightly flared. His boot-style shoes have narrow heels. The legend "Keep Britain Tidy" is barely visible on a waste-can attached to the lamp-post.[10]

The English "Mods" received the most "casualness," "feminine or masculine," "grooming of wearer," and "nationality" thematic comments. More than half of the respondents disapproved of the picture; another 23 per cent were undecided about it. Women remarked about overall taste and appearance; older respondents most disliked the picture.

PICTURE 2

In the foreground, a woman is seated at a desk, holding a telephone. The setting appears to be a busy office . . . several men in shirtsleeves and ties are visible in the background. The woman is wearing a low-cut black dress with a large white horseshoe-type collar and white cuffs on three-quarter-length sleeves.[11]

[10] *Life* (January 31, 1964), p. 31.
[11] "Necklines Make You Nervous?" *The Saturday Evening Post* (February 22, 1964), p. 28.

This picture prompted most of the "modesty" and "suitability for occasion" themes; two thirds to three fourths of the respondents, respectively, mentioned such themes. It was "disapproved" by the largest number of people. Respondents from the Midwest disapproved more often than those from the East Coast.

PICTURE 3

A girl wearing tight-fitting melon-colored slacks and a blouse in a lighter tint of the same color is posed by an

ornately carved doorway. She is looking back over her shoulder at the camera behind her. Her shoes are white canvas.[12]

Themes most often associated with this picture were "overall appearance and taste," "fit on wearer," "posture and pose of wearer," "suitability for figure of wearer," and "color." About 30 per cent more of the younger women respondents than older ones stated that they would wear the outfit.

PICTURE 4

A girl wears a low-cut sheath dress with little fit at the waistline. She appears to be dancing—a well-dressed man is with her, other couples and what may be a band

[12] "The Fair Young Hollywood Girls," *The Saturday Evening Post* (September 7, 1963), p. 23.

are behind her. The fabric in her dress is a large printed design in pink and white.[13]

Fifty per cent of the thematic responses were directed toward "modesty" of the dress. Most of the comments had an element of disapproval, indicating that informants felt that the garment was immodest even though the setting may have been appropriate.

The printed fabric in this picture received the second highest number of comments. Almost a third of the respondents noted the fabric. Almost 40 per cent more younger respondents liked it than did older people.

(*Courtesy of Milton H. Greene Studios*)

PICTURE 5

A model is wearing tight-fitting white lace slacks with low white boots. The slacks are cut lower than normal

[13] "Necklines Make You Nervous?" op. cit., p. 26.

at the waistline in the back, and the matching lace jacket is fastened at the neckline in the back by a satin bow, leaving the rest of the jacket free to show her bare back. The model wears large jeweled earrings and is shown standing in front of a mirror, her back facing the camera.[14]

The themes used most often for this picture were "suitability for occasion," "modesty," and "overall appearance and taste." More sexual appeal comments were noted for it than for any other picture. It was least favored by both sexes, and by the Midwesterners. Thirty-three per cent more in the older group disliked it than in the younger age group.

Measurement of Awareness by Questionnaire

Using a Scalogram Analysis, Arthur M. Vener[15] determined clothing awareness scores for 782 twelfth-, tenth-, and eighth-grade boys and girls in Lansing, Michigan. Types of questions ranked on five-point scales according to level of sensitivity to clothing in social life are as follows:

How much thought and attention do you think someone your age should give to clothes?

Do you ever want to know whether other people like or dislike your clothes?

I don't enjoy wearing my clothes unless my friends like them.

How often do you pay attention to the clothes you wear?

Findings include the following:

1. Girls demonstrate greater clothing awareness than boys.
2. Girls who participate more in organizational activity, i.e., belong to more organizations and hold some official

[14] *Life* (June 5, 1964), p. 127.

[15] For other details, see Arthur M. Vener, "Adolescent Orientations to Clothing: A Social-Psychological Interpretation," unpublished Ph.D. dissertation, Michigan State University, March, 1957.

position in these organizations, tend to demonstrate greater clothing awareness.

3. Girls who are more socially confident tend to be less aware of clothing.

4. Boys and girls who are more other-directed tend to be more aware of clothing. For girls only the statistical significance of the association and degree of association of these variables is much greater.

Measurement of Interest in Clothing

Closely related to awareness is interest in clothing; an index of interest developed by the author [16] makes use of questions fashioned around types of behavior revealing time, energy, money, thought, or attention devoted to clothing. A minimum of emphasis was placed on the actual amount of money spent for clothing so that economic status would not be the most important factor in the resulting score.

Questions used to measure time and energy spent on clothing included looking carefully at fashion advertisements, shopping for clothing or fabrics, planning a season's wardrobe, deciding in advance upon clothes for special occasions, checking clothing for needed cleaning and repair, helping friends select clothing, remaking old clothing, and reading fashion magazines.

To measure amount of attention given to clothing, questions were formulated on the following items: observing, when at a movie, the name of the costume designer and details of costumes; indulging in window shopping; choosing a high-style fashion magazine from an offering of many types; noticing how people in the street are dressed; working out ensembles that would be inter-

[16] Mary Lou Rosencranz, "A Study of Interest in Clothing Among Selected Groups of Married and Unmarried Young Women," unpublished Master's thesis, Michigan State University, 1948.

changeable; discussing style trends; and acquainting oneself with the incoming fashions.

Questions that related to the amount of money one would spend on clothing concerned the number of trips made locally or out of town to buy clothing, disposition of a gift of one hundred dollars, and frequency of buying a new formal dress.

Other questions indicated the range of types of clothes in a wardrobe, frequency of buying new clothes, interest in having others think the informant well dressed, and willingness to make special efforts to be well dressed.

Age, rural or urban background, occupation, and income had a significant positive relationship to total scores in the Clothing Interest Questionnaire. Education, marital status, number of children in the family, and membership in organizations also had a positive relationship to women's interest in clothing, but to a lesser degree.

The most discriminating question measured the range of types of clothing each person had in her present wardrobe. Although it is possible that the number of types of clothing would measure economic status as well as interest in clothing, a statistical test showed the relationship between this item and income not to be significant.

Questions next in their discriminative value measured attention given to clothing by reading fashion magazines, reading fashion advertisements in the newspapers, recognizing fashion designers, and recognizing brand names. Other valid measures were related to the time and energy used to make clothes when a woman could not buy what she preferred.

An adaptation of the Clothing Interest Inventory was used by Christopher K. Knapper [17] in a study of the relationship between personality and style of dress for males. Knapper's purpose was to determine whether or not there were systematic relationships between personality of the wearer and judged clothing style. A "clothing differential" using thirty-two scales was designed to measure the four factors of neatness, originality, trying to impress, and coordination. Peer ratings on the clothing differential were

[17] Christopher Kay Knapper, "The Relationship Between Personality and Style of Dress," unpublished Ph.D. dissertation, Division of Social Sciences, University of Saskatchewan, Canada, 1968.

obtained from eighty-eight males; these were intercorrelated with two measures of personality as well as measures of clothing interest, clothing satisfaction, socioeconomic status and rural/urban background.

Clothing measures obtained from the wearer himself correlated significantly with most of the personality dimensions; high clothing interest was related to extraversion and poor adjustment; high clothing satisfaction indicated a wearer who was outgoing and who coped well with social relationships.

Very few correlations between personality and peer ratings on clothing were significant. "This implies that whatever relationships exist between clothing and the personality of the wearer, it is unlikely that many of these relationships can be detected by most observers. Hence, perceivers who use clothing as a cue to personality are likely to make inaccurate judgments." [18]

Clothing interest and clothing satisfaction were related. "Wearers who were satisfied with their appearance saw themselves, and were seen by others as good, neat, original, coordinating dressers. Students with high interest in clothes rated themselves similarly, but paradoxically were seen by their peers as merely trying to impress." [19]

[18] Ibid., see abstract.
[19] Ibid.

Part Two

CLOTHING SYMBOLS

At all stages in the development of his civilization, man has used symbols. Wherever we look, be it art, language, literature, material possessions, religion, dreams, or visions, our worlds of the past and present are filled with symbolism. In general the symbolic is instrumental in giving value and meaning; though not universal it is usually crystallized in time and space. Some symbols conceived on a grand scale are used to link the human with the cosmic or to impose order on disorder; indeed, they are an enrichment of what is significant in life, and offer a continuity in communication and a sense-making shorthand.

Clothing symbols are so widely and so frequently used that we are often unaware of their true significance. Because it may represent or stand for something else we concentrate on the message and not the medium, which is clothing or some aspect of appearance. It is only when we break down the elements of a symbolic system that we become cognizant of the part that clothing plays in the total situation or cultural complex—how it modifies and is modified by the other components. However, if the dissection of a single clothing symbol is carried too far and is not considered in total context, the identity and meaning of the symbol may be lost. In our day-to-day living we do not have to analyze constantly or to have "instant replay" of a situation in order to appreciate and use clothing symbolism effectively.

In this discussion several dichotomies will be used to play up various facets that are involved in clothing and appearance symbolism. As a point of departure we will consider individuality as contrasted with conformity. Examples of famous historical style innovators as well as present day clothing individualists will be included. The uniqueness of the self expressed by clothing in our mass-produced milieu is as important today as at any time in history.

In the discussion of custom versus fashion we will examine the merit attributed and reverence shown to old and time-honored clothing and ornaments the world around. We will also scrutinize meanings that change as new values are assigned to new modes of clothing behavior. The vigorous critics as well as the eloquent supporters of fashion change will have their due.

Status variations from high to low will be examined in a variety of economic, religious, social, and political continua. Symbols range in kind, amount, elaborateness, costliness, and rarity, with strange reverses sometimes showing at the top or bottom of a status scale—the non-conspicuous consumers on the top compared with great emphasis on clothes among the low-income Puerto Ricans in New York City. Although we will spotlight such exceptions, the usual expectation of finding Veblen's conspicuous consumers in high status positions still holds true for most urban dwellers.

Another dichotomy is that of work and leisure. A brief look at the development of sportswear shows how it coincides with the development of leisure clothes.

Sex-related clothing is discussed on two planes of a very complex sphere: the masculine-feminine vector and the sex attraction to sex de-emphasis dimension. Clothing symbols may be changing faster in this area than in any other as we approach the end of this century.

The youth to age symbolism also has much verbal and pseudopsychological coverage in mass media today. Clothing looms large as a symbol of attitudes toward and acceptance or rejection of age positions.

Although taste may have as many definitions, and thus as many meaningful symbols, as there are people who examine the subject, there is a place for defining clothing and appearance as an expression of taste. If, indeed, accepted symbols of "good taste" are rare, there are countless symbols of indifference to taste.

A few measures of clothing symbols are included to show the little progress we have made in quantification and analysis of clothing symbols. This is an area that cries out for research tools.

8 Individuality and Conformity

One of Adler's major contributions to personality theory was the concept of the "creative self."

> Adler's self is a highly personalized, subjective system which interprets and makes meaningful the experiences of the organism. Moreover, it searches for experiences which will aid in fulfilling the person's unique style of life; if these experiences are not to be found in the world, the self tries to create them.[1]

Another aspect of Adler's psychology was its emphasis upon the uniqueness of personality. "Adler considered each person to be a unique configuration of motives, traits, interests, and values; every act performed by the person bears the stamp of his own distinctive style of life."[2] Adler felt that although every man has the same goal, that of superiority, not every man will utilize the same means in seeking to attain this goal.

In writing about clothing and the self, George Hartmann made these illuminating remarks:

> Clothes are, therefore, valuable (in the larger psychological sense which embraces more than the nar-

[1] Calvin S. Hall and Gardner Lindzey, *Theories of Personality* (New York: John Wiley & Sons, Inc., 1957), p. 117.
[2] Ibid., p. 118.

rowly economic) only to the degree that they enhance the value and experiences of the persons who wear them or who are otherwise affected by them. In other words, the subjective worth of any article of attire is proportionate to its contribution to some sort of extension or differentiation or enrichment of the self. The self with that piece of clothing must become a better self than it is without; otherwise, the item either makes no vital difference or fails to fulfill its function.[3]

This differentiation or enrichment provided by clothing is also reminiscent of one of the five basic needs that Eric Fromm suggests as rising from the condition of man's existence: "*the urge for transcendance* refers to man's need to rise above his animal nature, to become a creative person instead of remaining a creature."[4]

Let us examine some individuals who expressed themselves creatively and uniquely through their clothes. George Bryan Brummell, English fashion plate of the early 19th Century, has been described by various sources as dazzling, insolent, magnificent, romantic, practical, self-centered, unself-conscious, egotistical, haughty, and amusing, wearing the clothes of a dandy, that is, superbly suitable to the occasion and little more.

> The dandy is never shocked and never delighted. Indeed, it is his immunity from commonplace passions that makes it possible for him to impose himself upon society and carry egotism to a point where it is almost disinterested. He is intensely self-centered, yet also a stoic; for what moves him is not a vulgar concern with self-adornment, which measures its satisfaction by the approval of others, but a worship of perfection that is its own reward.[5]

In order to have his claim to magnificence, Brummell wore boots with blackened soles, a perfect neckcloth (whose tie was achieved only after hours of labor), and

[3] George W. Hartmann, "Clothing: Personal Problem and Social Issue," *Journal of Home Economics*, Vol. 41, No. 6 (June, 1949), p. 296.

[4] Eric Fromm, *The Sane Society* (New York: Holt, Rinehart and Winston, Inc., 1955), p. 36.

[5] Peter Quennell, "George Bryan Brummell," *Harper's Bazaar* (January, 1953), p. 93.

arrived in a cushioned sedan chair at the foot of a staircase or on the very threshold of a gathering that he expected to dazzle. Even when living in exile in France, in penury because of his gambling debts, he paid a washerwoman a third of his small income, for he still changed shirts three times a day and used gallons of hair oil and quarts of blacking.

Beau's two most significant contributions to dandyism were his inauguration of regular bathing and the fact that although he spent hours getting ready to appear in public, when launched in a drawing room, he never once glanced in a mirror or adjusted his clothes—he *knew* he was perfect!

Dame Edith Sitwell, a female whose individual approach to clothes is undeniable, on her seventy-fifth birthday wore a baroque red velvet gown, a black and gold turban, and a massive gold necklace. Her comments about her medieval attire were: "I think it's a mistake to dress like a mouse. Except when it comes to bravery, we are a nation of mice. We dress and behave with timid circumspection. Good taste is the worst vice ever invented." [6]

Bobby Fischer, the chess genius, expresses his feeling for clothes:

> Yes, I used to dress badly until I was about sixteen. But people just didn't seem to have enough respect for me, you know? And I didn't like that, so I decided I'd have to show them they weren't any better than me. They would say, he beat us at chess, but he's still just an uncouth kid wearing sneakers and blue jeans. So I decided to dress up.[7]

Bobby reported in an interview with Ralph Ginsburg that he would not touch ready-to-wear. He had suits made for him in Germany, Italy, Argentina, Trinidad, England, New York, and California. His shoes were handmade and his shirts cost $25.00 each.

Periodically fashion magazines note the "individual" response to fashion by quoting famous individuals. Examples: Mrs. Winston Guest buys designer suits and wears them happily for seven, eight, or nine years. She tends to underdress and buys few French dresses because

[6] Dame Edith Sitwell, *Time* (September 14, 1962), p. 44.
[7] Ralph Ginsburg, *Harper's Magazine* (January, 1962), p. 53.

Individualists—1970

they are too complex. She even buys reams of shirts at boys' departments. The great strength of her fashion personality lies in a simple fact: she knows what it is.[8]

In the same article Mrs. Henry Fonda is described as one who limits her clothing looks to three looks: the dress and jacket look for days, a series of dinner-skirt looks for entertaining at home, and a romantic look featuring glamorous evening dresses.[9]

[8] "Have You a Fashion Personality?" *Vogue* (April 1, 1959), p. 84.
[9] Ibid., p. 88.

In the 1960's, clothing personalities in the high fashion magazines included such young individualists as Nancy Sinatra wearing Pucci prints, Gernreich's high potency colors, Jax pants-suits, and pairs of leather boots,[10] or tall, rangy Vanessa Redgrave, "new heroine in lace, frills, and pants," or "a star in a star's color—bright chrome yellow."[11]

For an individual who really wanted to capture the center of the stage the new electrifying fashions that TURN ON and FLASH were bound to please. Dresses designed by Diana Dew were striped with light panels resembling ironed-flat neon tubes, which were wired at the hem and connected to a battery pack camouflaged into a dropped waist belt. Turn the switch and it lights; turn another and alternate the speed, and the tubes flash from right to left or left to right.[12]

Individuality in clothing in the 1970's is most widely expressed in the dress of young people. Avoiding the usual mass produced sources, young individualists buy from boutiques or army and navy surplus stores, search the attic for "old" clothes, or fashion their own from leather, patchwork quilts, and drapery fabrics.

Two black fashion individualists of 1970 are described in *Essence* magazine. Pat Evans, a model and trend setter, has eliminated her head of hair with a razor and now displays a well-shaped cranium that is her trademark. Shedding her hair has also changed her way of dressing: her clothes are now worn as costumes—and she has a different costume for each day. "More fantasy is needed in these troubled times," she says. "Clothes should be sensational and unusual without being complicated."[13] With a different approach to fashion, model Ramona Saunders wears her hair braided in front in eight tiny wisps, bound in leather thongs and hung with masses of little brass rings. "She sets off the hairdo with a lacquer red skirt, black satin shirt and black satin boots, as flat as a ballet slipper. She looks like a present day African princess."[14]

[10] "Sinatra Is Her Name," *Harper's Bazaar* (October, 1966), p. 144.

[11] *Vogue* (August 1, 1966), pp. 93–97.

[12] "Electrifying Fashion," *Home Furnishings Daily* (December 30, 1966).

[13] "Tastemakers," *Essence* (September, 1970), p. 30.

[14] Ibid., p. 47.

Conformity

Rudofsky says that the clothes we wear are "anachronistic, irrational and harmful." [15] Baker Brownell uses even stronger language:

> That men in a modern age will tolerate such clothing indicates, to say the least, an insensitivity and a stupid fear of change that is alarming. Can a worthwhile new world come of such a head of asses? It begins to seem doubtful.[16]

William H. Flower discusses the propensity to deform or alter the natural form which is practiced by primitive and barbarian peoples as well as civilized and refined societies. He observes that alterations on the human body, once made, cannot change as easily as fashions in apparel. He continues by reflecting:

> The origins of these fashions are mostly lost in obscurity, . . . but whatever their origin, the desire to conform to common usage, and not to appear singular, is the prevailing motive which leads to their continuance. They are perpetuated by imitation, which, as Herbert Spencer says, may result from two widely divergent motives. It may be prompted by reverence for one imitated or it may be prompted by the desire to assert equality with him.[17]

It is a well-known fact that most children from the age of entering school through early adolescence tend to conform in dress. The symbol of uniform dress helps in the socialization process and gives the child a protective badge. Elizabeth Hurlock says that, as he grows older, the adolescent's desire to identify with the herd shifts to a desire

[15] Bernard Rudofsky, *Are Clothes Modern?* (Chicago: Paul Theobold, 1947), p. 115.

[16] Baker Brownell, *Art Is Action* (New York: Harper & Row, 1939), p. 195.

[17] William Henry Flower, "Fashion in Deformity," in *Humboldt Library of Popular Science Literature*, Vol. 5, No. 28 (New York, 1882), p. 2.

Uniforms—Nautical Nurse
Stewardess with
Boots and Bubble

to identify with a small group.[18] One's popularity often depends upon being dressed like the group.[19] Stone found that early recollections of informants' wanting to wear a particular item of clothing almost unanimously cited appropriations of the dress of their peer groups.[20]

[18] Elizabeth Hurlock, *Adolescent Development* (New York: McGraw-Hill, Inc., 1949), p. 15.

[19] C. M. Tryon, "Evaluations of Adolescent Personality by Adolescents," *Monographs of the Society for Research in Child Development*, Vol. IV, No. 4 (1939), p. 83.

[20] Gregory P. Stone, "Appearance and the Self," in A. M. Rose, *Human Behavior and Social Processes* (New York: Houghton Mifflin Company, 1962), p. 108.

The use of the uniform is a case of almost complete conformity. Certain jobs for adults require uniforms for purposes of cleanliness (doctors, nurses, dentists, food service people), or convenience, in various service occupations. Uniforms can be used as symbols of authority (policemen, government officials, and to denote particular rank in the academic and military fields), or as symbols of submission (the livery of servants or slaves, prison stripes, the overalls of some military personnel).

The relationship of the uniform to symbols of authority poses several problems, which are outlined by Langner:

> After the uniform was invented to indicate that the men wearing it were all uniformly subject to the same rules of authority, humanity found itself in a dilemma. The uniform denoted uniformity, but there was also a need to distinguish the superiority of one or more persons in uniform over the others. Man's ingenuity came into play again, and he invented the insignia, the stripe, the epaulette, or some other variation in the uniform to indicate the difference in rank. How simple it seems today—but what a great invention it was when it was first made, since it has lasted through the ages and will continue long into the future. Thus we distinguish our "non-coms" from our commissioned officers and our lieutenants from our generals by their stripes and insignia.[21]

Another problem for the uniformed militia was conspicuousness: the bright colors (as, for example, the British Redcoats) and brilliant braid or brass trimmings stood out to such an extent that officers and other ranks made easy targets for the enemy. Today drab uniforms with less vivid insignia help to solve this problem in battle. Dress uniforms, however, may still reflect the romance and glamour of earlier times.

Conformity as expressed by religious garb is indeed an integral part of several religious groups. Many meanings given to the dress of Catholic sisters include the following: dress of a particular class of people (often peasants, thus, poverty), chastity, obedience, cloistered solitude, simplicity, and dedication to moral principles. Originally,

[21] Lawrence Langner, *The Importance of Wearing Clothes* (New York: Hastings House, 1959), p. 134.

habits were adopted deliberately in order to make the wearer inconspicuous, and therefore usually included features common to their particular country at the time. Worn unchanged in other countries and centuries later, those habits could not help but be conspicuous and, therefore, contrary to the original idea or symbolism of the founders.

Several orders of Catholic sisters have modified their garb and some newly established orders (this century) have adopted a "uniform" type of dress. In 1918 the first uniformlike attire was used by a new community founded in New Mexico for the purpose of doing missionary and social service work in the United States. This group is known as the Missionary Catechists of Our Lady of Victory; they wear a navy blue uniform garb, with white collar and cuffs, a simple navy blue veil, and a silver medal of Our Lady of Victory is worn on a silver chain around the neck.[22]

Not long after this the Social Mission Sisters, who came to the United States from Hungary, went about their religious duties in the slum areas of Cleveland wearing a habit that was also adapted to the sisters' special vocation. It consisted of a tailored black dress and a black hat "suited to the prevalent style." A gold ring, bearing the letters I.H.S., was the only insignia of their dedicated life.[23]

Another group, founded in 1931 for the purpose of helping the social outcasts of America, is known as the Society of Christ the King. The members wear a modern dress and hat and, in season, a coat. A crucifix worn on a neck chain identifies the members.[24]

In 1949 a community founded in Detroit, Michigan, called themselves the Home Visitors of Mary and to facilitate their work in "carrying the church to the doorstep" wear a dark blue dress, navy top coat, and simple round felt hat.

The symbolic use of clothing for group identity is a

[22] Elinor T. Dehey, *Religious Orders of Women in the United States* (Hammond, Ind.: W. B. Conkey Co., 1930), p. 822.

[23] Ibid., p. 835.

[24] Thomas P. McCarthy, *Guide to the Catholic Sisterhoods in the United States* (Washington, D.C.: Catholic University of America Press, 1952), p. 277.

prominent feature of the Amish. The prescribed garb admits the individual to full fellowship with the group. John Hostetler [25] notes that one of the most highly symbolic of all garments among the women is the Kapp or head cap worn by all women, even infants. At about age twelve, a girl wears a black cap for Sunday dress and a white cap at home. After she marries, a white cap is worn at all times. Different communities specify the shape, size, and style of cap, including the number of tucks and the fabric used. Women are not permitted to cut or curl their hair. Young girls braid their hair, but older girls and women wear their hair parted in the middle and knotted simply in the back. No facial make-up or nail polish is permitted.[26]

Because buttons symbolize the military to these peace-loving people, Amish women secure their black capes and aprons with straight pins; men fasten their suits and coats with hooks and eyes. Dress, then, keeps the insider separate from the world and also keeps the outsider out.

In *The Long March,* Simone de Beauvoir describes conformity of dress in modern China:

> Impossible to tell an intellectual from a worker, a char-woman from a capitalist's wife. This is in part owing to the notorious uniformity of dress . . . everyone wearing the self-same classical outfit of blue cotton. The fact is that in Peking blue trousers and jackets seem to be as ineluctable as black hair. [However] one must be labouring under a delusion to take them for an army of ants.[27] Homogeneity does not signify sameness . . . unity stems from a deeper source.[28]

Thus, we have run the gamut from criticism of conformity by Rudofsky and Brownell to an acceptance of it by various occupational, military, and religious groups to praise for it from Simone de Beauvoir.

[25] John A. Hostetler, *Amish Society* (Baltimore: Johns Hopkins Press, 1963), p. 136.

[26] Ibid.

[27] Simone de Beauvoir, *The Long March* (Cleveland: World Publishing Company, 1958), p. 53.

[28] This remark indicates Mme. de Beauvoir's sympathy with Red China. She wrote this after a visit at the invitation of the Chinese government.

Studies of Conformity

An investigation of relationships between conformity in dress and several color, design, and personality attributes was conducted at Utah State University among women students who were enrolled in a beginning clothing course. Findings confirmed that conformity in dress was related to an interaction orientation; students who placed high in conforming dress behavior were interested in maintaining harmonious relations with others. A negative correlation was found between conformity in dress and aesthetic value, from which the investigators concluded that students who conform in dress "do so in order to be accepted by and liked by those students around them and not because of an appreciation for form and harmony." [29] Individualism, on the other hand, was found to be characteristic of the aesthetic person in earlier studies made by Gordon Allport and his colleagues.[30]

Glickman found that the main requirement for clothing for young adolescents is that their clothing be approved by the peer group. "Above all else the boy wants his clothes to conform to the style accepted by his friends. Being different means being inferior." [31] What other boys wore was also considered to be "smartest" wearing apparel. Closely related to these findings was the fact that boys liked to wear their old clothes and disliked new ones, knowing that their old clothing was acceptable. Even clothing leaders were found to have a certain minimum degree of clothing conformity.

Aiken [32] related the concept of conformity in dress with personality inventories and value scales. Those rating high

[29] Lucy C. Taylor and Norma H. Compton, "Personality Correlates of Dress Conformity," *Journal of Home Economics*, Vol. 60, No. 8 (October, 1968), p. 656.

[30] Gordon Allport, Philip E. Vernon, and Gardner Lindzey, *Study of Values* (Boston: Houghton Mifflin Company, 1960).

[31] Albert S. Glickman, "Clothing Leadership Among Boys," Ph.D. thesis, University of Michigan, 1952, p. 36.

[32] Lewis R. Aiken, "The Relationship of Selected Measures of Personality in Undergraduate Women," *Journal of Social Psychology*, Vol. 59, No. 1 (1963), pp. 119–128.

in "conformity in dress" were found to be conscientious, moral, sociable, traditional, and submissive. Conformity in dress also correlated positively with economic, social, and religious values and negatively with aesthetic values.

9 Custom and Fashion

Another dichotomy relating to clothing symbolism would involve the extremes of long-time stability of styles compared with rapidly changing fashion. Since there are striking evidences of clothing customs in every culture, it is a difficult task to select only a few examples from such a kaleidoscope of clothing patterns.

Many symbols of long-enduring custom can be found the world over: Pakistani women in purdah (Persian for curtain or veil); polyandrous Tibetan wives wearing their yak-buttered hair in one hundred and eight braids (to commemorate the number of Buddhist books); shaved and barefooted Buddhist monks in flowing orange robes; Japanese children wearing costumes handed down for generations to honor Buddha's birthday, or red-robed Koreans celebrating the birthday of Confucius.

In the South Pacific, the chief of Tikopia has lime-bleached hair and blue tattooing on his body; nomadic men of Borneo *[1] wear necklaces and carefully trimmed bangs; a girl of the Crocodile Islands * has a quarter-skirt designed for use only when she is sitting down; men of the Torres Straits * wear grass skirts and masks made to resemble human lower jaws (a cannibalistic symbol); men of Mer wear cloth skirts and flowers in their hair; * a

[1] The starred examples are from Edward Weyer, Jr., *Primitive Peoples Today* (Garden City, N.Y.: Doubleday & Company, Inc., 1959).

Japan *India*

Custom

man in New Guinea wear his "bankbook" on his head, in the form of hollow sticks representing his property, a pig, a wife, a gold-lipped shell, or an ornamental ax; * or another in New Guinea's Telefolmin Forest sports a "fire-cord" for starting fire by friction and a headdress commemorating his passage of puberty rites.*

On the other side of the world lived the American Indians, each tribe easily distinguished by its individual clothing symbols—Mandan of the Dakotas in buffalo robes and ermine tails; the Sioux in splendid eagle headdresses and elaborate tobacco pouches; the Crow with unusually long hair, sometimes touching the ground with the help of

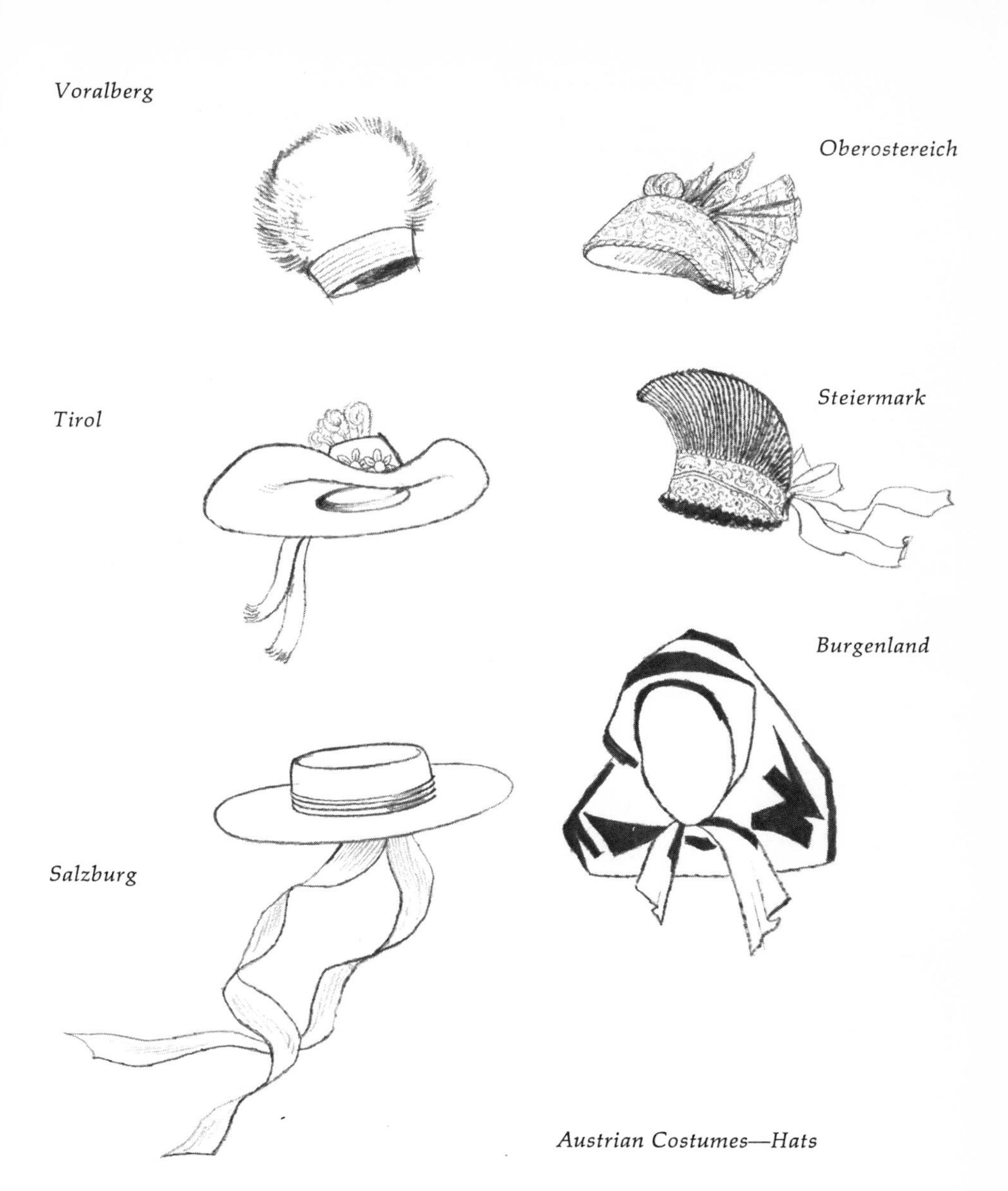

Austrian Costumes—Hats

spliced-in strands; the Navajo refulgent in bright woven patterns and beaded designs; the Cheyenne in frightening horned headdresses.

Among the less primitive cultures we find the voluminous hooded cloaks worn by Irish women, making them look like figures out of a Celtic twilight, and the traditional tartans of the Scottish clans—reds, blues, greens, and yellows dyed from vegetable roots and lichens, then woven in certain patterns or setts. Some national costumes have survived—in Sweden (handwoven striped skirts with bright red or yellow vests and white textured aprons); in Switzerland (the distinctive use of black, red, and white—puffed sleeves, ruffled collar, black laced vest, and small black hat). In Austria eight or nine distinct regional costumes[2] exist, including the Frastanz costume (a black wheel cap, bodice with a lot of lacing, colorfully stitched bib with red ribbon decoration, and long blue skirt), and a Gras costume of bright-colored silk with very long three-cornered shawl and pleated gold horn-shaped dress cap. Men's costumes in some sections of Austria are particularly colorful—the Tyrolean type has a very wide belt decorated with feather quill embroidery, worn over stitched leather knickerbockers, a blue waist-length coat, red vest, and green ribbon hat; in Carinthia, men wear wide felt hats decorated with flowers; they also wear flowers or fruit on their coats and have a bright red tie; near the Hungarian border men wear long white skirts with fringed hems, long wide sleeves, red embroidered vests, and black hats with white plumes.

Rudofsky states that we in the United States are cheated by our short historical background and are envious and susceptible to the relics of the past that other nations possess in profusion. We do consider costumes and armor as charming but when we try to exhibit such charm we miss our mark:

> The dolled-up men and women who double as ethnical exhibits and museum guards in such neohistorical places as Williamsburg, amount to little more than licensed impostors; rather than representing a link with the past, they add an uncalled-for note of Hallowe'en.[3]

Rudofsky goes on to say that ancient Japanese costumes were rich and exotic—"women in artichoke-like court dresses so ample that one of them filled a small apartment; men in what one might call self-transcendent pantaloons twice as long as their legs, the surplus being dragged on

[2] See Rudolf Fochler, *Costumes in Austria* (Munich: Verlag Welsermuhl Wels, 1965).

[3] Bernard Rudofsky, *The Kimono Mind* (Garden City, N.Y.: Doubleday & Company, Inc., 1965), p. 42.

the ground."[4] Yet, however exotic, sartorial do's and don't's were in existence. The more than two hundred and sixteen varieties of dress were prescribed not by tailors but by lawmakers. Eighteen categories of princes, thirty ranks of officers, and on down to the lowest personage in the country all had detailed rules to follow regarding shape, color, texture, size of stitching, and number of knots in their clothing code.

Other examples of sumptuary laws go back in recorded history to the empires of Greece and Rome.[5] These ordinances were in part to keep people from displaying wealth, but also to contain customs in dress and not let them get out of hand. Most of these attempts were doomed to failure for they were either ignored, opposed, or seldom enforced; thus they gradually became obsolete.

The treatise on the rules and duties of monastic life called *Ancren riwle,* written in the thirteenth century, has some interesting regulations relative to clothing customs versus the fashionable attire of the times. It is believed to have been written by Simon of Ghent for the anchoresses of Tarente.

> The garments should be of such a shape and all their attire such that it may be easily seen to what life they are dedicated. . . . If ye would dispense with wimples, have warm capes, and over them black veils. She who wishes to be seen, it is no great wonder though she adorn herself; but, in the eyes of God, she is more lovely who is unadorned outwardly for His sake. Have neither ring, nor brooch, nor ornamented girdle, nor gloves nor any such thing that is not proper for you to have. . . . Anchoresses err in their headdress no less than ladies. They say that it belongs naturally to a woman to wear a wimple. Nay, the Holy Scriptures neither had, nor do they speak of wimple; but of coverings for the head. The apostle said to the Corinthians, "A woman shall cover her head." Cover, he saith, not wimple.[6]

[4] Ibid., p. 224.

[5] "Sumptuary Laws," *Encyclopedia Americana,* 1955 edition, Vol. XXVI, p. 18.

[6] *Ancren riwle,* a treatise on the rules and duties of monastic life. Translated into English by M. B. Salw (Notre Dame, Ind.: University of Notre Dame Press, 1956), p. 14.

Transition to Fashion

In many cultures it is also apparent that there is a transition between custom and fashion. Even in the traditional saris of India, evidences of fashion are seen in the fabric, where a completely new print may appear or a hand-painted design becomes the vogue or a change of color is the new and different mode. Fashion is also seen in the use of jewelry in India.

Among the Amish, described earlier, the changes are slower and still prescribed:

> The style of dress changes from generation to generation only when some items become impossible to acquire and genteel substitutions are made—but only after due deliberation and approval by the religious leaders of the sect.[7]

In an investigation of the meaning of religious dress today Miller and Roach [8] found that "tradition" was the highest ranked reason among lay people, but that group "identification" was most important for Catholic sisters. In addition, they found that 65 per cent of the sisters preferred change, as did 63 per cent of the lay respondents. About 20 per cent wanted some small modification. According to one sister, "The religious habit should be in keeping with the needs of the times. Religious habits that lack simplicity often repel rather than attract others to their ideals." [9]

In an analysis of children's drawings, Wayne Dennis points to the trend away from traditional dress by several groups of children whose culture normally prescribes traditional dress. Only 35 per cent of the children of the Brooklyn Hassidim drew pictures of men in traditional dress. These people are mainly post-World War II immigrants from Hungary who are dedicated to preserv-

[7] Charles S. Rice and John B. Shenk, *Meet the Amish* (New Brunswick, N. J.: Rutgers University Press, 1947), p. 4.

[8] Sister Mary Claudelle Miller, S.C.L., and Mary Ellen Roach, "Religious Garb: Significant or Sentimental," *Journal of Home Economics*, Vol. 48, No. 9 (November, 1966), p. 731.

[9] Ibid., p. 732.

Children's Drawings

ing a pious Jewish way of life. "This way of life among other things, prescribes for males the wearing of curls before the ears, the wearing of a black, broad-brimmed hat, and, as early as possible, the growing of a full beard." [10] Since 65 per cent of the drawings were modern in appearance, Dennis predicts that many Hassidic boys will "defect" from the traditional garb.

Similarly, in drawings made by Chamala Indian children who were attending rural primitive schools and themselves wearing native costume, only 30 per cent of the men pictured were wearing native dress.

In a similar study, 25 per cent of the Navajo children sampled drew men in native dress, while 21 per cent of Orthodox Israelis, 11 per cent of children from Taipei, and 9 per cent of children from a Japanese village drew men in native attire.

> It must be remembered that boys do not make or buy their own clothes. They cannot wear modern clothes if their parents do not provide them. The reasons their parents do not do so are two-fold: the first is that parents may disapprove of modern dress.

[10] Wayne Dennis, *Group Values Through Children's Drawings* (New York: John Wiley & Sons, Inc., 1966), p. 46.

The second reason is that if parents approve of modern dress, nevertheless they may not have the money to buy modern clothing, nearly all of which is machine-made and must be paid for in currency. Traditional dress is usually homemade, and is made possible only by an increase in income. We predict, on the basis of drawings, that when the standard of living of any group now wearing traditional dress but drawing modern dress improves, modern dress will be worn.[11]

Fashion

The exact beginnings of fashion are lost to us. Many authorities will cite the Renaissance as the time of the appearance of this phenomenon. However, in the usual sense, fashion has several identifiable aspects that are quite well expressed in this definition—fashion is a continuing process of change in the styles of dress that are accepted or followed by substantial groups of people at any given time and place.[12] The important elements are continuing change, the acceptance of styles, and the identity of a special time and place. In general, changes are gradual with minor innovations each season.

Helen Brockman provides us with another definition of fashion: "a style that is accepted by enough women to make deviation from it noticeable or obvious." [13] Nystrom, too, emphasizes numbers of followers. "Of the multitudes of styles past and present, only those which are followed by groups of people are fashions. A style followed by an individual means nothing." [14]

Brockman also emphasizes change in the visual aspects of fashion, saying that the eye becomes indifferent to an

[11] Ibid., p. 46.

[12] Jeannette A. Jarrow and Beatrice Judelle, *Inside the Fashion Business* (New York: John Wiley & Sons, Inc., 1965), p. 3.

[13] Helen L. Brockman, *The Theory of Fashion Design* (New York: John Wiley & Sons, Inc., 1965), p. 30.

[14] Paul Nystrom, *Economics of Fashion* (New York: The Ronald Press Company, 1928), p. 19.

Fashion Classics

unchanging stimulus and needs something new for continued stimulation. Ronald Amey, an American designer, says that fashion is of the moment with an expectation of tomorrow. It is always a set of changing proportions.[15]

The term "high fashion" is sometimes used to label fashions of limited appeal because they are too expensive, sophisticated, or extreme for the average person. The term "fashion cycle" is sometimes applied to the duration of a style, while at other times its use may imply the return

[15] Comments at Clothing and Design Seminar, Pennsylvania State University, College of Human Development, in April, 1967.

of a style. However, these so-called style revivals are never complete repetitions—only certain elements reappear.

Some fashions satisfy such basic needs or have such wide appeal that they remain a fashion for long periods of time. Dr. Paul Nystrom [16] noted such fashion classics as flesh-colored hose for women, wrist watches, shirtwaist dresses, and low shoes. Other more recent classics include cardigan sweaters, Chanel-type suits, printed silk scarves, short white gloves, knit dresses, and stoles. Certain designers have been given credit for initiating classics that can be worn for twenty years or more—a Mainbocher gown worn by Mrs. Julien Chaqueneau [17] in 1955 had been worn regularly for the ten years 1936 to 1946, then for any special occasions from 1946 to 1955. The gown that Mrs. Rose Kennedy wore to her son's inauguration was another example of a dress that looked fashionable over a period of many years.

Yet most critics of fashion and fashion change have in mind the dialogue between Don John's followers in Shakespeare's *Much Ado About Nothing:*

BORACHIO: . . . Thou knowest that the fashion of a doublet, or a cloak, or a hat, is nothing to a man.
CONRADE: Yes, it is apparel.
BORACHIO: I mean, the fashion.
CONRADE: Yes, the fashion is the fashion.
BORACHIO: Tush! I may as well say the fool's the fool. But seest thou not what a deformed thief this fashion is?

. . . .

. . . how giddily a' turns about all the hot bloods between fourteen and five-and-thirty? sometime fashioning them like Pharaoh's soldiers in the reechy painting; sometime like god Bel's priests in the old church-window; sometime like the shaven Hercules in the smirched worm-eaten tapestry, where his codpiece seems as massy as his club?
CONRADE: All this I see, and I see that the fashion wears out more apparel than the man. . . .[18]

[16] Nystrom, op. cit., p. 21.

[17] *Life* (April 18, 1955), pp. 91–92.

[18] William Shakespeare in "Much Ado About Nothing," Act III, Scene III. As printed in *Works of Shakespeare*, Vol. 5 (Boston: The Jefferson Press, 1907), p. 66.

Other critics will stress the fickleness of fashion. Lord Spencer in 1792 made a bet with Sir Edward Chetwynd that he could set a fashion that would be the prevailing mode within a period of six months. The proposed fashion was to be a form of dress wholly meaningless and unnecessary. Spencer then took a pair of shears, cut off the tail of his long coat, put on the unhemmed, unfinished garment and went for a stroll. Within three days several young men were seen in the streets wearing similar "Spencers." In two weeks all London was wearing the garment and in two months all England, including men, women, and children.[19]

Duration of Fashion

How long does a fashion last? How long is the symbol of newness present? Different authorities will give different answers to these questions. Nystrom says that fashion cycles in dress accessories such as "flowers, scarfs, costume jewelry, handbags, tend to run but a season. Fashions in color, designs and materials, as a rule, require a year. Fashion cycles in silhouette . . . seem to run for several years."[20]

Writing in 1961, Leland Gordon[21] stated that the average life of a style is two years—"the first six months is used for introduction, the second six months the style is in vogue and the last year its status diminishes." He also suggests that public reaction varies at each stage.

One style that did not last anything like two years was "the sack" of 1958. Part of its unpopularity was due to criticism by the public. Marya Mannes, a critic's critic, was very vocal in her opinion.

[19] Alice Morse Earle, *Two Centuries of Costume in America* (New York: The Macmillan Company, 1903), p. 802.

[20] Nystrom, op. cit., p. 29.

[21] Leland J. Gordon, *Economics for Consumers* (New York: American Book Company, 1961), p. 128.

"Smack"[22]

I am taken aback
by the sack.
Filled with unease
by the chemise.
They cloak
a pig in a poke,
provoke alarms
at the disguise of charms
dear to the male. Enshroud
the contours proud
while they expose
hose—and knees
that fail to please.

Why then must we
submissively
accept the sack
because some maniac
couturiers in Paris lack
a love of form?
Pervert the female norm
so they can sell
a gunny sack, a funny
sack, a dressmaker-in-
the-money sack
that looks like
hell?

Revivals of styles of earlier periods do occur, but always in a different form or with some changes. Examples of style revivals that made the fashion scene in the late 1960's were lavish beaded dresses like those of the 1920's and 1930's, Victorian nightgowns—now sold as evening wear as well as sleep wear—capes from the turn of the century and from the 1930's, dresses of sequins and net from the 1880's. The shift or chemise of 1958 differed from the styles of the 1920's in the special accent on back fullness and back interest, the tightness near the hem, the frequent use of collars, and the longer lengths of the earliest designs (1957).

According to Gordon, among the factors favoring new fashions are democracy, adequate income widely diffused, transportation and communication, advertising, leisure (the display of new fashions), and a philosophy of change (a liberal attitude):

> Fashion is stronger than the individual consumer, the producer or group of producers. It would appear that the control of fashion rests with the consumers collectively. Advertising does not start or stop a fashion but spreads the acceptance of the fashion already in progress.[23]

[22] Marya Mannes, "On the Sack," in *Marya Mannes in Subverse* (New York: George Braziller, Inc., 1959), p. 15.
[23] Gordon, op. cit., p. 130.

Gordon also emphasizes the few styles that become fashionable. Out of the thousands (possibly as many as two hundred thousand) of models shown in Paris each season, only two hundred are brought to the United States and only twenty of these will be copied to the extent that they are made fashionable.

Fashion Leaders Today

What kind of women are fashion leaders as opposed to fashion followers? Some clues to the answer to this question are found in research by Margaret Grindering.

She reported that self-identified early fashion adopters were women with a high degree of fashion interest, that they were likely to use mass media as a source of fashion information, and that they looked to nationally and internationally prominent women as a comparative frame of fashion reference. Reverse characteristics were true of women who identified themselves as late adopters of fashion.[24]

How do fashion leaders view themselves? Zoe Hagy found several interesting definitions of fashionable women given by a selected sample of known fashion leaders. Most definitions included the words *good taste, well-groomed,* and *attractive.* Awareness of current fashion was deemed to be important, but also the adaptation of fashion to the individual, the creation of a look of one's own was stressed. Here is an extract from the pen of a fashion connoisseur:

> A fashionable woman is an alert, lively, informed woman—these qualities reflecting in her bearing. She is always well-groomed and has a sense of taste which results in her wearing the "right" clothes for the "right" occasion. She must be undogmatic in her approach to fashion but capable of achieving a "personal signature" in her selection of clothing, just as she does in her choice of perfume.

[24] Margaret P. Grindering, "Fashion Diffusion," *Journal of Home Economics*, Vol. 59, No. 3 (March, 1967), p. 173.

A second——

> She is a modern girl, at ease and comfortable in any situation. Keeping her own personality, she should be able to project a mood of mystery and danger, or health and sports, even be swinging and sexy, but always in good taste and above all with a sense of humor. Fashion is a love affair with beauty and fun!

And a third——

> A fashionable woman is a goose—the object is style.[25]

John Fairchild calls women on the Best Dressed List "the Impeccables"; beyond them are two "fashion goddesses"—Mrs. William S. Paley and Mrs. Loel Guinness.[26] Mrs. Paley in her aristocratic and gracious way is "cool-easy-without-noise." She is the "only one who can wear a Chanel and make it a Paley style." [27]

Gloria Guinness, graceful as a dancer with a long, long swan neck, has always been an improviser. "Years ago when I was poor I would buy a beautiful piece of jersey, cut a hole in the top, put it over my head and tie a beautiful sash around my waist. Everyone asked me where I bought my dresses." [28]

One of the most eloquent pleas for the continuation of fashion appears in Lawrence Langner's *The Importane of Wearing Clothes.* His case for fashion follows:

> Should we abolish fashion if we could? The alternative to fashion is the uniform, against which humanity eventually tends to rebel. Man has risen from the animal world by his faculty of reason and invention, and has differentiated his clothes from man to man, and from generation to generation. If there is to be a new goal for humanity, the uniform man or robot, then by all means do away with fashion, for it

[25] Zoe Benedict Hagy, "A Study of Fashion Awareness and Motivation of Selected Socially Prominent Women," unpublished Master's thesis, University of Missouri, January, 1968, pp. 67–68.

[26] John Fairchild, *The Fashionable Savages* (Garden City, N. Y.: Doubleday & Company, Inc., 1965), p. 146.

[27] Ibid., p. 148.

[28] Ibid., p. 151.

is the enemy of the stereotyped individual, the mass-produced mind and the unthinking human product of the propaganda machine. But since the world progresses by the progress of its individuals, as well as by its masses, there is reason for optimism in believing that fashion, which is the product of individual taste, exercised without compulsion, will continue to exist as it has in the past as a constructive force in the world of the future.[29]

[29] Lawrence Langner, *The Importance of Wearing Clothes* (New York: Hastings House, 1959), p. 299.

Status

A third dichotomy involves the various clothing symbols representing a certain kind of status or high position contrasted with symbols denoting a low status.

Clothing Symbols of People in High Positions

Leaders, heads of state, kings, and emperors all use some clothing symbol to emphasize their position. A few far-flung examples would include, first of all, the crown, symbol of a royal head of state. Many monarchs have inherited priceless crown jewels; perhaps some of the most exotic are the Pahlevi and the Kiyani Crowns of the Shah of Iran. Queen Elizabeth of England has some eleven diamond tiaras to wear in place of her coronation or official crowns. Quite another kind of symbol would be the white turban of a Druse sheik (indicating high religious office), or the flaunting headdresses of lions' manes worn by Masai warriors, the copper circles on a Zulu warrior's head (meaning he has killed enemies), or the tall two-faced masks worn by the high-status magic men of New Guinea.

Crowns and Status Headdresses

The use of necklaces or other ornaments is found the world over. The clothing of royalty for state occasions usually includes precious jewels sewn somewhere on the garment. Here is a description of a gown worn by Queen Sirikit of Thailand:

> On a gold-leafed Thai bed, the Queen wears a dress of twenty-carat gold embossed in crystal, and appears to be paved in diamonds—canary and white diamonds —on her hair, her throat, her wrists, her tapering fingers.[1]

Prophet Jones of the Church of Universal Triumph in Detroit, Michigan, posed in a white mink coat made of seventy-five rare pelts with a scarlet silk lining that cost

[1] "The Golden Court of Thailand," *Vogue* (February 15, 1965), p. 85.

his followers $12,900.[2] He also carried a gold-headed cane and a bracelet containing eight hundred and twelve diamonds.

Some status symbols worn by more primitive peoples: Meo women north of Thailand wear thick loops of silver around their necks, huge copper anklets are worn by African Wamba women (the original purpose was to keep a wife from running away, now it is a means of displaying wealth); shells are worn around the neck to indicate the economic status of the upper class in New Guinea; and silver ornaments are worn by the Navajo.

To see really lavish jewelry we have to go to the entertainment world, the world of movie stars, of café society. For example, Debra Paget used to paste star sapphires on her forehead; she also bought a strawberry-colored Cadillac which she encrusted with five hundred dollars worth of jewels. Other celebrities enjoy having jewels not only on their person but around them. Doris Duke is reported to have had a jade-inlaid bathroom and pearls in her dressing room. Jeweled hairdresses by Alexandre of Paris have been known to incorporate $2.3 million worth of jewels. Many celebrities have three-thousand-dollar jeweled dresses by Balenciaga or Bohan. Richard Burton's recent purchase of the Cartier Diamond for more than a million dollars proclaims his idea of an appropriate symbol for his wife, Elizabeth.

At times colors, fabrics, and symbols signify a certain high status, such as for example, the purple worn by Roman senators, the yellows and oranges beloved by Louis XIV, the Sun King, the sun symbol of the Emperor of Japan, or the use of red in some Eastern cultures. High-status persons in Okinawa wear silk fabrics in purple and white. In the United States during the seventeenth century, only the upper classes were permitted to wear silver and gold thread, slashed sleeves, embroidered caps, belts, ruffs, and gold and silver girdles.[3] In our times, low status is attached to the color blue when it describes blue-collar *jobs* as opposed to white-collar *occupations.*

Furs such as ermine are usually reserved for royalty because of their expensiveness or rarity. Alligator leather

[2] "Prophet's Mink," *Life* (March 30, 1953), p. 65.

[3] Marion Day Iverson, "Color in Pilgrim and Puritan Dress," *Antiques*, Vol. 61 (1952), pp. 240–241.

is an upper-class symbol. Billie Sol Estes felt that his hand-stitched alligator oxfords ($135 per pair) were "status" shoes.

Prohibitions relating to the use of color, ornaments, furs, and fabrics are eloquently set forth in Spanish sumptuary legislation in the reign of Alfonso X of Castile. These laws were decreed in A.D. 1258:

II. The King may wear as many suits of clothing as he wishes. . . .

IV. The King commands: that none of his notaries, archers, falconers, gatekeepers, or any other men of his or the Queen's households may wear [or use] white furs, sendal, gilded or silvered war saddles, gilded spurs, scarlet stockings, gilded shoes, or hats ornamented with gold or silver thread or silk—except the senior servant of each office.

V. The King commands: that all the clergy of his household be tonsured . . . and that they may not wear bright red, green, or pink; that they may not wear stockings except of black, pale green, or dark brown; that they may not wear sendal, except for prelates and canons [who may use it] as lining; that they may not wear bright red or yellow tunics, shoes with strings, or closed or detachable sleeves; that they must wear conservative clothing except for prelates or the canon of a cathedral; that they must use red or white saddles and bridles, except for prelates whose [saddles] may be blue or canons whose [saddles] may be red wool without other colors; that they may use breast leathers of silver except any that are suspended. . . .

XIV. No grandee, knight, or any other man whomsoever may have more than four suits of clothing each year; and those may not bear ermine, drawn work, silk, gold or silver thread, elaborate needlework, gold embroidery, pelts, trimmings, or any regal or elaborate material whatever except fur and cloth; one suit of clothing may not be covered with another; no one except the King may wear a scarlet rain cloak; no one may have more than two mantles per year and a rain cloak should last for two years; no one may wear sendal or silk except the King or a noble knight (except as lining in clothing); no one may wear marten furs except the King, a noble, a grandee, or a bridegroom if he is the son of a grandee; no one may wear silver, crystal, buttons, long chains, ermine, or otter on their cloaks or robes except around the edges of their mantle; and no grandee may wear traveling costume in court.[4]

Coming a little close to our times and forebears, we find this act of the General Court of Massachusetts in the year 1651.

> We declare our utter detestation and dislike that men and women of meane condition should take upon themselves the garb of gentlemen by wearing gold or silver lace or buttons or points at their knees or to walk in bootes or women of the same rancke to weare silke or tiffany horlles or scarfes, which though allowable to persons of greater estates or more liberal education, yet we cannot but judge it intollerable in persons of such like condition.[5]

Many persons were persecuted for violations of this law. In 1673 thirty women in the towns of Springfield, Hadley, Hatfield, and Westfield were noted as "persons of small estate who use to wear silk contrary to law." Later, thirty-eight women were brought to court for wearing silk, long hair, or other extravagances.[6]

Symbolic meanings of ornaments can change in time. Here is an interesting example of a low-status symbol acquiring a higher status:

> Nose rings are a favorite form of self-adornment in many parts of the world. Those worn by the Kuna and San Blas Indian women of Panama are symbolic of servitude. Long ago, before these Indians had ever seen a white man, they made part of their living by raiding other tribes. They were not actually at war with their neighbors. They merely wished to secure a supply of fresh meat, for at that time, they were cannibals.
>
> On these raids they killed any man who resisted capture, carried male prisoners to their villages to

[4] "Excerpts from Decrees of Jan. 28, 1258, by Alfonso X," *Business History Review*, Vol. 37 (Spring/Summer, 1963), pp. 99–100.

[5] Edward Newton and Herman Richley, "17th Century New England," in *The School in American Social Order* (Boston: Houghton Mifflin Company, 1963), p. 46.

[6] Ibid.

be kept and fattened for future food, and brought the female captives home to serve as slaves or wives. It was not easy to keep these women from running away, so the cannibal Kunas pierced their noses, passed cords through the holes, and strung the captives together for safe keeping. Today, civilized farmers keep strong bulls under control by a similar nose ring and rope method.

Having thus been provided with a hole in her nasal septum, it was second nature for the captive woman to make good use of it later by adorning it with a ring or a pendant. At first, it was a badge of servitude, for it indicated the wearer had been literally "led by the nose." But after a time the women changed all this. Compelled by necessity to learn the language of their captors, these women preserved their original dialect by teaching it to their daughters. This led to a dual language for these tribes, that of the women being unknown to the men.

Almost before they knew what was happening, the men discovered that the women were gaining the upper hand. They could understand everything the men said, but the men could not understand a word of what the women were talking about when they conversed in their feminine tongue. Before very long the women were the real rulers of the tribe.

Today, the Kuna and San Blas women own everything the tribe has except the weapons of their men. The women select their own mates. They lay down the law to the chiefs, who are mere figure-heads. Thus the nose rings worn by the women would seem eventually to have become signs of superiority instead of badges of servitude.[7]

Another example of a changing symbol is found in Arabian anklets weighing a pound and a half each. They, too, were in origin symbols of slavery, and, connected with a short chain, made running away impossible. "Through the silversmith's cooperation they evolved into fashionable adornments, and finally became emblems of rank." [8]

Small feet have long been a symbol of status. The Chinese lily foot was bound when the girl was very young and made her foot so deformed that she could not walk.

[7] A. Hyatt Verrill, *Strange Customs, Manners and Beliefs* (Boston: L. C. Page & Company, Inc., 1946), pp. 32–35.

[8] Bernard Rudofsky, *The Kimono Mind* (Garden City, N. Y.: Doubleday & Company, Inc., 1965), p. 165.

Chopine—1590

Thus she could not work, therefore must be waited on, hence was of an upper class. This practice lasted for some eight hundred years.

Shoes, too, have been status symbols. The chopine or stilted shoe worn for several centuries reached the height of twenty inches in 1430. Women wearing them had to be supported while walking or standing—of course, such shoes were worn only by the leisure classes.[9]

Periods of pointed toes have come and gone, probably reaching their extreme during the fourteenth century, when points were so long that they had to be tied up to

[9] Ibid., p. 169.

the leg. (Both men and women wore them.) Laws were enacted limiting the length to twenty inches for upper classes—middle classes could only have shoes with toes six to twelve inches long.

Recently Dichter noted some psychological associations relating to shoes and status:

> The first shoe in a person's life is highly significant. With the possible exception of trousers for boys and dresses for girls, shoes contribute more to the child's self-esteem than any other article of clothing. The significance of shoes is attested to by a great many fairy tales. To be barefoot often means being deprived, not fully recognized. When Cinderella gets her beautiful clothes, new slippers take a prominent place. When she loses one at the dance, the prince finds it and then finds her. In the story of the seven-league boots, the proud possessor of the wonder shoes can take great strides, hurdle all obstacles.
>
> Shoes are not just articles of clothing. The saying, "You can never fill his boots," expresses the way shoes indicate the stature and caliber of a man. A man who is "down at the heels" feels psychologically let down, depressed, down and out.[10]

In ancient China, fingernails sometimes were allowed to grow as long as six inches. In 1942, an American magazine advertisement showed nails that were an inch and a half in length. Both of these examples show that the owner cannot do manual work.

Today, well-established and socially secure individuals can afford to set their own styles and ignore the usual low-status symbolism of garments they wish to wear.

The popularization of blue jeans for girls started with wealthy coeds and afterward became "acceptable among others for whom the saving in money was much more important." [11] A few garments transcend all social strata, however. The trench coat is "worn by dad, or lad, dowager or damsel, bricklayer or baker." [12] Flat shoes can be found in wardrobes of women of all classes.

[10] Ernest Dichter, *Handbook of Consumer Motivation* (New York: McGraw-Hill, Inc., 1964), p. 104.

[11] James N. Morgan, *Consumer Economics* (Englewood Cliffs, N. J.: Prentice-Hall, Inc., 1955), p. 312.

[12] Stewart Henderson Britt, *The Spenders* (New York: McGraw-Hill, Inc., 1960), p. 60.

Barber and Lobel [13] found that in the American social class system the upper or "old money" families did not depend upon fashion and sometimes were even eccentric in dress. Advertising appeals to this group used "distinguished," "well-bred," and "aristocratic" types of descriptive copy. Ranking just below the old money families we find the followers of high fashion who look to Paris and other cosmopolitan design houses. They seek sophistication by looking chic but never ostentatious.

Vener's study measuring clothing importance for men had similar findings. Men of the highest social groups did not show the highest estimate of clothing importance, for clothing decreased in importance in the highest status categories. The author interprets the low estimates in part by stating, "The highest status individuals may have already attained their status goals, therefore, clothing as a symbol of success, or as a means to a higher status goal, is of little consequence in the social life of these people." [14]

For the high fashion class the vocabulary is likely to include such descriptions as *strict, severe, stark, plain, unadorned, rigorous,* while lower down on the scale clothes are described as *cuddly, charming, winning, adorable,* and *lovable.* Eve Merriam [15] describes a fashion totem pole with many contrasts.

Lower	*Upper*
Beads, beads, beads	Simple string of pearls
Frothy red net dress with large satin bow and flowers	Little black nothing dress
Plastic purse shaped like a shoebox with butterflies and shells impaled between the layers	Plain satin clutch
Gold lamé bathing suit	Grey wool jersey tank suit
Coat; mink outside	Coat; sable inside
Black in winter; white in summer	White in winter; black in summer
Chiffon handkerchief	Kleenex

[13] Bernard Barber and L. S. Lobel, "Fashion in Women's Clothes and the American Social System," *Social Forces,* Vol. 31 (1952), pp. 124–131.

[14] Arthur M. Vener, "Stratification Aspects of Clothing Importance," unpublished Master's thesis, Michigan State College, 1953, p. 84.

[15] Eve Merriam, *Figleaf* (Philadelphia: J. B. Lippincott Company, 1960), pp. 77–78.

Eve Merriam's descriptions suggest that the upper classes do not engage in conspicuous consumption in the usual sense of the term. In most cases they are playing down clothing rather than using it as a gaudy or expensive symbol.

> Too often conspicuous consumption has been dismissed by reference to the common idea of "keeping up with the Joneses". . . . Conspicuous consumption does not imply a mad pell-mell consumptive race. . . . We do not attempt to keep up with someone in a recognized higher status position. This would be social climbing in a vulgar fashion and if found out would lead to social disaster. We do, however, consume those items of a grade and expensiveness called for by one in our allotted status position. It is conspicuous consumption because it involves those items which are primarily in the public view—our houses, our entertainment, our automobiles, our children's schooling, our clothing.[16]

A publication celebrating New York City's fifty years of fashion leadership describes the contrast between high and low social groups—in 1900 upper classes were swishing around in custom-made dresses costing $750 to $1,000 while the "woman of moderate means had only about three dresses—her 'best silk,' her everyday dress, and a housedress. They were carefully nurtured, remodeled, and worn several years." [17]

With respect to numbers of clothes, even though the upper-uppers of today are less conspicuous than formerly, the average clothes inventory of a woman on the Best-Dressed List is still of staggering proportions.

Laura Riley made this survey for *Ladies Home Journal* in 1958:

A Look into the Closet of One "Best-Dressed" Woman [18]

5 fur coats and 6 less important fur items	42 blouses
28 long evening and ball gowns	29 sweaters
	225 pairs of gloves
	89 pairs of shoes

[16] David Hamilton, *The Consumer in Our Economy* (Boston: Houghton Mifflin Company, Riverside Press, 1962), p. 73.

[17] City of New York, *Golden Anniversary of Fashion 1898–1948*, Mayor's Committee for the Commemoration of the Golden Anniversary of the City of New York.

[18] Laura Date Riley, "America's Best-Dressed Women," *Ladies Home Journal* (March, 1958), pp. 66–67.

14 cocktail, dinner, or short evening dresses
19 suits
10 light wool afternoon dresses
8 cotton or linen day dresses
6 cloth coats
1 fur-lined cloth coat
4 separate jackets
3 dress-and-coat ensembles
8 short printed silks and chiffons for afternoon and on into cocktails
35 housecoats and negligees
37 nightgowns
8 bed jackets
37 hats
93 scarves (and light stoles)
23 slips and 8 half slips
16 panties
18 brassières and 4 strapless brassières
17 girdles
5 dozen pairs of stockings
28 handbags
3 umbrellas
1 pair of plastic rain boots (no raincoat)
117 handkerchiefs
45 pairs of earrings
38 necklaces
28 clips and pins
16 bracelets

For an outstanding male example of upper-class consumption we must go back to 1888. During the last century E. Berry Wall wanted to have the title "King of the Dudes." On an August day in 1888 he got his title.

> Twilight was falling over Saratoga Springs, New York. At the fashionable United States Hotel, Berry Wall strolled onto the piazza, his cane jauntily held, his mustache trimmed to a fare-thee-well, his high-winged collar in place. It was his fortieth complete costume change of the day. The band struck up "Hail the Conquering Hero Comes" and everyone knew that Wall was the dudes' king. He had announced the day before that he would change clothes forty times between breakfast and supper and half of Saratoga bet that he could not. Now at the foot of the steps none other than John L. Sullivan stood raking in cash, for he had backed Berry's claim. Nobody grudged Berry Wall his triumph, for a gentleman's dress was far from simple. To accomplish his sartorial feat, he had to button forty sets of high spats, link up forty pairs of cuff links, secure forty starched shirt collars on forty studs and fix two score different stickpins into two score different silk cravats. He had eaten lunch, taken afternoon tea, and enjoyed a leisurely stroll down Saratoga's Main Street into the bargain.[19]

[19] "Gay Old Days of High Living," *Life* (December 28, 1959), p. 14.

Some contemporary social class differences related to concepts and attitudes concerning fashion were cited in a study by Mary Aslakson. Here, women whose husbands had white-collar occupations were compared with those who had blue-collar jobs. Significantly more white-collar than blue-collar wives discarded clothes because they were out of style, thought that the silhouette made an article fashionable, thought that short skirts looked to be in better proportion, bought in specialty shops, noticed if the person's clothes suited the person's personality, noticed the general appearance of other people's clothes, felt confident and at ease when wearing fashionable clothes, and thought their husband's opinion about clothes counted most. On the other hand, young women whose husbands were in the blue-collar occupations noticed the neatness and cleanliness of clothes, thought that their mothers were the most interested in clothes of all family members, and that their mothers' opinions regarding the informants' clothing choices counted most; young blue-collar wives also thought that their own clothes were average, and thought that a secretary's job demands more fashionable clothes than any other occupation.[20]

McLuhan captures the status symbols of car, clothes, and color in this news item, showing the parts that fit the total scheme:

> It was terrific. There I was in my white Continental, and I was wearing a pure-silk, pure-white, embroidered cowboy shirt, and black gabardine trousers. Beside me in the car was my jet-black Great Dane imported from Europe, named Dana von Krupp. You just can't do better than that.

Furthermore, says McLuhan, "the car has become an article of dress without which we feel uncertain, unclad, and incomplete in the urban compound." [21]

In the days before the automobile the numbers and types of carriages were status symbols. A well-furnished

[20] Mary Aslakson, "Concepts of Fashion in Clothing and Home Furnishings," unpublished Master's thesis, University of Missouri, 1962.

[21] Marshall McLuhan, *Understanding Media* (New York: Signet Books, 1966), p. 194.

Newport stable might have between twenty and thirty carriages. The one reserved for occasions of state had grooms riding the near-side horses and two footmen in full family livery on the step behind.

> The color scheme of family horse livery was carried over to coachmen, grooms and mounted footmen so that the Vanderbilt maroon, Mrs. Astor's bottle-green, and Mrs. Hermann Oelrichs' deep tan with red piping identified the turnouts to the knowing and announced their occupants to the world as clearly as the coat of armor engrossed on the carriage doors.[22]

> Jim Fisk had a six-in-hand with black and white horses. Two Negro grooms made the lead horses in white livery; two white footmen on the rear step wore black livery. The effect was nothing less than spectacular.[23]

C. Wright Mills states that frequently the sales clerk borrows prestige from his customers and that "sometimes the prestige source includes the merchandise itself or the store, but its center is normally the customer. In addition, some sales people like the feeling of power in manipulating the customer's appearance and home." [24]

Bond Street in London, England, is a good example of Mills's observations. For about a quarter of a mile, extending from Piccadilly to Oxford Street, the shops are arranged in a tight little enclave of richness without ostentation that exudes craftsmanship, good taste, luxury, and high prices. "Within the deep carpeted interiors are fastidious but highly knowledgeable men and women dealing with the public (some of them would probably faint if you called them clerks) who won't even use the word—*sell.*" [25] Instead of using the term *sell,* that crass and commercial word, such circumlocutions as these are used:

[22] Lucius Beebe, *The Big Spenders* (New York: Pocket Books, 1967), p. 191.

[23] Ibid., p. 192.

[24] C. Wright Mills, "The Middle Classes in Middle-Sized Cities," in R. Bendix and S. Lipset, editors, *Class, Status and Power* (New York: The Free Press, 1966), p. 280.

[25] Margaret Conlin, "Bond Street Is for the Rich and Elegant," *St. Louis Post-Dispatch* (September 19, 1966).

We recently supplied one of our clients with. . . .
We were able to provide Her Royal Highness with. . . .
We were happy to find for Sir Jones one of our. . . .[26]

A study in a southern Michigan city revealed that the middle and upper classes were more likely to know the clerks in clothing stores than were the lower classes. Furthermore, only a third of those claiming membership in the upper or middle classes said they would like to dress like sales clerks, as compared to more than half of the women in the lower classes who said they would like to do so.[27]

Social Mobility

In relation to mobility, the actual change or the desired change from one social class to another, Ruth Gates [28] found that the movement from one status group to another had little effect on clothing behavior. The upwardly mobile valued the buying of clothing to conform. One group of aspirationally mobile women owned more prestige items than those who did move up the social scale. Perhaps what this really means is that one dresses as what one aspires to be; after one "arrives" the symbols are less important.

In a study of children's color preferences, red was a greater favorite among children in poor areas than among the children in well-to-do neighborhoods during their earlier years; the reverse was true of green. Differences due to social status tended to be overcome as the children advanced in age and school attainment.[29]

[26] Ibid.
[27] Gregory P. Stone and William H. Form, "The Local Community Market: A Study of the Social and Social-Psychological Contexts of Shopping," Agricultural Experiment Station Bulletin, No. 262, Michigan State University (1957), p. 52.
[28] Ruth E. Gates, "Clothing Behavior Associated with Types of Mobility, and with Extrinsic-Reward Orientation Among a Specified Group of Non-Employed Wives," Ph.D. thesis, Pennsylvania State University, 1960.
[29] S. E. Katz and F. S. Breed, "The Color Preferences of Children," *Journal of Applied Psychology*, Vol. 6 (September, 1962), p. 256.

Indeed, the original Horatio Alger hero generally followed the pattern of changing his attire when fortune came his way. "One of the first things the hero usually does to celebrate his good fortune is to buy a nice, new suit and a watch." [30]

In a rather facetious manner, Vance Packard [31] emphasized some of the changing symbols of status in a status quiz. Among the personal effects items were these:

1. Executive-length socks, which come up to the knee, having become popular, because they spare an executive the indignity of revealing a bit of skin to an underling. If husband of house wears executive socks. . . .
   Count ten ______
2. White shirts used to be Status, but now they're not. Does husband dare to wear colored shirts anywhere, anytime? Count five ______
3. President Kennedy didn't wear button-down collars, so now they're "out." If you have thrown them all away. . . . Count five ______
4. It is no longer Status to have your clothes made in London. But if you have something made in Hong-Kong. . . . Count five ______
5. Do you travel with "matched luggage?". . . .
   Count five ______

Another bit of advice on how to get to the top is contained in a United Press release called "Society Now Ruled by the 1,000 Mobile Successors to the 400." These jet-set people, sometimes known as "the beautiful people," are seen at charity balls, discothèque openings, theater benefits, galas at the opera and symphony, and the seasonal openings of supper clubs. They are international nomads but unlike the café society of old they prefer quiet dinner parties. Today's society must have the following:

(1) Money, a lot of it and not necessarily old. If spent freely on peer socialites, celebrities and publicity sources no one will ask where it came from except the Internal Revenue Service.

[30] R. Richard Wohl, "The Rags to Riches Story," in *Class, Status and Power*, op. cit., p. 503.

[31] Vance Packard, "What's Your 'Status Status?' ", *This Week* Magazine (July 28, 1963), p. 10.

(2) Flair, an indefinable quality that encompasses good looks, dash, taste, verve, the instincts of a gambler, mobility, basic social graces, humor and a dilettante knowledge of the arts (after all, you may be seated next to Lennie Bernstein at your next dinner engagement).
(3) Mobility, a jet age must. If you can't be where the action is—Seville when Jackie's there, Schloss Mittersill at ski-time, Acapulco for Merle's costume ball, Mrs. Merriwether Post's Adirondacks house party—give up!
(4) Persistence, in abnormal quantities. The dropouts in today's society are legion. Money and health, husbands and columnists can all run out on you. Where are the Brenda Fraziers of yesterday? Flash! Where are the Baby Jane Holzers and Edie Sedgwicks of only yesterday? Pop!!
(5) Vanity, which goes without saying. This most human of weaknesses is the 1,000's greatest strength. For as Jonathan Swift observed of go-go Georgian society: "The strongest passions allow us some rest, but vanity keeps us perpetually in motion." [32]

Clothing Behavior in Lower Status Positions

Barber and Lobel reported that the middle and lower classes dislike the daring and the unusual in clothes. They want respectable clothes that everyone is wearing. They stress femininity and prettiness as desirable qualities in a style.[33]

Another picture of the shopping behavior of the lower-class woman was drawn from data collected in Chicago, Louisville, Trenton, and Tacoma over a period of twelve years:

> Many working class women exhibit extremely narrow horizons in their choices of shopping places. In

[32] "Society Now Ruled by the 1,000," *St. Louis Post-Dispatch* (Sunday, December 4, 1966), p. 22H.
[33] Barber and Lobel, op. cit., p. 130.

comparison with middle class women, they are very provincial shoppers. The working class wife confines most of her shopping expeditions to those neighborhood stores where experience has taught her that she will neither be "taken" nor "ignored." She prefers to make her big ticket purchases through "connections," such as relatives or long-time friends who run businesses themselves. Partly this reliance on relatives or friends has a real bargain or discount as its object. Equally, however, such reliance is a means of avoiding the unknown in stores or salespeople, where the outcome of the purchasing venture can be viewed much less optimistically. The working class wife's preference for a personalized world and her discomfort with the impersonal influence her shopping as they do other aspects of her life.[34]

The authors go on to say that women claimed preferences for simple, plain garments, yet their actual behavior belied their stated choices.

> We know that the working class women are often among the fanciest, frilliest, and fussiest dressers on any given occasion. We know that their conscious, superego-directed apparel goals are sometimes betrayed; that a fancy dress somehow gets into their closets and gets worn to a party. If working class women reject such clothing in a hypothetical test, it is partially because they are aware of the strictures placed by style experts against too much frilliness in clothing; and because they too share in the general feminine intelligence which upholds the advantages of simple, versatile clothing. . . .
>
> Our Chicago study showed that the overwhelming majority of women at all class levels believe they dress less fancily than the average woman. Since this is obviously impossible, we are driven to the conclusion that women try to believe "the dresses are frillier on the other side of the room." [35]

In describing status incongruence, Malewski states the proposition: "People whose status is very high and stable

[34] Lee Rainwater, Richard Coleman, and Gerald Handel, *Workingman's Wife* (New York: Oceana Publications Inc., 1959), p. 163.

[35] Ibid., p. 198.

pay less attention to behavior as the visible symbol of their higher status." [36] The reverse of this statement appears to be true when one examines the importance of the visible symbols of clothing as used by lower-class Puerto Ricans both at home and in New York City. Oscar Lewis [37] describes the kinds and costs of clothing and jewelry owned by two Puerto Rican women, stating that they spent from two to three times as much on clothing as on household goods. Felicita Rios, while earning from $1,400 to $1,700 a year, had an inventory that included "25 dresses, 7 skirts and 7 blouses, 12 pair of shoes, 7 brassières, 22 panties, and 3 gold rings."

The author continues by saying that "the emphasis upon clothing and appearance was too widespread a pattern to be explained by the occupational requirements of a prostitute. In part it may also have been caused by inferiority feelings and the reparative needs and by imitation of the Puerto Rican middle class, which stresses the importance of clothing." [38]

In New York City, Felicita's sister and husband bought $3,035 worth of clothing and jewelry on an income of $8,000 (37 per cent of their income). Obviously, clothing was very important even though their income was higher than those of their Puerto Rican relatives. Some of their possessions included: [39]

Soledad		*Benedicto*	
27 dresses	$304	5 suits	$530
3 suits	44	10 pair pants	165
11 skirts	43	23 shirts	124
11 blouses	26	25 undershirts	?
11 slips (half)	17	25 undershorts	?
16 panties	8	4 pair shoes	77
7 pair of shoes	45	40 pair socks	?
2 wrist watches	115	2 watches	280
		1 gold chain	225
		3 gold rings	495

In a clothing study of low-income ($3,000 and below) Negro and white women, Marilyn Hunter found that

[36] Andrzej Malewski, "The Degree of Status Incongruence and Its Effects," in *Class, Status and Power*, op. cit., p. 307.
[37] Oscar Lewis, *La Vida* (New York: Random House, 1965), p. XXXVII.
[38] Ibid.
[39] Ibid., p. XL.

Negro women thought that clothes were more important than did white women; more Negro women also felt that people judged them by their clothes. One of the most interesting trends of the study pointed to the fact that Negro women had significantly more garments than the white women owned—these comprised numbers of casual dresses, formal dresses, coats, dressy suits, and blouses.

The Negro women had more dresses given to them as hand-me-downs than did the white women. When purchasing dresses, Negro women paid more for their street and business dresses, house and casual dresses, and formal and cocktail dresses than the white women did. The Negro women received most of their hand-me-down dresses from employers. No white woman in the study had clothes from employers.

More of the white women reported that their favorite dress was plain with no design. Many of the Negro women reported that their favorite dress had lace or a metallic thread—none of the white women made this statement. More of the white women knew a name for style and fiber content of their favorite dress than did Negro women. On the other hand, more Negro women reported that their favorite dress was a warm color while most white women reported that their favorite dress was a cool color.

Although the Negro group had more clothing, the investigator suggests that in such a study one should also know whether items enumerated are actually wearable, in that they fit the figure or the occasion at which they are worn. In other words, there probably is a difference between number of clothes in one's possession and clothes in a wearable wardrobe.[40]

Sioux Indian parents with meager incomes feel that they must dress their children in new, stylish, and clean clothes. Murray and Rosalie Wax report that peer group approval is so desired that children will not wear clothes that are criticized by their schoolmates. The demands of children of very young ages surprised the investigators as they reported:

[40] Marilyn Kay Hunter, "A Comparison of Clothing Between Negro and White Women of Low Socio-Economic Status," unpublished Master's thesis, University of Missouri, January, 1967.

My boy (third grade) doesn't want to wear his jeans. They kind of lost their color—they're kind of light blue like. He says, "That's faded; that's old; they'll laugh at me; I can't wear that."

My girls (fourth and fifth grade) they have to change anklets every day. . . . They say, "Can't you ever wash our anklets white?" And oh, I get mad at them. And they say, "Can't you iron better? Our dresses are wrinkled and we can't wear them."

We don't want them to dress in a faded dress or jeans because they really make fun of each other. So we have had a hard time. We practically go broke. [41]

[41] Murray and Rosalie Wax, "Formal Education in an American Indian Community," supplement to *Social Problems*, Vol. II, No. 4 (Spring, 1964).

Work and Leisure

Clothing, ornaments, tattoos, or tribal markings have probably indicated man's work status since the beginning of history. Indeed, lack of clothing may have signified the positions of slaves and captives in many parts of the world. The importance of clothing to work is perhaps second only to the importance of dress as a symbol of social status.

Mark Twain recounts many situations where occupational clothes make the man; further, he states that clothes are the man and without them he is a "cipher, a vacancy, a nobody, a nothing."

> A policeman in plain clothes is one man; in his uniform he is ten. Clothes and title are the most potent thing, the most formidable influence in the earth. They move the human race to willing and spontaneous respect for the judge, the general, the admiral, the bishop, the ambassador, the frivolous earl, the idiot duke, the sultan, the king, the emperor. No great title is efficient without clothes to support it.[1]

The garb of the priest is described as having both evidences of a servile status and a vicarious life. Priestly

[1] Mark Twain, "Clothes Are the Man," from *Mark Twain at Your Fingertips,* edited by Carolyn T. Hornsberger (New York: Beechhurst Press, Inc., 1948), p. 321.

vestments are in Veblen's terms "ornate, grotesque, inconvenient, and, at least ostensibly, comfortless to the point of distress. . . . In economic theory, the priest is a body servant, constructively in attendance upon the person of the divinity whose livery he wears."[2] The point is also emphasized that he is expected to refrain from the usual product-producing efforts.

Rudofsky, likewise, describes encumbering ecclesiastical robes and military uniforms as recognized symbols of respect for those particular vocations. He further states that they embody the principle of tightness or restriction of movement and that they intensify the owner's personal awareness of the symbol he is wearing. "The tension of muscles and nerves due to clothing apparatus, reflects itself in a change of behavior. The outstanding example of that personal transformation is the military style of machine-like motion."[3]

Women, too, use clothing as occupational symbols. Martha Hyer is reported to have said that she never feels more like a movie star than when she wears a fur coat—this symbol of glamour and luxury is what she believes the public expects of an actress.

The other extreme is the woman who deglamorizes herself by playing down her femininity and reducing herself to an office. Murray Wax says that she tries to "minimize her natural shape, smell, color, texture, and movement and to replace these by impersonal neutral surfaces." He further states that these types of women often are found as a part of bureaucratic authority.[4]

Yet many women seeking employment in male-dominated occupations have real justification in trying to dress to please their prospective employers. Here is an instance where a woman was denied a job because of her dress:

> We had one young woman come down here from one of the Big Ten. She had the M.A. and was working on her doctoral dissertation and we would have very much liked to have gotten her, but when she saw

[2] Thorstein Veblen, *The Theory of the Leisure Class* (New York: Modern Library, 1934), p. 183.

[3] Bernard Rudofsky, *Are Clothes Modern?* (Chicago: Paul Theobold, 1947), p. 156.

[4] Murray Wax, "Themes in Cosmetics and Grooming," *American Journal of Sociology*, Vol. 62 (May, 1957), p. 592.

the Dean, he turned her down. He did not like the way she was turned out, thought she was too stylishly dressed. We had thought she looked very lovely.[5]

On the other hand, studies have shown that males tend to dress up for job applications even when their jobs do not require such clothing. In a study called "The Social Significance of Clothing in Occupational Life," Form and Stone found that three fifths of the white collar group dressed up for their job interview; one fifth of the manual workers took some care in clothes to impress their future employer.

A composite of various occupational clothing symbols and cues reported in this study is presented in Table 1.

The important cues for occupational identity were types of clothes—uniforms, overalls, and suits. Obviously, more people used clothing to identify manual occupations than white-collar occupations. The condition or cleanliness of garments was also an important indication of type of work to the respondents. Expressive symbols such as neatness, taste, and total effect were also used in identifying workers. White-collar workers used more symbols and more types of cues for occupational identification of the wearer than did manual workers.

In the Clothing TAT (see pages 69–80) occupation of the characters pictured was used in thematic responses of the storytellers for all seven cards. The types of occupations mentioned ranged from teacher, minister, lawyer, coach, social worker, junior leaguer, to chorus girl, gangster, and prostitute. Occupation was noted most often in Cards IV, VI, and VIII.

Another informative study that deals with occupational images[6] elicited responses from 1,045 students to seven occupational life styles. These students projected numbers and types of clothing in addition to many other consumption practices for an assembly line worker, a carpenter, a bookkeeper, a salesman, a sales manager, a teacher, and a doctor. Table 2 shows the projections in numbers of suits, overalls, and items of formal wear.

[5] Theodore Caplow and Reece J. McGee, *The Academic Marketplace* (New York: Science Editions, Inc., 1961), p. 125.

[6] Howard A. Rosencranz, "The Relation of Social References to Occupational Life Styles," unpublished Ph.D. dissertation, Michigan State University, 1960.

TABLE 1 PERCENTAGE DISTRIBUTION OF CLOTHING SYMBOLS, CUES, AND EXPRESSIVE ITEMS USED BY VANSBURG MEN TO IDENTIFY THE OCCUPATIONAL AFFILIATIONS OF OTHERS [7]

Symbols, cues, and expressive items	*White collar workers*	*Manual workers*	*Totals*
Type of garment:			
Uniforms	50	24	35
Overalls, coveralls, aprons, work clothes	23	24	24
Suits, sport clothes, and tuxedos	23	7	14
Fabric cues:			
Marks on clothing— grease, paint, dust	27	21	24
Dirty or clean clothes	18	31	25
Good quality, expensive, or tailored clothes	18	21	20
Expressive cues:			
Well-dressed or dressed up	18	21	20
Neatly dressed or presentable	9	14	12
Conservative vs. flashy and loud clothes	23	3	12
Other cues:			
Shoes, adaptations to clothes (special pockets), trade-marks, and other labels	27	3	14
Hands dirty or clean	9	3	6
Tools of the trade: rulers, briefcase, etc.	9	—	4
Totals*	254	172	210
Number of respondents	22	29	51

* Some respondents identified more than one type of garment, symbol, or expressive item.

Although people do not follow occupational symbols or stereotypes to the letter, the person who dresses in a manner very unlike his occupational group or profession probably does not like his profession. "If a man is a banker and doesn't dress like one (expensive and conservative), then I conclude he does not really think of himself as a banker,

[7] William H. Form, and Gregory P. Stone," The Social Significance of Clothing in Occupational Life," Michigan Agricultural Experiment Station Technical Bulletin, No. 247 (1955), p. 18.

TABLE 2 PERCENTAGE DISTRIBUTION OF PROJECTED NUMBER OF SUITS, OVERALLS, AND FORMAL WEAR FOR SEVEN OCCUPATIONAL GROUPS

Occupation	*Average number of suits*	*Average number of overalls*	*Tuxedo or formal wear for male*
Assembly line worker	2.6	5.0	no
Carpenter	3.0	6.0	yes (5%)
Bookkeeper	3.7	2.4	yes (5%)
Salesman	4.2	2.3	yes (20%)
Sales manager	5.8	2.4	yes (80%)
Teacher	4.5	2.5	yes (40%)
Doctor	5.8	2.3	yes (80%)

or at least not a good one. He probably secretly believes he ought to be something else. He has problems." [8]

Successful men from the business and communications hierarchy often have their clothes made in Savile Row in London in order to project the image of elegant, formal, and conservative tailoring. The actor Clifton Webb reported that he had his clothes made in London because "English tailors make clothes for gentlemen," [9] and it is only recently that actors have been admitted to the rank of gentlemen.

On the college campus, sometimes future occupational aspirations are evidenced by the students themselves. At least, there persist on some campuses the following stereotypes—the "aggie" wears a cowboy hat and a blue denim jacket, the artist wears longer hair and casual clothes, the "Greek" boy is in a blue jacket with his fraternity crest, the "Greek" girl wears a Villager and monogrammed jewelry. The college professor is thought to be in baggy tweeds or is seen at rare ceremonial occasions in his academic robe, hood, and mortarboard.

At the other end of the occupational scale, the assembly line worker tends to disengage himself from his occupational role. He says, "I am not what I do; do not judge me by what I do for a living," and turns to his nonworking

[8] Dr. William Jennings Bryan, Jr., "Clothes Tell What You Are," *St. Louis Post-Dispatch* (March 31, 1965), p. 38.

[9] Russell Lynes, *A Surfeit of Honey* (New York: Harper & Row, 1957), p. 69.

life for values and identity.[10] This often includes his clothes, as can be observed in the case of workers who keep work clothes in lockers at the plant and change before working and again before returning home.

A sensitive description of the work clothing of the rural working man of several decades ago is recalled by James Agee:

> So far as I know, overalls are a garment native to this country. . . . They are the standard or classical garment at the very least of the southern rural American working man: they are his uniform, the badge and proclamation of his peasantry. . . .
>
> Perhaps little can be said of them after all: yet something. The basis: what they are: can best be seen when they are still new; before they have lost or gained shape and color and texture; and before the white seams of their structure have lost their brilliance. . . . A new suit of overalls has among its beauties those of a blueprint: and they are the ways of a working man.
>
> The shirts too; squarely cut, and strongly seamed; with big square pockets and with metal buttons: the cloth stiff, the sweat cold when it is new, the collar large in newness and standing out in angles under ears; so that in these new work-clothes a man has the shy and silly formal charm of a mail-order-catalogue engraving.
>
> The changes that age, use, weather, work upon these.
>
> They have begun with the massive yet delicate beauty of most things which are turned out most cheaply in great tribes by machines: and on this basis of structure they are changed into images and marvels of nature.
>
> The structures sag, and take on the look, some of use; some, the pencil pockets, the pretty atrophies of what is never used; the edges of the thigh pockets become stretched and lie open, fluted, like the gills of a fish. The bright seams lose their whiteness and are lines and ridges. The whole fabric is shrunken to size,

[10] Bennett M. Berger, "The Sociology of Leisure: Some Suggestions," in Erwin O. Smigel, editor, *Work and Leisure* (New Haven, Conn.: College and University Press, 1963), p. 34.

which was bought large. The whole shape, texture, color, finally substance, all are changed.[11]

Leisure

The Greeks believed that leisure was concerned with activities worthy of a free man: politics, debate, philosophy, art, and athletic contests—all expressed a style of life. Leisure was the schooling or cultivation of oneself so that he could express the highest values of his culture. Work was productive activity "below the dignity of a free man, fit for only slaves and women." [12]

The industrialized West conceives of leisure as time that is not devoted to paid occupations and "leisure activities are viewed as primarily re-creative and restorative." [13]

In many older civilizations the number of days of leisure often amounted to half the year. The Roman passion for holidays reached its peak in the middle of the fourth century when days unlawful for judicial or political business numbered 175.[14]

At the turn of the century Thorstein Veblen discussed the clothes of the leisure class, which were too ornate, too expensive, and too confining to allow the wearer to participate in useful work. Well-versed in the complex systems of etiquette developed by persons with time to do so and time to learn their complexities, the lady of means wore time-consuming attire: corsets to be laced, clothes to be hand wrought and cared for by servants. Dress was also in Veblen's eyes a conspicuous waste of goods, but waste according to a social standard. In his scientific objectivity, he considered this paradox:

[11] James Agee, "The Importance of Clothing to Poor Whites," in *Let Us Now Praise Famous Men* (Boston: Houghton Mifflin Company, 1960), p. 267.

[12] Berger, op. cit., p. 24.

[13] Ibid.

[14] Ibid., p. 109.

Leisure Class Clothes in Veblen's Time

> It is true of dress in even a higher degree than most other items of consumption, that people will undergo a very considerable degree of privation in the comforts or necessities of life in order to afford what is considered a decent amount of wasteful consumption; so that it is by no means an uncommon occurrence, in an inclement climate, for people to go ill clad in order to appear well dressed.[15]

Veblen goes on to cite the corset as a prime example of a garment designed to impress upon the beholder the fact

[15] Veblen, op. cit., p. 168.

that the wearer does not and cannot habitually engage in useful work.

Now and then female critics have cried out against the corseted, idle woman. The English feminist, Barbara Bodichon, found "the lady class of America more utterly idle than anywhere outside the harems of the east. A huge population of young ladies cluttered up the boarding houses, waiting to get married." [16]

Perhaps the holiday or festive garments can be considered the first leisure clothes. Practically all societies have some garb or decorative ornament set aside for festival times. Thackeray is eloquent when describing this type of attire in England in his day:

> Thus, then, my beloved Bob, I would have your dining-out suit handsome, neat, well-made, fitting you naturally and easily, and yet with a certain air of holiday about it, which should mark its destination. It is not because they thought their appearance was much improved by the ornament, that the ancient philosophers and topers decorated their old pates with flowers:—it is not because a philosopher cares about dress that he wears it; but he wears his best as a sign of a feast, as a bush is the sign of an inn. You ought to mark a festival as a red-letter day, and you put on your broad and spotless white waist-coat, your finest linen, your shiniest boots, as much as to say, "It is a feast; here I am, clean, smart, ready with a good appetite, determined to enjoy. . . ." You must have proper pumps willing to sprint and whirl lightly, and a clean pair of gloves, with which you can take your partner's pretty little hand.[17]

Russell Lynes comments on more recent formal wear: [18]

> The tuxedo, known to the more expensive trade as the dinner jacket, and to the French as le smoking, is not the conservative object it once was. For one thing it weighs about a pound and a half less than it did

[16] Andrew Sinclair, *The Better Half* (New York: Harper & Row, 1965), p. 114.

[17] William Makepeace Thackeray, "Mr. Brown's Letters to His Nephew," published in the *Works of William M. Thackeray*, Vol. XIV (Philadelphia: J. B. Lippincott Company, 1884), p. 235.

[18] Lynes, op. cit., p. 69.

fifty years ago, and it can be bought in colors that haven't been seen on dressed-up men since the days of lace cuffs, jabots, and silk and you can buy tuxedos in such edible tones as "blueberry," "strawberry," "grape," and "banana." This fruit-salad approach to formality is evident in men's shops everywhere, but no more so than at Brooks Brothers of New York, traditionally known as a stronghold of the conservative and an institution as proper as a girl's seminary.

In England, Ferdynand Zweig says that he can tell how a man spends his leisure by the way he dresses—that if he meets a well-dressed young man he knows he is interested in dances, shows, and films. A pub-goer is apt to dress shabbily with cloth cap and muffler, partly because there is a tradition of shabby clothes among pub-goers.[19]

Russell Lynes also notes the various at-home leisure activities that have resulted in changing attire for middle-class men in particular.

> Do-it-yourself is the biggest thing ever to hit the blue-jeans industry. Manufacturers of work clothes have a brand-new market among what used to be called the white-collar class for pants named "steadies," "slimerees," and "Taper Twills," and for work shirts, denim jackets, and work shoes. The phenomenal sale of men's blue jeans is a rare instance of a fad that was first taken up in the East by cowboy-minded teenagers and became a general fashion for their elders, both male and female.
>
> The eagerness with which the suburban male approaches the out-of-doors not only impels him into the garden in work clothes; it also makes him want to eat his barbecued spareribs in the back yard dressed like a bird of paradise. For some reason food seems to taste better to him if he has on blue canvas shoes, brick-red or canary-yellow slacks, and a pastel sports shirt which hangs free, like a young matron's maternity smock, outside the pants. These are symbols of leisure and the good life as advertised by Hollywood. They are also symbols of the revolt against the conformity that is imposed on men by the daily routine of business. Here, supposedly, the free-wheeling spirit is given wings. The country squire becomes the

[19] Ferdynand Zweig, *The British Worker* (London: Penguin Books, 1952), p. 160.

Oriental potentate in fine raiment, and the effect is as quaint as the peasant costumes of any nation.[20]

Sportswear As an Example of Leisure Clothes

Riding Clothes—1914

The acceptance and development of sports by and for women has been mirrored in the clothing devised for these leisure-time activities. During the eighteenth and nineteenth centuries the only sport women were allowed to take part in was riding. Eighteenth-century riding costumes were "a kind of long cassock buttoned down the front so that it could be opened to let the skirts fall over their high riding boots. This costume was considered too indecent and unbecoming to be depicted in paintings." [21] The introduction of the side saddle allowed the woman to ride her horse gracefully and still keep her feet covered. Women did not again ride astride until after World War I.

After the Civil War croquet swept the American nation, closely followed by tennis. At first the playing of tennis was refined. "There were no overhead strokes, no smashes, no back court drives. Women held the trains of their long dresses daintily and were never expected to run after the ball." [22] Later, when mothers of eligible young ladies found that tennis provided a way for young people to get together, the sport mushroomed. "The number of women on the courts was legion. The result was a veritable upheaval of the laws of fashion." [23]

In the middle nineties, women played in a tight corset, a long trailing skirt, and a blouse with voluminous sleeves. Often they added an elaborate befeathered or beflowered hat.[24] "The most modern part of her dress was her shoes

[20] Lynes, op. cit., p. 72.

[21] "Sports and the Upper Classes," *CIBA Review*, 1965/4, pp. 11–21.

[22] Oliver Jensen, *The Revolt of American Women* (New York: Harcourt, Brace and World, 1952), p. 124.

[23] Ibid.

[24] James Laver, *Taste and Fashion* (London: George G. Harrap and Company, 1937), p. 222.

Tennis—1910

which were of black canvas with india-rubber soles, but even they had high heels." Eventually, skirts and washable blouses became the right attire for tennis and consequently fashionable. Copies of men's stiff straw boaters replaced those decorated with flowers.[25]

The newspaper media followed society onto the tennis court, to the links, and to the fashionable watering places. There was a relatively small but important summer resort business for the wealthy in the 1890's. Such summer resorts as Saratoga Springs, New York, and White Sulphur Springs, Virginia, had been fashionable even before 1825.[26] However, people of leisure were few and whatever the

[25] *CIBA Review*, op. cit., p. 15.

[26] Jesse F. Steiner, *Americans at Play* (New York: McGraw-Hill, Inc., 1933), p. 5.

state of a man's affairs, he felt obligated by public opinion to spend his time in some sort of public or private business. Until leisure attained a more respectable status, those who could afford it in conspicuous fashion disguised their indulgence at "health" resorts that profited by the trade in valetudinarianism, whether real or affected, but, in every case, costly.[27]

After the Civil War, Newport, Long Branch, Nahant, the White Mountains, and other places as far south as Florida and as far west as the Rockies were attracting seasonal crowds of vacationists that increased by the year. The annual trek southward to winter resorts began to assume considerable proportions during the nineties, and specialized clothes were introduced for resort wear.[28]

Country clothes came about when the locomotive created the need. The steam engine made traveling to various watering places easier. These country clothes tended to be of lighter colors and in thin and washable fabrics such as silk and linen and cotton.

The tailored look was revived in the eighties with the shirtwaist. Hall notes that the shirtwaist "costume was given additional impetus by the increasing vogue for sports of all kinds.[29] Charles Dana Gibson immortalized the "Gibson Girl"[30] wearing a woman's mannish shirtwaist having a deep pleat over each shoulder, with a high stiff collar and stiff starched cuffs. A variation of the blouse with softer collar and tie continued for many years to be worn by all women who took sports seriously.[31]

The first bathing costumes are described by Laver as being voluminous with "ample pantaloons and a thick roomy dress with long sleeves and reaching to the throat. The whole outfit was adorned with frills and flounces which when wet must have made it even heavier."[32]

Bathing was usually segregated, with women having their own beach or men and women being admitted to the

[27] Marshall B. Davidson, *Life in America*, Vol. II (Boston: Houghton Mifflin Company, 1951), p. 15.

[28] Steiner, op. cit., p. 8.

[29] Carrie A. Hall, *From Hoopskirts to Nudity* (Caldwell, Idaho: The Caxton Printers Ltd., 1938), p. 83.

[30] Ibid., p. 84.

[31] Max Von Boehn and Oskar Fischel, *Modes and Manners of the Nineteenth Century*, Vol. IV. (New York: E. P. Dutton & Co., Inc., 1927), p. 219.

[32] Laver, op. cit., p. 218.

Gibson Girl Shirtwaist—1895

beach at certain and separate times. The bather could dress at home, get into a horse-drawn vehicle that was closed, be driven to the beach, and be backed out into the ocean and into the arms of a waiting superintendent who helped in the adjustment to the water and watched to see that the bather didn't stray too far. "By mid-century, the pleasure of sea bathing was an accepted, healthful sport for men, women and children. As late as the 1860's three to five minutes spent in the water was considered by physicians a long enough time from which to derive benefit. In the last two decades of the century, sea bathing was accepted not as a health measure but as a recreation and so thought was given to an appropriate costume." [33]

By the middle 1880's women's bathing costumes had become a little more daring. Some of them consisted of what was apparently a one-piece garment, reaching from the knees to the throat, and with very short sleeves. Sometimes the top of the suit was decolléte about as much as an evening dress of the period, and the trouser leg had risen to within several inches above the knee. Many women bathers added a skirt of knee length, and this costume remained unchanged, with a very few variations, for years to come.[34]

But with time the bathing costume dropped away piece by piece, until it became topless in the 1960's. Payne suggests that "the bathing costume is one of the first straws in the wind indicating the eventual break with tradition regarding concealment of the body and the evolution of garments appropriate for varied activities." [35]

The bicycle, which first appeared in the mid-seventies, had a tremendous influence on clothing and "the fact that women became cyclists imposed an entirely new set of problems, which were to go on agitating both fashion designers and moralists for many years." [36]

Victorian prudery was reluctant to admit that women had legs. But to cycle a woman had to have the use of these two appendages, and their existence had to be admitted. It was impossible for her to wear the long skirts that sufficed for skating, croquet, and tennis. Long skirts were not only inconvenient but were also a safety hazard. The woman cyclist was forced to adopt the knickerbockers of the male cyclist or to wear a shorter skirt. Women did both. Parisian women quickly adopted bloomer costumes—these consisted of a "very wide pair of knickerbockers; stockings, with boots or shoes; a simple shirt with collar and tie and a soft felt hat with no trimming. Later the

[33] Turner R. Wilcox, *Five Centuries of American Costume* (New York: Charles Scribner's Sons, 1963), p. 145.

[34] Laver, op. cit., p. 219.

[35] Blanche Payne, *History of Costume* (New York: Harper & Row, 1965), p. 518.

[36] Laver, op. cit., p. 89.

knickerbockers were superseded by a divided skirt."[37] Elegant ladies often wore a bolero over a white blouse and held their hats in place with a tightly drawn veil. In addition, their cycling garb was generally cut from navy blue or black cheviot with stockings to match.[38]

Sarah Bernhardt gave this opinion of trouser-skirts for women: "I think that the bicycle will have more far-reaching effect on our mode of life than is readily apparent. All these young girls and women roving around are abandoning to an appreciable extent their roles in the household."[39] The Women's Rescue League was vitally interested in these young girls and warned that "thirty percent of all fallen women had at some time been bicycle riders."[40]

Davidson sums up the bicycle's contribution in this way:

> During the score of years that the sport maintained its great popularity it did more than anything else to bring a free, wholesome companionship to men and women. It played a large part in liberating women from bondage of Victorian clothes and behavior. . . . At the turn of the century, the census bureau declared that "few articles ever used by man have created so great a revolution in social conditions as the bicycle".[41]

After 1900 the automobile entered the life of women of fashion. "It was not until the turn of the century and the appearance of the limousine, with its luxurious appointments, that motoring was considered a part of the life of the grande dame."[42]

Since the unpaved roads required the use of garments for protection, fashionable people had an opportunity to develop specialized clothes just for motoring. These included motor veils, hats, caps, coats, capes, gauntlets, gloves, and goggles. The veil was one of the most unique parts of the costume, for early vehicles had no windshields to break the strong draft of wind, even though speeds were only about fifteen or twenty miles an hour. Some veils

[37] Hall, op. cit., p. 70.
[38] *CIBA Review*, op. cit., p. 20.
[39] Ibid., p. 10.
[40] Jensen, op. cit., p. 126.
[41] Davidson, op. cit., p. 65.
[42] Hall, op. cit., p. 86.

were voluminous, filmy, soft creations swathing picturesque hats, framing faces, and tying under chins in frothy, airy aureoles.

A definite change in silhouette was directly credited to the motor car—the change from smooth-fitted coats to loose, roomy, large-sleeved wraps styled for utility and comfort. To quote from a leading fashion magazine: "They are wraps that move not with your movement, but which allow you to move in them freely." These, the magazine continues, are "the most rational cloak models of late years." [43]

> By the opening years of the 20th century, Americans were taking their recreation in dead earnest. Step by step the working hours of most people had grown fewer and their leisure greater, and their hunt for amusement more intense. Having fun, according to one critic, had become the crowning ritual of American life. Billions of dollars were involved in the business of supplying it through moving pictures, automobiles, radio, professional sporting events, sporting equipment for amateurs, vacation equipment and facilities and endless other means.[44]

Closely following the leisure and sports boom, clothes to enjoy them in were created. By the mid-1920's stores had opened special departments for sports clothes; these were soon divided into active and spectator apparel. A new word came into our vocabulary in 1928—"spectator sports" frocks, designed for the woman who was merely an observer at sports events.[45]

Skiing, too, heralded profound changes in sportswear. This advice was given to modern skiers by *Vogue:*

> Dress in layers: better two thin leotards than a single thick one. Better two thin cotton undershirts than one thick sweater. Silk underwear and gloves under shirts and mittens in icy weather. . . . Keep socks and ski boots meticulously dry. . . . Woolen caps are warmest and most professional. Ski teachers

[43] Doris Jane Brockway, "Social, Political and Historical Influences Reflected in Twentieth Century Costume," unpublished Master's thesis, University of Washington, 1939, p. 55.

[44] Davidson, op. cit., p. 4.

[45] Brockway, op. cit., p. 144.

hate the bunny look of a junked up hat; they prefer a cowboy or stocking cap pulled way down over the forehead. . . . The less paraphernalia the better. All those big belts with zippers add bulk and shorten a trim skiing look. Keep the minimum of makeup in zipper pockets. A well-cut jumpsuit gives you freedom of movement . . . makes you look tall and sleek.[46]

The word après-ski now signifies a whole new category of ultraglamorous leisure clothing. No word at present symbolizes a wider scope of elegance in leisure.[47]

[46] *Vogue* (November 1, 1969), p. 78.

[47] The author is indebted to Margaret W. Watts for many hours of library research on leisure and sportswear.

12 Symbols of Masculinity and Femininity

Clothes are used by most societies to distinguish between males and females; even in those groups where both sexes wear a skirt there is a difference in length or style. Usually the headdress or hairstyle is different for males and females. In addition, there may be a difference in the number and types of ornaments.

Jivaro women in South America wear a simple rectangle of woven material, the upper edges of which go under the left arm and over the right shoulder, where the two corners are held together by a wooden pin. It is taken in at the waist by a simple belt and hangs below the knees. Men wear a short skirt but add many ornaments and painted designs to their bodies. Males also wear a fur and feather crown, are very fastidious about their lustrous black hair, and never travel without a "vanity" case.[1]

The Chavantes, most feared of Brazilian Indians, wear very little clothing. Yet there are still male and female differences, women wearing a simple fig leaf and bead necklace, while men are ornamented by wooden ear skewers, cord wrappings on wrists, ankles, and neck, and a yellow penis cone.[2]

[1] Edward Weyer, Jr., *Primitive People Today* (Garden City, N. Y.: Doubleday & Company, Inc., 1959), pp. 91–92.
[2] Ibid., p. 121.

Tuareg men and women wear voluminous desert costumes covering most of their bodies. Tuareg men, however, wear veils and white turbans, while the women show their faces.[3] In another part of Africa, the Masai differentiate the sexes by ornaments for the women and headdresses and shields for the men. Metal armbands from wrist to elbow on the right arm and from elbow to shoulder on the left arm adorn Masai women for life. Men, in their warrior role, wear flaunting headdresses of lions' manes or ostrich plumes and carry shields with clan designs.[4]

In the Judaeo-Christian tradition of the Old Testament, *Deuteronomy* 22:5 states Moses' proclamation that "a woman shall not wear that which pertaineth unto a man, neither shall a man put on a woman's garment; for whosoever doeth these things is an abomination unto Jehovah thy God." Among the many Anglo-Saxon admonitions Philip Stubbes proclaimed in *The Anatomy of Abuses,*

> Our apparell was given as a signe distinctive to discerne betwixt sexe and sexe; and therefore one to weare the apparell of another sexe is to participate with the same, and to adulterate the veritie of his owne kinde.[5]

An interesting historical account of sex differences in children's clothing is recorded in Philippe Aries' *Centuries of Childhood:*

> But two other tendencies were to influence the development of children's dress from the seventeenth century on. The first emphasized the effeminate appearance of the little boy. We have seen earlier that the boy in "bib and tucker," before the age of "the robe with collar," wore the same robe and skirt as the girl. This effeminization of the little boy which became noticeable about the middle of the sixteenth century, was at first a novelty and barely hinted at. For instance the upper part of the boy's costume retained the characteristics of masculine dress; but soon the little boy was given the lace collar of the little girl, which was exactly the same as that worn by the

[3] Ibid., p. 142.
[4] Ibid., p. 183.
[5] Quoted by Lawrence Langner in *The Importance of Wearing Clothes* (New York: Hastings House, 1959), p. 63.

> ladies. It became impossible to distinguish a little boy from a little girl before the age of four or five, and this costume became established for something like two centuries. About 1770 boys stopped wearing the robe with collar after age four or five, but until that age they were dressed like little girls, and this would be the case until the end of the nineteenth century: This effeminate habit would be dropped only after the First World War, and its abandonment can be compared to that of the woman's corset as symptomatic of the revolution in dress corresponding to the general change in manners.
>
> It is interesting to note that the attempt to distinguish children was generally confined to the boys: the little girls were distinguished only by the false sleeves, as if childhood separated girls from adult life less than it did boys. The evidence provided by dress bears out the other indications furnished by the history of manners: boys were the first specialized children.[6]

Lindsmith and Strauss report a more modern example of sex identification and children's clothing. In this situation a five-year-old acquaintance of the authors attended a party during which children of both sexes bathed in the nude. When the child was asked how many boys and how many girls were at the party she answered, "I couldn't tell because they had their clothes off." [7]

In a study of two hundred boys and girls between the ages of four and twelve, Conn and Kanner [8] found that clothing and dress were the first criteria by which these children differentiated the sexes. Typically, little girls were associated with dresses and little boys with suits and pants. In addition, overalls, underwear, shirts, and neckties were considered to be appropriate for boys while petticoats, slips, blouses, skirts, and ribbons were associated with girls.

Vener studied one hundred and twenty children from the ages of thirty to sixty months using lists of sex-linked

[6] Philippe Aries, *Centuries of Childhood* (New York: Alfred A. Knopf, Inc., 1962), p. 58.

[7] Alfred Lindsmith and Anselm Strauss, *Social Psychology* (New York: Dryden Press, Inc., 1950), p. 427.

[8] J. H. Conn and L. Kanner, "Children's Awareness of Sex Differences," *Child Psychiatry*, Vol. 1 (1947), p. 327.

items. In general, he found that female items were easier for his sample to identify. His explanation is as follows:

> In contemporary American culture there are very few male articles which are as distinctly masculine as female articles are distinctly feminine. A father would never use lipstick, a brassière, or hosiery, whereas a mother might wear underwear that looks similar to men's briefs, or she might use a razor, a handkerchief, or don a shirt.[9]

Rudofsky remarks on the ceremonial dress of religious leaders, particularly those who wear robelike garments. He states that "the encumbering ceremonial robes of priests, which lend a good deal of dignity to the wearers, have conserved their female quality, since the priest's garment is the symbol of his renouncement of virility." [10]

Psychological researchers have used Freudian symbol interpretations to explain male and female traits. But Leon Levy found reasons to doubt their universal value. In a study of sex symbolism and symbolism of the sexes he found no relation at all for children of about ten years of age, a high occurrence of such a relation at the college age; no relation for early adolescents; and a slight relations possibility for educated adults of above college age.[11]

Gerard DeWit, using fifty stimulus words, found definite symbols of femininity to be "a rose, a flower, a bracelet, a dustpan, butterfly, a jewelcase; and as definitely masculine symbols: a stick, a necktie, a pocket, an eagle, a gun, a sabre, a hammer, and a machine." [12]

> It seems that despite their emancipation and a factual, legal equality in politics, business, and industry, women are still essentially considered by both sexes to be beautiful, attractive homemakers with a tinge of delicate flightiness, and the man is essen-

[9] Arthur M. Vener and Audrey Weese, "The Preschool Child's Perceptions of Adult Sex-Linked Cultural Objects," *Journal of Home Economics*, Vol. 57, No. 1 (January, 1965), p. 49.

[10] Rudofsky, *Are Clothes Modern?* (Chicago: Paul Theobold, 1947), p. 156.

[11] Gerard A. DeWit, *Symbolism of Masculinity and Femininity* (New York: Springer Publishing Co., Inc., 1963), p. 13. See page 238 for more description of this study.

[12] Ibid., p. 75.

> tially considered to be an esthetically unappealing, strong, courageous fighter and a protector and the creator of a craftmanship requiring technical knowledge of the world.

In comparing sex-differential findings of his study, DeWit notes that male participants gave

> a higher number of masculine than feminine meanings, indicating a more self-centered attitude; a higher number of "objects used" associations indicating a greater inclination towards simple associative thinking; in the dominant majority of sex symbols given, a much greater inclination towards immature obscene thinking. The female participants, on the other hand, show by a greater number of analogy appearance reactions, especially in relation to their own sex, that feminine beauty is more valued by women than by men; by a higher number of character analogy reactions, a keener interest in the psychological aspects of the masculine and feminine existence; and by a higher number of unexplained masculine reactions, most likely a better integration of sexually symbolic aspects into the symbolism of the whole person.[13]

He goes on to suggest that women probably have a more mature attitude than men toward the symbolism of the sexes.

Margaret Mead stresses the cultural settings and meanings attached to symbols of masculinity and femininity.[14] Most societies have an "ideal" female and an "ideal" male type. Yet within each group there are a few individuals who

> insist on playing the role of the opposite sex in occupation or dress or interpersonal sex activities. Whether full transvestism will occur seems to be a question of cultural recognition of this possibility. . . . Peoples may provide sex-reversal roles for both sexes—as among the Siberian aborigines, where sex reversal is associated with shamanism; they may permit it to men but deny it to women; or they may not provide any pattern at all.[15]

[13] Ibid., p. 79.

[14] Margaret Mead, *Male and Female* (New York: Mentor Books, 1955), p. 103.

[15] Ibid.

The Mohave Indians recognize both male transvestites and female transvestites. The transvestite duplicates the behavior pattern of his adopted sex at an early age. When the child is given toys or garments of his true sex, he throws them away. "Then people prepare a shirt of shredded bark for the boy and a breech-clout for the girl. . . . Female transvestites (hwame) are like lewd women who also throw away their house-keeping implements, and run wild." [16]

Throughout recorded history, women have indeed adopted men's clothes for a variety of reasons: during wars for practical purposes, or as in the French Revolution, when some female revolutionaries wore trousers "not as a fighting aid so much as a visual indication that sex differentiation no longer existed." [17] Some reform groups in America in the 1850's, including the women of Modern Times, Long Island, and females of Berlin Heights, near Cleveland, were free-love colonies "who indicated their freedom by their dress." [18] Or, sex-linked imitations satisfy that old tyrant, fashion. Going back to the Egyptians of the Old Kingdom, elegant women imitated masculine fashions.[19] In 1940 a college girl "would be just about ostracized if she wasn't practically indistinguishable from a Princeton sophomore." [20]

Although Rudofsky has said that more women than men have worn trousers throughout history, we have for many centuries associated trousers with men. The trouserlike bloomer promoted around the 1850's was in part a symbol of female attempts to achieve equality with men; the boyish look of the flapper also reflected the emancipation of women, here de-emphasizing hips and bosom. However, both of these attempts were followed by feminine-type garments—bloomers were followed by wide sweeping

[16] Robert C. Owen, J. F. Deetz, and A. D. Fisher, *The North American Indians: A Sourcebook* (New York: The Macmillan Company, 1967), p. 413.

[17] Alice Morse Earle, *Two Centuries of Costume in America*, Vol. II (New York: The Macmillan Company, 1903), p. 766.

[18] Marie Bishop, "That Was New York," *The New Yorker*, (June 29, 1940), p. 44.

[19] Mila Contini, *Fashion* (New York: The Odyssey Press, 1965), p. 23.

[20] Jane Cobb, "Girls Will Be Boys," *The New York Times Magazine* (November 3, 1940), p. 10.

Beach Pajamas—1920's

skirts and the styles of the twenties were succeeded by Empire-type fashions highlighting the midriff and breasts.

Yet today we see many reversals of the trouser-skirt pattern for men and women. Pants for women in late years have evolved from the bloomer girls of 1850 to the sophisticated "celebrity" slacks of Marlene Dietrich, the slacks of World War II women defense workers to the sportswear vogue of the fifties and sixties. Even the names of women's pants present an impressive list—shorts, bermudas, jamaicas, minishorts, microshorts, slacks, jeans, pedal pushers, culottes, slim jims, toreadors, knickers, stretch pants, bell bottoms, harem pants, beach pajamas, and most recently, hot pants. Sports and active leisure activities probably gave the greatest impetus to pants for women in the initial phases of this movement. Now pants-suits for street and office wear and evening pants are adding new dimensions to the picture. Even the designs for "space" clothes show how pants are the only practical type of garment for space travel, thus adding the prospect of still wider use of bifurcated garments for women.

The first recent suggestion for skirts for men may have come from beachwear designed in the early 1950's—with wrap-around sarong-type cover-ups proposed for after-swim wear. In December, 1966,[21] a Munich men's shop showed miniskirted males. (Along with the skirt, the boy model was wearing a shirt and necktie made of checked fabric that matched the skirt and high laced boots.) Jacques Esterel's collection in the spring of 1967 included a plaid kilt suit for men called a "Mirontone." (In this case the model was also wearing red stockings and shoes with ankle straps.)

The treatment of the hair is another recent reversal of the usual male-female symbols. Not only the long flowing locks, but also the time and money spent on hair preparations and styling are a break with the past for the boy. Schools make headlines when they send boys home for haircuts, make them wear hair nets or bathing caps in their swimming pools. Lest anyone think that today's schools are the first to cry out against boys' hair, consider the following from 1649:

> Forasmuch as the wearing of long haire after the manner of Ruffians and barbarous Indians, hath begun to invade New England contrary to the rule of Gods word wch sayth it is a shame for a man to wear long haire, as also the Commendable Custome generally of all the Godly of our nation until within this few yeares Wee the magistrates who have subscribed this paper (for the clearing of our owne innoceny in this behalfe) doe declare & manifest our dislike & detesta-

[21] *Columbia Missourian* (December 12, 1966).

Greece 1970

Germany 1966

Skirts for Men

> tion against the wearing of such long haire, as against a thing uncivil and unmanly whereby men doe deforme themselves, and offend sober & modest men, & doe corrupt good manners.[22]

Harold Rosenberg claims that, in America, masculinity is primarily associated with the out-of-doors and "with such certain outdoor trades as cattle driving, railroading, whaling, and trucking." These occupations are assumed to possess such masculine traits as "toughness, resourcefulness, love of being alone, fraternity with animals, attractiveness with women and the urge to abandon them." The derived clothing symbols are boots and saddle, lumber jackets and shirts, sailors' caps, pipes, and guns. Beards used to be material evidence of maleness: today they are frequently an appurtenance of masquerade. In fact, the look of masculinity is now largely a myth. "A person uncertain of his sexual identity dresses up in boots, bandanna, and riding breeches not so much to fool the public as to parade his ambiguity." [23]

Girls today are being compared with English gentlemen of the mid-eighteenth century. "One look at the men in Sheridan's *School for Scandal* at New York's Lyceum Theatre, and you'll see the resemblance—the George Washington's hairdo, the knickers, the white stockings, the buckled shoe." [24] James Laver relates the miniskirt to the doublet or tunic and tights worn by men in Elizabethan times.

The popular ideal of the teenage girl who really didn't look like the feminine ideal of the past was exemplified by Twiggy. However, Marshall McLuhan gives us an interesting insight into her appeal. "Her power is incompleteness; any person with a very undefined, casual, spontaneous image requires the viewer to complete it." [25]

In another article McLuhan and Leonard state that the new "sex symbols" poke fun at the super female—that boyish-looking Twiggy is to Sophia Loren as an X ray to a Rubens painting. "Not a realistic picture, but a deep, in-

[22] Paul Sann, *Fads, Follies and Delusions of the American People* (New York: Crown Publishers, Inc., 1967), p. 252.
[23] Harold Rosenberg, "Masculinity: Real and Put On," *Vogue* (November 15, 1967), p. 106.
[24] *Women's Wear Daily* (November 28, 1966).
[25] "Twiggy: Click Click," *Newsweek* (April 10, 1967), p. 65.

volving image. Not a specialized female, but a human being." The article describes an incident in which a college administrator was completely baffled by a young person whose sex he could not determine by outside appearances. McLuhan and Leonard say that in the most "technologically advanced societies, especially urban Britain and America, members of the younger generation are making it clear—in dress and music, deeds and words—just how unequivocally they reject their elders' sexual world." The young men with the long flowing hair are really saying: "We are no longer afraid to display what *you* may call feminine. We are willing to reveal that we have feelings, weaknesses, tenderness—that we are human." [26]

In England, during the last decade, males have been adopting clothing and hair styles that were formerly thought to be feminine. In part, this was a mechanism for gaining attention, for being noticed. Not only such singing groups as the Beatles and the Rolling Stones, but also males in the arts and theater favored this feminine look. An interesting description of Mary Quant's first meeting with the man later to be her husband and business partner follows:

> His arrival had an enormous effect on everybody . . . to begin with there was his appearance. He was very lean and long. He seemed to have no clothes of his own. He wore his mother's pyjama tops as shirts, generally in that colour known as "old gold" which usually comes . . . in shantung.
>
> His trousers also came out of his mother's wardrobe. Beautifully cut and very sleek fitting, the zip was at the side and they were in weird and wonderful variations of purple, prune, crimson, and putty. The trouble was that they came to a stop half-way down the calf of the leg so there was always a side gap of white flesh between the tops of the Chelsea-type boots he wore and the end of the trouser leg.[27]

In the late 1960's not only the artist-types but also quite ordinary men were more swept up in the "Peacock Revolution." These splendid trappings included Nehru jackets

[26] Marshall McLuhan and George B. Leonard, "The Future of Sex," *Look* (July 25, 1967), p. 56.

[27] Mary Quant, *Quant by Quant* (New York: Ballantine Books, Inc., 1967), p. 9.

worn with golden chains or medallions, shirts with lace cuffs, all-over embroidery, fur coats, velvet dinner jackets, double-knit suits, and above all color, color everwhere. What did all this kaleidoscope of color and form show? Of course, there are as many explanations as there are scents of the new colognes and perfumes worn by the now fragrant male: symbols of affluence, images of success, signs of the influence of mobility and world travel, vibrant expressions of the youth cult, or just "doing your own thing." James Laver contends that a nation's rank and power are related to the way men clothe themselves. He believes that when a nation ceases to be powerful, as happened to Britain in the 1950's, "people are no longer restrained from expressing themselves flamboyantly." Conversely, he argues that this can also happen in a powerful nation as the United States, "when people are overwhelmed by the complexity of political and social problems, crime racial disorders, balance of payments, etc." [28]

Again, Laver deplores the fact that boys and girls are dressing so much alike that in some cases it is difficult to tell them apart:

> In a patriarchal society—one in which the man is dominant—the clothes of men and women are vastly different. But in a matriarchal society the clothes worn by the two sexes become more and more alike.[29]

He also feels that men first lost major symbol of dominance when they lost their top hats.

Rudofsky has an interesting observation relating to the possible diminishing of maleness and femaleness in garments:

> The slide fastener, still in its teens and sometimes awkward, is of singular interest for it might put an end to an age-old custom born from superstition; the distinction between male and female clothing by buttoning right and left. There is no doubt as to the dual character of present-day clothes. Any piece of fabric can be charged with sexuality by simply working it into a precise shape. The resulting form might deter-

[28] As reported by Bernard Gavzer, "Colorful Fashion Plumage," *St. Louis Globe-Democrat* (April 11, 1968), p. 4C.

[29] James Laver, quoted by Jane Clark in *St. Louis Globe-Democrat* (February 1, 1967).

Male Peacocks—1970 and 1700

mine the actual sex. . . . The overlap of a blouse, a jacket or a coat determines the sex of the article. By buttoning a garment on the right side, it becomes suitable for men only and definitely unsuitable for women. Whatever the quaint explanations of folklore are, the right side of the body has always been male, the left side female; this orientation survived despite its irrationality. As the slide fastener can do without an overlap, this leaves us without a cue to the sex of clothing.[30]

Rudi Gernreich, after a sabbatical year, predicted the complete unisex look for males and females in the 1970's —shaved heads and bodies, then thinly applied body make-up for both sexes. His models wore identical outfits—black and white monokinis—topless for both male and female models. In his 1970 line all sexual variations were eliminated in his leotards, miniskirts, and pants-suits for both men and women. He feels that by wearing the same clothes, males and females "enhance their bodily differences." [31]

Jacques Esterel also promoted the unisex look in the 1970 Paris spring fashion openings. His several unisex creations included identical skirted numbers with buckskins and telescopic sleeves. He described another of his look-alike designs as having a "negligee snob" look.

Diana Trilling says:

> And gone—or going— . . . is the social-sexual differentiation between men and women in terms of dress and hairstyle. While I confess to having no love for the shared slovenliness of so many young men and women, since I see in it a depreciation of their pride in themselves as persons, I welcome the unisexual appearance of the sexes if only for its criticism of a culture in which sexually differentiated styles of hair and dress, designed not by God but by man, were treated as if they were biological actualities. As I see it, or at least as I hope it, whatever reduces the false separations between men and women is bound to reduce their suspicions and hostilities, and thus permit them a fuller expression of their human potentiality. Free of the cultural detritus of our sexual differences, perhaps we can come to a sounder and happier knowledge of our distinctive maleness and femaleness than is now permitted us.[32]

Will unisex ever become the norm? Besides the vast tradition of sex differences reflected in the clothing of

[30] Rudofsky, op. cit., p. 126.
[31] "Modern Living," *Time* (January 26, 1970), p. 39.
[32] Diana Trilling, "Female Biology in a Male Culture," *Saturday Review* (October 10, 1970), p. 40.

Unisex

practically all peoples everywhere, we have two rather subtle factors to take into account, both overlapping into the psychophysical spheres. The publication of the Museum of Contemporary Crafts describing their exhibit of "Body Covering" in the spring of 1968 reads as follows:

> Men and women dress differently because of differing sensual demands from the surface of their bodies. Once freed from primitive conditions, i.e., an igloo or a space capsule, these differences become apparent. An overall physical sensitivity makes clothes a source of sensual pleasure for women and their putting them on and their taking them off are rituals which men should take very seriously. It is only necessary to

> watch the symphonic process of taking off clothes, unfolding petticoat after petticoat, the anticipating gift-wrapping, well understood by little girls with dolls. These sensual rituals have insured that permanent emblems of femininity have often been the fasteners, the ribbons, buttons and bows.[33]

Mr. Weatherson goes on to suggest that man by contrast wears clothing less for sensual pleasure and more for displaying physical and economic resources for the age-old purpose of frightening the enemy, and will continue to do so. Unisex, beware!

Ernest Dichter[34] reports male and female differences relating to the symbolism of fibers. Cotton was seen by women as being fresh, clean, cool, and very feminine. Women also thought that cotton was "sexy in a quiet way." Men, on the other hand, felt that cotton was cheap, shoddy, and lacked durability. Cottons were neither "soft" enough for the intimate life nor hard enough for the everyday work life, according to men.

Both men and women felt that wool was least feminine, that it made women appear businesslike, urban, sophisticated. According to Baker, linen was thought to be clean, wholesome fun. The delicacy and lightness of lace makes it a women's fabric with an air of elegance, aloofness, yet soft femininity. Dichter and Baker call silk the most feminine and sensuous of all materials—"It shines and reflects the play of light." It is very soft and clings to a woman's body. This characteristic brings out the seductive qualities of its wearer.[35] Everyday speech acknowledges the standard of excellence for silk when we say "as fine as silk." Special value is attached to hair that is "silken." Silk evokes "images of places, of kings and queens and princesses, images of graceful oriental luxury."[36]

In choosing symbols or props for advertising illustra-

[33] Alexander Weatherson, *Body Covering*. Exibition at the Museum of Contemporary Crafts of the American Craftsmen's Council, 29 West 53rd Street, New York, April 6–June 9, 1968, p. 7.

[34] Ernest Dichter, *The Strategy of Desire* (Garden City, N. Y.: Doubleday and Company, Inc., 1959), pp. 106–108.

[35] Stephen Baker, *Visual Persuasion* (New York: McGraw-Hill, Inc., 1961).

[36] Dichter, op. cit., p. 108.

tions, the following have been found by Baker to have a sex of their own:[37]

> Male–potato, tree, black, train, wool, dog, square
> Female–tomato, flower, white, silk, cat, circle
> Neuter–apple, grass, gray, auto, linen, horse, triangle

A radio comedian carried the femininity symbol into the automobile world by describing a new Feminine French Auto with lavender sidewalls, low-cut radiator, and mini-fenders, which used, not gasoline in a tank, but perfume dabs behind the headlights.[38]

Bernice Fitzgibbon theorizes on the feminine appeal of sewing and its present-day importance:

> America's femaler females are sewing more than at any other time in our history. Women know in their bones it's fittin' and proper and feminine to sew. They also know that sewing impresses a man silly. A man thinks any girl with a thimble is automatically sweet, pretty, clever, industrious, thrifty, will be a perfect life companion and a perfect mother of his children. There's something utterly, innately, irresistibly feminine about sewing; psychologists come right out and say girls who sew are femaler females. It you want to reduce a man to blithering helplessness, you should cry on his shoulder or sew on his buttons. Sewing restores the delicate male-female balance. In the twinkling of a needle's eye, a man is Joe Piltdown with a caveman's club. Mentally, he's got the gal by the hair of her head. Actually, she's got him in the palm of her hand. Yes, needlework is still the woman's bailiwick.[39]

The revival of the art of sewing in the early 1970's included some busy, talented, and feminine women who were also in the public eye. The glamorous opera and supper club star Marguerite Piazza says she likes to do things with her hands and has joined a sewing circle in Memphis. Laura Greene of singing, comedy, and television commercials sews for both practical reasons as well as pleasure: "I can

[37] Baker, op. cit.
[38] *Don MacNeil Breakfast Club*, February 6, 1967.
[39] Bernice Fitzgibbon, *Macy's, Gimbels and Me* (New York: Simon and Schuster, 1967), p. 266.

get so much better fit that I sometimes even buy clothes and redesign them myself."[40] Leslie Uggams, singer and entertainer, finds sewing relaxing; her most-liked creations are pants outfits, skirts, and at-home wear.

But feminine clothes can be misleading in that they do not correctly symbolize the woman under the clothing. Queen Elizabeth I's wardrobe of several hundred dresses, her lavish use of jewels, and her legendary walk over Sir Walter Raleigh's cloak, spread to shield her feet from the muddy ground, did not completely mask the ruthless qualities that were necessary to keep her firmly in control of the monarchy at one of the most challenging periods in English history.

A modern example of an outward feminine, submissive appearance masking the true woman beneath is to be found in the girls of present-day Vietnam.

> Like butterflies they have floated in and, folding the panels of their *au dais* around their slim, straight bodies, have settled on the couch. But for the flicker of a hand as the ceiling fan whips at their long dark hair, the two girls have not moved for the past half hour. Poised, expressionless, they have watched the two American men—particularly the one who leans forward and speaks with the intensity of a new arrival in Viet Nam.
>
> "Where you come from?" one of the girls asks suddenly.
>
> "Washington. I'm here just for a short time on a State Department study group. I . . ." The young man over-explains himself in an attempt to compensate for his inattention to the Vietnamese, whom, after all, he has come to study. Where do you come from, what do you do, I mean, how do you spend your day, have you brothers and sisters?
>
> The girls giggle and twitter, punctuating their answers with sharp little gestures. The American pushes himself to the limit of what he concludes must be a near-vacuum. He retreats, smiling vaguely.
>
> "I should have told you about them," his friend remarks later. "Tri Minh owns two bars on the toughest street in Saigon. She is a self-made millionaire at the age of twenty-four. The other girl is twenty-two and

[40] "Look Who's Sewing," *Harper's Bazaar* (October, 1970), p. 138.

not quite so rich; she has spent the afternoon with Tri Minh arranging a loan to buy an ice plant in Da Nang."

In Viet Nam all of the butterflies stamp. American experts are puzzled. They have been puzzled since the advance guard of economists, social engineers, and institution builders came to Viet Nam only to discover that their operations depended on the whim of Mme. Ngo Dinh Nhu. Perhaps because the alternative was too fearful to contemplate, they dismissed Mme. Nhu as an exception, as a monstrous aberration from the stereotype of the submissive Oriental woman. In truth she was the norm.[41]

[41] Frances Fitzgerald, "The Power Set," *Vogue* (February 1, 1967), p. 154.

13 Symbols of Sex Attraction

Most of us would agree that part of the reason for wearing clothes is to appear attractive to the opposite sex. This idea applies to the origins of clothing as well as to contemporary practices. In most discussions of sex attraction, the concept of modesty emerges. However, modesty has both positive and negative relations to sex attraction; although modesty often acts as a restraint on behavior, it often works at cross-purposes with itself, as Flugel states so well:

> The real point to bear in mind is that modesty is essentially correlated with desire. Its purpose is to fight desire, but in so doing it rekindles it, so that a circular process is inevitably set in motion. Nature has, in fact, provided that modesty can never finally attain its end except through its own disappearance—hiding under the cloak of modesty there are often to be found certain subtle components of the sexual urge itself . . . modesty is, therefore, not merely an obstacle to the clear apprehension of external reality; it also fosters something in the nature of internal hypocrisy, and thus stands condemned on a double charge of distorting the appearance both of our bodies and our minds.[1]

[1] J. C. Flugel, *The Psychology of Clothes* (London: Hogarth Press, 1930), p. 192.

Cunnington also aptly describes the duality of prudishness:

> The prude is necessarily highly sex-conscious, so that the dread subject is detected in a thousand innuendoes, in inanimate as well as animate forms, for a multitude of objects become to the prude, symbols of it. The prude is continually training his (or her) . . . mind towards it. He does not admit, of course, that the subject fascinates him, but in fact he derives a peculiar satisfaction in detecting those systems in others which he professes to condemn.[2]

The Victorian attitude toward nudity was evidenced not only in the heavily robed figures of the living, but in the decorative arts as well. In the mid-1800's the Ladies' Academy of Art in Cincinnati hired an artist "to conceal the 'parts' of their European statuary." In 1890 a small college in Ohio, upon unveiling the sight-unseen purchase of a statue of Apollo, experienced "wild screams and a precipitate scattering of the students, who fled in all directions, leaving the god master of the situation. . . . It was decided to resort to heroic measures. . . . When a pair of fine velvet knee breeches were completed the famed Apollo was decently clothed with them; and there he stands, clad as no god was ever before adorned, a monument to the . . . ingenuity of the students." [3]

Ideas about modesty change with time. In the 1960's, skirts inched their way to mid-thigh, and acceptance followed several inches behind high fashion promotion. Other fashions, including lower necklines and bare-backed pajamas were considered "improper" one year but were selling in stores across the country the next. In fact, the bare-backed pajama found its way into the counter book of a pattern company by December, 1964, thereby bringing the outfit within means of any woman who could sew (the original cost $800).

As many observers have noted, the female body has usually been exposed one part at a time. The main trend

[2] C. Willett Cunnington, *Feminine Attitudes in the Nineteenth Century* (New York: The Macmillan Company, 1936), p. 275.

[3] As reported in Mary Cable and the Editors of American Heritage, *American Manners and Morals* (New York: American Heritage Publishing Company, Inc., 1969), p. 271.

of the fifties and continuing into the sixties involved the bustline. As early as 1953, French movie star Martine Carol was censored for her film, *Caroline Chérie,* in which she bounced about in low-cut bodices. During the same decade Jayne Mansfield, Sophia Loren, Marilyn Monroe all came under fire for bare bosoms. But the shocker of the sixties had to be the topless bathing suit. Even the naked bodies of "Hair" and "Oh! Calcutta!" caused less furor.

The topless bathing suit was just too extreme to gain acceptance in 1964; it was treated as a joke in most quarters, though there were reports of sales, of women wearing it, and of arrests of said wearers. However, the topless suit did make the abbreviated bikini seem modest

1926 Cartoon

1964 Topless

Approaches to Nudity

by comparison. Most of the bathing suits for sale in 1965 were abbreviated two-piece designs.

The topless bathing suit did indeed inspire many reflections on modesty itself. A *Life* magazine writer philosophized:

> The topless suit isn't lewd, though the attitude with which it is worn may be. Sex isn't what a woman puts on—or what she takes off either. . . . In some of the highest civilizations women have gone topless in public. The fashion was at its most distracting during Crete's Minoan period around 1600 B.C. It staged repeated and artful comebacks in the royal courts of Europe through the 18th Century.[4]

Anthropologist Eric Dingwall sees the bustline emphasis as a different symbolic reference. "Abnormal interest in the breasts is a symptom of the increasing emotional infantilism in the culture of the United States. It reveals an exaggerated devotion to the mother."[5]

The "no-bra" look was the subject of much concern during the late 1960's. But, again, this idea was not really new. In 1954 Elizabeth Hawes promoted a bra-less look in her book, *It's Still Spinach*. She felt that a whole generation of women had ruined their pectoral muscles by binding their breasts after World War I to conform to the boyish look. In defense of her position she gave an interesting description of one of her acquaintances who did not wear a bra:

> One of those women who is so attractive there are always six men near her panting a little, a woman about fifty-five . . . has rather small but quite pendulous breasts. She never wears a bra. She wears rather loose-topped clothes and the slight sway of her breasts under folds of material is most seductive. If your breasts hang down . . . and you have the rare courage to remove your bras completely, wear loose-topped clothes like the lady. Get your sweater several sizes "too big." . . . After a while you will get less self-conscious about not looking like that surreal

[4] Shana Alexander, "Fashion's Best Joke on Itself in Years," *Life* (July 10, 1964), pp. 56–62.

[5] Eric J. Dingwall, *The American Woman* (London: Gerald Duckworth & Co., Ltd., 1956), p. 138.

character in the brassière ad and can wear tight tops when you feel like it.[6]

Stephen Baker explains that the average American goes about sex with a great deal of caution. Even the advertiser must keep in mind that sexual furtiveness is part of our culture and in order not to offend potential customers and their deep-seated inhibitions, he must assure us that sex really isn't so bad after all. For example, Maidenform found it possible to present sex "in its most basic form if properly ensconced in an atmosphere of fantasy."[7]

Legs, which were alluring in the twenties and again in the sixties, have had their share of critical comment. Feminine legs have been draped or veiled for most of history. Victorians did not use the word *leg* but substituted the word *limb.* In an earlier age a fiancé's gift to his royal bride (silk stockings) was chastized and rebuffed by the statement, "The Queen of Spain has no legs."[8]

With both the midi look and pants threatening to cover the female leg in 1970, one designer voted against using pants for airline hostesses even where the practicality of pants could have been a strong point. Jean-Louis says:

> A great number of airline passengers are men and men have what you call a psychological block against seeing women in pants. I am sure that a little leg showing will remain an important feature of airborne fashion for many years.[9]

Shoes and feet have been used as symbols of sex attraction by many peoples. The story of Cinderella is full of hidden significance. The diminutive shoe itself is a classic example of fetishism; the mutilation of the stepsister's foot is a further evidence of cruelties endured to please a desired mate. In China the small foot was so desired in the middle of the last century that the "young bride's shoe is exhibited before the bridegroom's parents and figures as

[6] Elizabeth Hawes, *It's Still Spinach* (Boston: Little, Brown and Company, 1954), p. 140.

[7] Stephen Baker, *Visual Persuasion* (New York: McGraw-Hill Inc., 1961).

[8] Havelock Ellis, "Erotic Symbolism," *Studies in the Psychology of Sex* (New York: Random House, 1936), p. 26.

[9] "Long Look for a Wide Jet," *Mainliner*, United Airlines (August, 1970), p. 23.

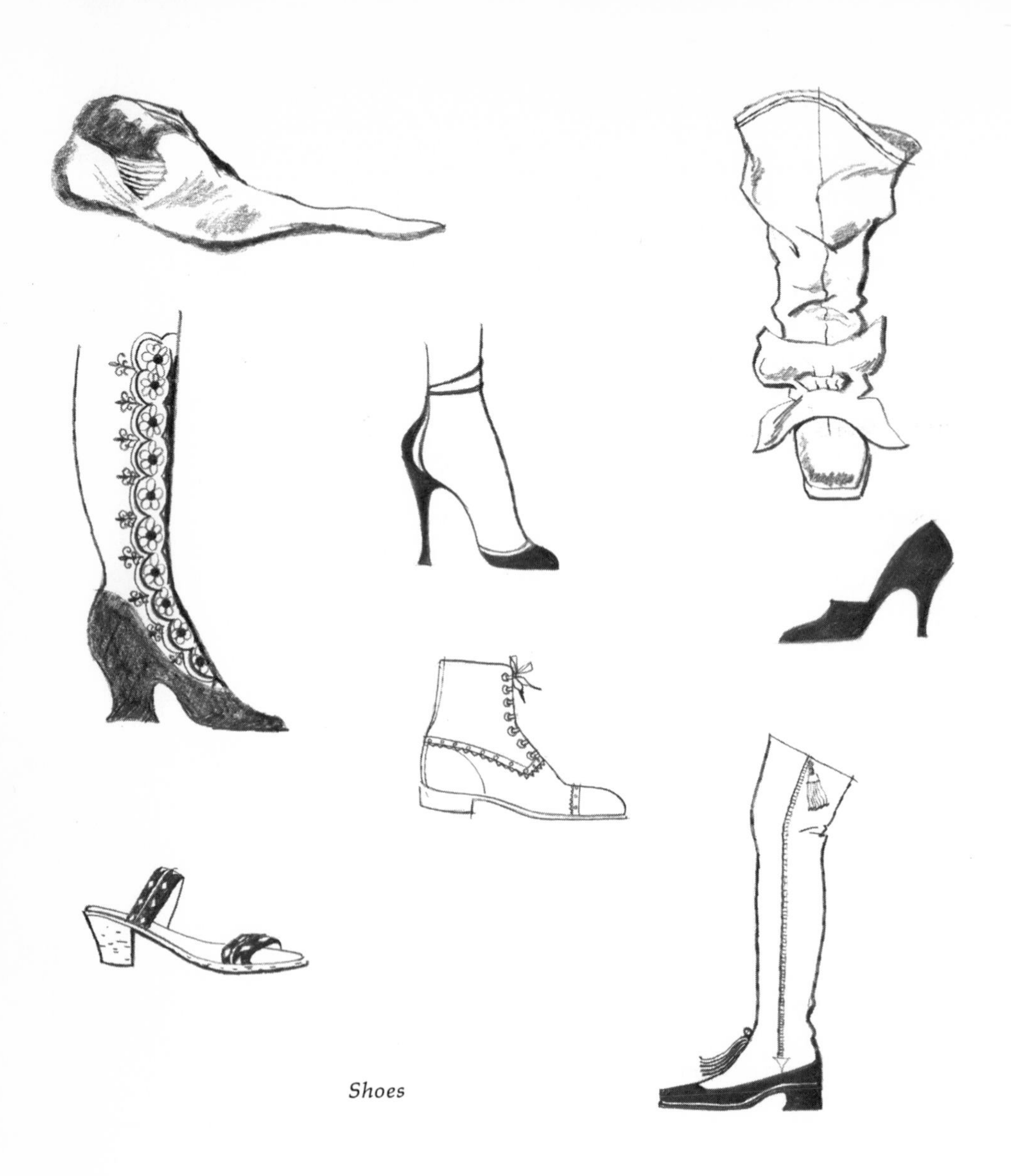

Shoes

one of the deciding arguments in determining the price of purchase." [10] Chains and anklets have been designed and used since Biblical times in Palestine and in many Arab countries. Havelock Ellis describes the appeal of fetters thus: "The feet became the chief focus of this fascination, and the basis on which a foot-fetishism or shoe-fetishism

[10] Bernard Rudofsky, *Are Clothes Modern?* (Chicago: Paul Theobold, 1947), p. 166.

tends to arise, because restraint of the feet produces a more marked effect than restraint of the hands." [11]

In the Middle Ages the pontaine or long-toed shoe was fashioned into a claw, a beak, or a phallus. Gisèle D'Assailly reports that in the fourteenth century pointed shoes extended to such lengths that they had to be reinforced with whalebone.[12] Pope Urban V issued condemnations against the lascivious nature of these shoes.[13]

The high-heeled shoe which makes a woman walk with helpless gait has been admired by ancient Chinese, Europeans, and modern Americans. Rudofsky assails the practice in searing prose:

> Contrary to what might seem to be the eminent seductive qualities of woman—her primary and secondary sexual characteristics—it is female bearing that attracts man most. Since the anatomical difference between man and woman does not produce different ways of walking, a specific feminine gait has been artificially engineered with the help of various and often ingenious implements. Extreme weight and height and more recently non-essential heels were added to a woman's shoe in order to throw her body out of balance.[14]

Italian courtesans of the fifteenth and sixteenth centuries favored the chopine which reached the height of 20 inches. The early eighteenth century Queen of Spain, wife of Philip V, had to walk with the support of two pages when she wore chopines.[15] Popes and governments banned such stilts, but to no avail; the fashion endured for at least three centuries. The frank admiration of the male for woman's birdlike tripping assures a place for high-heeled shoes even in fashions yet to come.

The use of sexual lures including the high-heeled shoe were often censored. In the fifteenth century the English Parliament issued this edict:

[11] Havelock Ellis, "Love and Pain," *Studies in the Psychology of Sex*, Vol. 1, Part 2 (New York, 1936), p. 158.

[12] Gisèle D'Assaily, *Ages of Elegance* (Paris: Librairie Hachette, 1968), p. 51.

[13] Lawrence Langner, *The Importance of Wearing Clothes* (New York: Hastings House, 1959), p. 205.

[14] Rudofsky, op. cit., p. 172.

[15] Ibid., p. 170.

Beauty Spots

> Any woman who, through the use of fake hair, Spanish hair pads, make-up, false hips, steel busks, panniers, high heeled shoes or other device, leads a subject of Her Majesty into marriage, shall be punished with the penalties of witchery.[16]

During the reign of Louis XV, satin or black velvet beauty spots appeared all over a woman's face:

> One was not enough. The coquettes would stick on seven or ten of them at a time giving them various names according to the place chosen: "passionate" at the corner of the eye; "gay" in the middle of the cheek; "saucy" on the nose; "coquette" on the corner of the mouth; "kisser" over the upper lip; near the temple was the "majestic." "Playful" was over a dim-

[16] D'Assailly, op. cit., p. 75.

> ple; "hidden" over a spot . . . and "murderess" on the breast. Sometimes these patches took the shape of a star or cresent moon.[17]

Beauty spots returned in the "Gay Nineties," during the 1920's and in the 1960's. Contemporary spots are likely to be gold, silver, or gemlike and may appear on all parts of the body including the back and legs, and especially the knees.

Long hair for women has often been considered to be seductive. Primitive and civilized men alike have succumbed to the lure of long hair. Puerto Rican men say they prefer long hair whatever the age or size of the female. One reporter found that Puerto Rican women spend much time on their hair, often wearing extreme evening-type hair styles during the day.[18]

Much of the time and money once allotted to hats was diverted to wigs, hair pieces, and falls in the 1960's. The top of the head was so important an item in women's sexual appeal that hairdressers not only became household words, but also held court in luxurious establishments. Grateful clients showered them with gifts and invited them to be part of the society of the Beautiful People.[19]

Nudity

Throughout history we have had trends toward nudity but the bare look would be followed by fashions that covered and concealed, so that the wearer directed, then diverted attention by covering and subsequently exposing various parts of the body. Hemlines and necklines have moved up and down, but seldom in opposite directions at

[17] Ibid., p. 122.

[18] Diane Meade, unpublished research paper, University of Connecticut, January, 1970.

[19] Marylin Bender, *The Beautiful People* (New York: Coward McCann, Inc., 1967), pp. 258–263.

the same time; that is, short skirts and low necklines were not worn together until the 1960's. It would indeed seem that a true revolution is taking place and that the bare look is approaching the nude look even for streetwear. No longer restricted to the beach, the home, or to the performing arts, nudity is now nearly on the street. It must of course be understood as a reflection of a way of life, a demonstration of freedom of expression, a symbol of a break with the past as well as a symbol of sexual attraction. Sex symbolism is probably less important in the nearly nude look of today than it was when the ankles were bared.

In 1966, in the name of fashion *and* charity, Susan Stein and Amanda Burden suggested "Nothing" to the question "What shall we wear?" for the New York Shakespeare Festival.[20] Linda Hackett in sheer white harem pants and low, low neckline used "spirit gum and something else" to keep her bosom in place after Band-Aids didn't work. Starlet Pamela Tiffin wore a strapless jeweled bra under a one-shoulder toga slashed to the hip. Christina Paolozzi Bellin in white crepe with diaphanous midriff kept wishing she were nuder. "You can't even tell I'm naked," [21] moaned the girl who made her fame by being scratched from the Social Register in 1962 for posing nude from the waist up in *Harper's Bazaar*. Stopping the show was Gloria Steinem in an Esterel creation of five bands of chinchilla held together by transparent black net over a body stocking. Thus, the ballgoers were backless, frontless, bottomless, and topless, though not in a single gown.

Designers besides Rudi Gernreich who have helped to promote nudity are Yves St. Laurent (with his sheer flesh-colored chiffon with clusters of shimmering bangles), Bill Blass (designing with fishnet), Giorgio di Sant'Angelo (creating vests and body necklaces with nothing underneath), Pauline Trigère (using transparent cotton chiffon), and Courrèges (predicting super nonclothes including a bridal gown of white kid gloves and not much else). Most of these designers claim freedom of expression as their aim,[22] or as Gernreich says, "Skin if it's attractive can be

[20] As reported in "Modern Fashion," *Time* (June 24, 1966), p. 94.

[21] Ibid.

[22] "Sex and the Arts," *Newsweek* (April 14, 1969), p. 68.

Nudity at the Charity Ball

part of the design." [23] Other designers express an increasing appreciation of the sensual; not just the pure hedonist philosophy of eat, drink, and be merry but the welcoming of "anything that delights the eye and the senses." [24]

From Havelock Ellis to Rudofsky there is a warning note about nudity. Both of these philosophers leave no doubt that it is the adorned or the partially concealed body and not the absolute naked body that acts as a sexual excitant. Critics of some of the current nude Broadway plays are bored by too much nudity: " 'Oh! Calcutta!' is not only inelegant but also anti-erotic. The sheer expanse of skin in time becomes a bore." [25] Critic Susan Sontag has an aversion to pornography because it can be a "crutch for the psychologically deformed" and suggests that "the place we assign to pornography depends on the goals we set for

[23] Cynthia Lindsay, "Wither the Bra," *McCall's* (November, 1969), p. 90.

[24] Paul Sann, *Fads, Follies and Delusions of the American People* (New York: Crown Publishers, Inc., 1967), p. 259.

[25] "Sex as a Spectator Sport," *Time* (July 11, 1969), p. 62.

our own consciousness, our own experience."[26] Ernest Dichter feels that instead of nudity being a new kind of immorality, we are "finally going back to some of the Greek ideals of 2,000 years ago where the human body was considered beautiful and nothing to be ashamed of."[27] Thus whether we see beauty or ugliness in nudity or attraction or repulsion depends upon the symbolic interpretation of the individual perceiver.

We should also keep in mind that nudity can mean the inferior status of a slave or captive. The removal of garments has also traditionally been a sign of respect in the presence of royalty or other exalted personages. Today, removal of the hat, gloves, or shoes is still practiced by many peoples as symbols of respect or worship.

What is considered as attractive to the opposite sex differs depending upon time, place, socioeconomic status, culture, and personality. Bared arms were considered to be disgusting at the time of Henry VIII;[28] Puritans were repelled by actual body exposure and by elaborateness of dress, and the unsightly or ill-formed body inspired disgust rather than desire.[29]

H. L. Mencken described the failure of women in trying to lure male attention by overdoing and overdressing:

> Women, when it comes to snaring men, through the eye, bait a great many hooks that fail to fluster the fish. Nine-tenths of their primping and decorating of their persons not only doesn't please men; it actually repels men. I often pass two days running without encountering a single woman who is charmingly dressed. Nearly all of them run to painful color schemes, absurd designs and excessive over-ornamentation. . . . It is color that kills the clothes of the average woman. She runs to bright spots that take away from her face and hair. She ceases to be woman clothed and becomes a mere piece of clothing womaned.[30]

[26] Quoted in "Sex and the Arts," op. cit., p. 70.

[27] Ernest Dichter, "Psychology of the Seventies," *American Fabrics*, Issue 86 (Spring, 1970), p. 37.

[28] Flugel, op. cit., p. 56.

[29] Ibid., p. 57.

[30] H. L. Mencken, "Appendix on a Tender Theme," *Prejudices, Second Series* (New York: Alfred A. Knopf, Inc., 1920), p. 238.

Genevieve Dariaux has compiled two interesting lists related to what attracts male admiration of the female:

What Is Really Attractive to Men

full skirts, tiny waists, and a long-legged look
clothes that are in fashion, but not avant-garde; men follow the fashion trends more than you realize, and even the *Wall Street Journal* prints articles about fashion
furs, and a general air of luxury
almost any shade of blue; white; very pale and very dark gray; certain men hate to see their wives in black; others adore it
perfume—but modern men appreciate lighter perfumes than their fathers did, subtle sophisticated blends rather than the simpler scents
collars on suits and coats

What Men Think They Like
(but only in the movies)

revealingly tight and aggressively pointed bosoms
false eyelashes
"femme fatale" lingerie
musky oriental scents
spike heels
yards of black fringe and miles of red chiffon flounces [31]

In short, men enjoy being envied, but they hate feeling conspicuous. They particularly dislike vulgarity in the women they love.

Sexual Attraction of the Male

Although less information is available concerning masculine clothing as sex symbols, this, too, is an important area of consideration. Historical examples include the slender waisted man of Crete who wore tight belts decorated

[31] Genevieve Dariaux, *Elegance* (Garden City, N. Y.: Doubleday & Company, Inc., 1964), p. 221.

with "spirals and rosettes made of gold, copper, or silver"[32] accenting their slim waistlines, and early Roman males who spent hours on their toilet:

> Their hairdressers known as "tonsores" curled their hair with little tongs. These gentlemen also used make-up and went so far as to apply beauty patches and use perfume extravagantly.[33]

An historian from Mainz records in 1367:

> Fashion became so ridiculous that young men wore coats so short that they failed to cover their private parts front or back. When they stooped over they exposed their bare posteriors. What a scandal![34]

An old English law passed in 1475 suggests that exposure of the private parts was a privilege reserved for the upper classes. "Nobody below the rank of Lord, Esquire, or Gentleman may wear a coat, cape, or smock so short that when he stands erect, it fails to cover his private parts and buttocks in which case he pays a fine of 20 shillings."[35]

During the fifteenth century forerunners of tights, known as "Polish leathers," were adopted by men because of their ability to give shapeliness to the legs and slimness to the feet. Leg-revealing hose were worn throughout the sixteenth century. A further example of male exhibitionism can be seen in the codpiece, a special bulging portion of hose that housed the male genitals. The codpiece was a necessity because of the tightness of the hose and trunks, but became more of a sex symbol when it was made of a "vivid or contrasting color, . . . which was further embellished by padding in such a way as to simulate a perpetual erection."[36] Rabelais describes the male costume of his day as follows:

> Trunk-hose was either tight or baggy, long or short, always hacked or gashed with bows of gold cloth, satin or taffeta showing through. And always the cod-

[32] D'Assailly, op. cit., p. 24.

[33] Ibid., p. 34.

[34] R. Broby Johansen, *Body and Clothes* (New York: Reinhold Book Corporation, 1968), p. 124.

[35] Ibid.

[36] Flugel, op. cit., p. 27.

piece, rounded and jutting out, merrily secured with two handsome gold buckles held in place by two enamel hooks.[37]

Males have resorted to padded shoulders and padded calves, they have covered their torsos with decorations, they have even worn corsets to copy the ideal figure of the time. Tattooing and mutilation seem to have been characteristic of the male rather than the female sex.[38] Height, being a desired male trait, is sometimes accomplished by high heels or in contemporary times by invisible lifts inside the shoe.

One group of the West African Fulani have an annual beauty contest for young men. Lips are underlined in black, cheeks are painted red, white triangles are drawn on mahogany skin. Creative arrangements of beaded bands, original headpieces of ostrich feathers, metal disks, and rings are all used in the beauty competition for men.[39]

Today, men are also involved in the race toward nudity. Male fashion magazines feature brief bikinis, see-through fishnet slacks, trunks, and shirts, dressy shirts slashed to the waist, and one-shouldered zebra-striped tops. Men also try to appeal sexually to other men. Mary Quant gives us a vivid description of the waiters in a restaurant owned by herself and her husband, on a certain New Year's Eve:

> The waiters were in full drag . . . the most tremendous drag you can imagine. They were dressed in women's clothes, wearing false eyelashes, tiaras, jewels, goodness knows what. One of them was impersonating Anna Magnani with huge false bosoms. . . . Then in walked the most beautiful boy, fantastically slim and elegant. He swept down the stairs wearing a marvellous white satin ball dress with a full train and tiara. He had a white mink wrap round his shoulders. He looked like the most marvellous model girl. We found out that his photograph had, in fact, appeared many times in a famous fashion magazine showing hats. . . . They all joined in a can-can and when it came to the uproarious climax, one of them, dancing on the bar top, bent over and threw up his

[37] Reported in D'Assailly, op. cit., p. 73.

[38] Flugel, op. cit., p. 43.

[39] Jacques Maquet, "The Quest for Beauty in Dahomey," *Vogue* (December, 1967), p. 274.

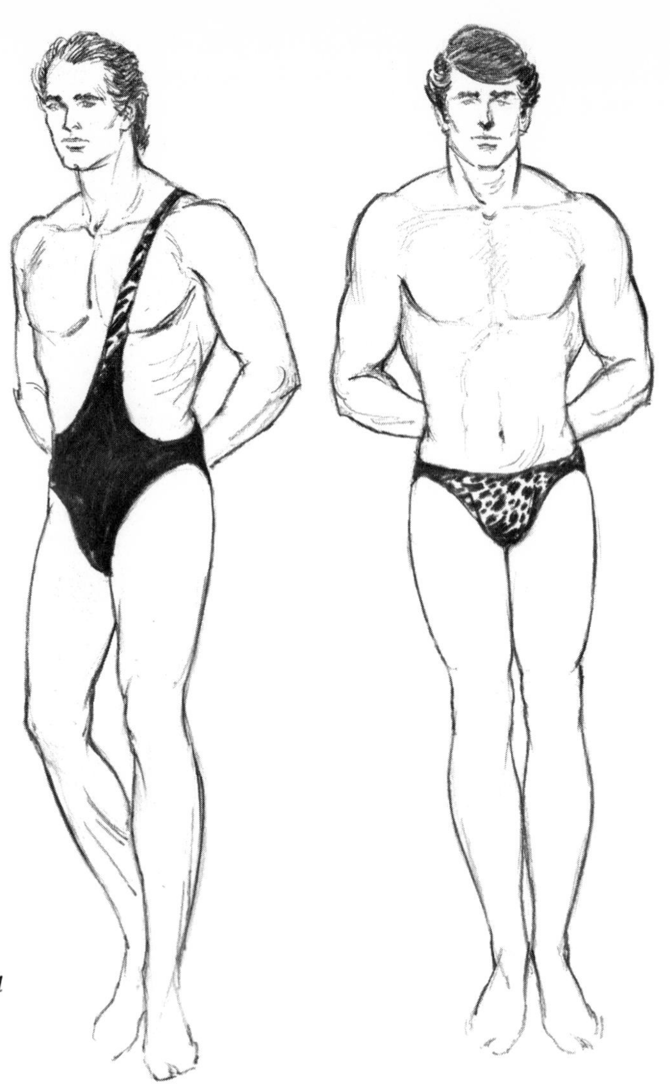

Male Sex Appeal

skirts as the real can-can girls do. He had a lighted candle thrust in his bottom! How he had managed to keep it alight under his skirts, I can't think.[40]

Robert Riley, a design research consultant to the Brooklyn Museum, believes that contemporary trends in men's clothes are launched by homosexuals and adolescents. Be-

[40] Mary Quant, *Quant by Quant* (New York: Ballantine Books, Inc., 1967), p. 67.

cause they exhibit the most overtly behavioral patterns, they dress to be sexually attractive. They are the leaders of the sexual revolution. On Seventh Avenue a homosexual doesn't have to camouflage himself. "He can flaunt." [41]

Sex De-emphasized

Clothes have been used to hide the sexual organs from early antiquity. At times clothing accomplishes this purpose; at other times it calls attention to the sexual organs or at least arouses curiosity. Very voluminous or loose-fitting clothing probably de-emphasizes best, which may well be the reason for certain religious orders continuing the use of such apparel through the centuries. The use of the word *robe* has no sexual connotation, and, indeed, robes worn for religious, academic, legal, or government functions rarely call attention to sex identification or enhance sexual attractiveness. The person performing the ceremonial duty is sexless at that moment in time.

Women have dressed in male-inspired copies in order to gain acceptance in the business world of the last century. In part, male clothes were more practical and efficient than fashionable women's wear of the early twentieth century, but the woman worker also tried to use these clothes as symbols of the qualities of honesty, seriousness, loyalty, efficiency, and capability associated with male workers. Probably in all times the clothes of the worker, including slaves, are less apt to inspire sexual advances, for the simple reason that the work must be done without any dallying or horseplay. Thus, in our world of work, we also play down sex.

The early feminists who preached equality of the sexes wanted to be treated as individuals and not as females. Angélique Martin wrote that she did not want to see women treated "as mere hatching and breeding machines whom they scornfully send back to their nurseries and

[41] Bender, op. cit., p. 97.

kitchens, forbidding them to aspire to anything else."[42] The notorious Dr. Mary Walker dressed in men's clothes all her life and promoted the equality of the sexes by founding a female colony called "Adamless Eve" to prove that the anatomy of a woman was similar to that of a man.[43]

Rudi Gernreich says of his unisex look today:

> Our aesthetics will change and center more on the body than on its adornment. Nudity will be much more prevalent. . . . Sexual honesty involves only the body itself. . . . [It] should not be judged on a basis of clothes. It is a spiritual thing—and a physical thing.[44]

Pleasure in Pain

Part of the sexual factor in clothing is related to pain and discomfort. Flugel describes the "supported" type of person who feels pleasurably strengthened and supported by especially tight or stiff clothes.[45] Rudofsky feels that much in clothing relates to perverted self-gratification:

> Psychologists are familiar with the autoerotic mechanism of body constriction. The masochistic tendencies which have been discovered in wearing exceedingly narrow waitsbands, belts, jackets, and bodices are two fold: to derive pleasure directly from pain of constriction, but also to enjoy the want of freedom.[46]

It is more difficult to foresee the enjoyment of pains with our accent on comfort and function today; perhaps the "nude" look will cause psychological pain to those of us less well endowed.

[42] Quoted in Andrew Sinclair, *The Better Half* (New York: Harper & Row, 1965), p. 259.
[43] Ibid., p. 261.
[44] *Time* (January 26, 1970), p. 39.
[45] Flugel, op. cit., p. 99.
[46] Rudofsky, op. cit., p. 156.

Youth and Age

America today is alive with symbols of youth, not the least of which are expressed through clothing and grooming. Our special "accent on youth" runs the gamut from babyhood to the elderly. Designers and retailers promote specialized clothes for infants, toddlers, preschoolers, schoolchildren, preteens, subteens, teens, mods, hippies, young career groups, and young marrieds. Most of these items have developed within the last twenty-five years, with the most radical changes for boys occurring during the past ten years. Words like "young," "youth," or "youthquake" appear in eight out of ten clothing advertisements.

At the turn of the century, children dressed much like miniature copies of adults. When they came of age during their adolescent years they changed clothing styles abruptly. For boys, knickers and long pants had special significance. Girls who reached young womanhood put up their hair, lengthened their dresses, and wore long stockings and shoes with heels.

Some primitive tribes introduce clothing for the first time to young people in elaborate puberty ceremonies called rites of passage. The new privilege of wearing certain clothes or ornaments often follows ordeal by torture. Among the San Blas Indians of Panama, the ceremony starts when the girl secludes herself in a small hut where she endures four days of almost continuous cold-water showers.

> As many as eight shifts cooperate in pouring water over the girl during the day, and four in the evening. By nightfall of the first day the girl, wearing only a loincloth, is shivering uncontrollably. Her only respite comes after dark, when she is allowed to add some clothing to the loincloth. . . . The most sacred part of the ceremony involves painting the girl black from head to foot to protect her from evil spirits who might be attracted to her beauty and subject her to a fatal disease. This occurs on the fourth day. . . . The painting signalizes the girl's attainment of young womanhood and gives her status comparable to when we address a young girl as "miss." After having her hair bobbed at sunrise the next day (it will be completely cut at a later ceremony), she is permitted to pull down the shelter in which she has been confined and to mingle with her friends. There is feasting and drinking, chants and songs.[1]

From the other side of the world we have this example. In Russia during the reign of the last Czar, Nicholas II, his eldest daughter, Olga, was given a full-dress ball to celebrate her sixteenth birthday:

> Before the dance, Olga's parents gave her a diamond ring and a necklace of thirty-two diamonds and pearls. These were Olga's first jewels, intended to symbolize her coming into young womanhood. Olga was dressed in pink in her first ballgown. With her thick blond hair coiled for the first time in womanly style atop her head, she arrived at the dance, flushed and fair.[2]

In India today children and young girls wear "frocks," that is, skirts and blouses much in the western style. On becoming a young lady most Indians don the sari. However, college girls in northern India might wear a pantlike garment, the *salwer,* or a type of shift called a *kameez,*

[1] Edward Weyer, Jr., *Primitive People Today* (Garden City, N.Y.: Doubleday & Company, Inc., 1959), p. 81.

[2] Robert K. Massie, *Nicholas and Alexandra* (New York: Dell Publishing Co., Inc., 1969), p. 179.

but return to the sari for dress-up or formal wear. Generally speaking, bright colors are associated with the very young while dull colors and white are usually worn by older women.[3]

The youth movement was seen in Europe during the early part of this century. In the United States the 1920's reached an all-time high in youth mania, only to be outdone in the 1960's. Although many parallels can be drawn between the two decades, history does not repeat itself exactly in clothes and other appearance features. If one considers short hair, popularized by Chanel, Irene Castle, and Anita Loos during the twenties, it was not as short as the Mia Farrow cut nor did it have the Spanish-looking long side lock worn by many fashion models in 1965. Besides, many young girls of the 1960's wore their hair long and straight. The long flowing hair, sideburns, and beards of the boys of the 1960's were very unlike the trim heads of the 1920's. Because the symbolically rebellious hair styles of young boys were much more drastic than anything boys had done in the past several decades, they produced opposition from authority. An eloquent case is made by the father of a long-haired schoolboy who was suspended from school:

> The school authorities are trying to tell my son not to be himself but to conform to their socially prejudiced image of what a boy should be. They throw up smoke screens about classroom discipline problems and laboratory safety hazards caused by long hair. But my son is a disciplined boy from an orderly home, who does not threaten society. He only asserts certain very personal rights as he explores his way to manhood. In an unstable time of changing political, social and sexual pressures, hair becomes a symbol to young people. By shearing it the school officials would like to cut off rebellion, perhaps even symbolically emasculate a new kind of young American who is painfully disturbing to the older generation.[4]

In the sixties, dresses reached new heights of abbreviation so that panty hose and the body stocking had to be invented. The rolled hose and teddy of the twenties were

[3] Information from Indian graduate students at the University of Missouri.

[4] "The GH Poll, Have Schools the Right to Enforce Haircuts?", *Good Housekeeping* (September, 1968), p. 16.

no part of the sixties' scene. Nor were boots and pilgrim shoes a repeat of the twenties. What the two decades did have in common was an expression, an overall look that was sleek, sophisticated, and worldly.[5] There was an overriding cry from youth for freedom to be themselves, to "do their thing," and to be different from older people (over thirty).

Although the cultural patterns and sanctions of the older generation rarely coincide with those of the younger generation (at least in America), the accelerated rate of change makes conflicts increasingly more likely. Parents are often unable to understand the standards of a social order that has changed so much since they were children.[6] As the chasm grows feelings grow in intensity. Irving Penn, fashion photographer, says:

> It's spitting in the eye, protesting against bourgeois values and generations of the past, against the Establishment.[7]

In England, the Mods were an eloquent expression of fads and fashions for youth alone. These clothes originating on Carnaby Street were as important for boys as for girls; in addition, they projected a total look from head to toe. The Mods were very much aware of the symbols they wore. In 1966 both boys and girls responded to a survey by stating that their knee-high boots and Prince Valiant bobs symbolized first a declaration of identity with their peers and secondly a declaration of rebellion against adult authority.[8] Teenage fads were carefully calculated to scandalize the square adult world and nothing could kill a fad faster than its being picked up by the wrong people (translation: adults).[9]

Mary Quant describes the Chelsea Girl—the type who buys and wears her clothes. The main thing is that the Chelsea Girls have a "life is fabulous" philosophy and that

[5] For an interesting discussion, see "Accent on Youth" in Karlyne Anspach, *The Why of Fashion* (Ames: Iowa State University Press, 1968), pp. 277–309.

[6] J. S. Coleman et al., *The Adolescent Society* (New York: The Free Press, 1961), pp. 2–3.

[7] Reported in Paul Sann, *Fads, Follies and Delusions of the American People* (New York: Crown Publishers, Inc., 1967), p. 258.

[8] Joseph Morgenstern, "What U. S. Teenagers Are Really Like," *Newsweek* (March 21, 1966), p. 74.

[9] Ibid., p. 15.

Youth Clothes

although they may be opinionated and extravagant, they are alive and ready to try anything new. Mary Quant says:

> It is their questioning attitude which makes them important and different. They conform to their own set of values but not to the values and standards laid down by a past generation. But they don't sneer at other points of view. . . . They are not interested in status symbols. They don't worry about accents or class; they are neither determinedly county nor working-class. They are scornful of pretence of any kind. . . . The voices, rules and culture of this generation are as different from those of the past as tea and wine. And the clothes they choose evoke their lives . . . daring and gay, never dull.[10]

[10] Mary Quant, *Quant by Quant* (New York: Ballantine Books, 1967), p. 171.

Quant goes on to say that at one time girls under twenty yearned to look like experienced, sophisticated thirty-year-olds. Then, round-faced teens practiced sucking in their cheeks to gain seductive hollows, dreamed of having sophisticated black dresses and very high heels. "All this is in reverse now. Suddenly, every girl with a hope of getting away with it is aiming to look not only under voting age but under the age of consent." [11]

What of American fashions? What is young on this side of the world? For girls it is miniskirts, bell bottoms, pants-suits, jump suits, the long overgrown sweater, the long trailing scarf, fringe, beads, floppy hats, tams, knee-high boots, knee socks, bright colors, gypsy skirts and head-bands, wild patterns, funky colors, chain belts, oversized zippers, and panty hose.

Another question we might ask is how young and to what age levels does the youth movement reach? Fashion and clothes awareness seem to be careening backward in time so that mere children are participating in "peacock parades." Marylin Bender says that girls in their early teens are among the avant-garde fashion cultists and display the most literal interpretation of fads, be they bizarre jewelry, short skirts, or unisex.

> "When you're older (17 and 18), you want to dress more conservatively," explains a 14 year old, "because by then you've been as sophisticated as you want at 14 and 15 and you realize how ridiculous it is. And besides you'll be going to college where everybody is the same and you don't want to give them the wrong impression about yourself." [12]

Psychologist Alexander Weatherson says that the young are geared to a faster, more impatient way of life so that the shorter, narrower, temporary styles are instant clothes, "as instantly taken up as taken off." [13]

Youthful distrust of permanence in part allows them to wear styles of the past out of context (funky or old attic varieties), in order to disclaim the values of the older

[11] Ibid.
[12] Marylin Bender, *The Beautiful People* (New York: Coward McCann, 1967), p. 254.
[13] Alexander Weatherson, *Body Covering* (New York: Museum of Contemporary Crafts of the American Craftsmen's Council, 1968), p. 8.

generation. Youthful clothes, then, are idealistic, unique, but fulfilling temporary aspirations in a search for future ideals.[14]

Middle Age

Whatever the numerical age limits of middle age, and these differ with individuals, social class, and culture, it is that time of life when the person is past the full bloom of youth. In spite of the preoccupation with youth in America there is also an admiration of well-preserved middle age. Most of the men and women on the Best-Dressed Lists are middle-aged. The younger sets in the White House (Lynda, Luci, Tricia, and Julie) did not become fashion ideals in the way that Jackie Kennedy did. The Europeans, especially the French, see the real symbol of womanhood in early middle age, describing this time of life as a "soft green meadow" on the "crest of a wave," or the magnificent years. The woman in her thirties still has a beautiful, strong body; she is free from the frustrations and trials of youth; she has grace, charm, and sophistication; she is no longer a technician but a craftsman. As Françoise Sagan put it:

> At thirty a woman is no longer a collection of scattered admirations arranged in découpage. At thirty she can begin to be what she dreamed she could be. At thirty she knows what the teen years were meant for: a preparation for something fascinating to come. She needed those early years, and she needed the dream stage of adolescence. . . . Glory comes only to those who have dreamed of it.[15]

If she has an awareness of clothing, she now has elegance, for she knows herself inside and out and she has developed the ability to shape clothes around a central theme. She has had time to develop a very personal way

[14] Ibid.
[15] Françoise Sagan, "The Fascinating Thirties," *Vogue* (July, 1963), p. 31.

of dressing and of creating a style of her very own. She no longer needs to follow fashion blindly, but she adapts the best of fashion to her body and being. Elegance is always suited to age.

In later middle age the body must be kept trim; it must be toned up to remain beautiful. This is not a new idea, far from it. In 1389, Isabeau of Bavaria took baths of asses' milk and stayed hours in the sweating rooms, after which "cupping glasses" were applied to make her look slim. "So as to appear younger, both she and her ladies-in-waiting used ingredients composed of crocodiles' glands, boar's brains, wolf's blood mixed with all kinds of strange oils." [16]

Contemporary men and women now take advantage of the many exrecise routines that are offered in the privacy of salons and are detailed almost daily in newspapers and magazines. *Miss Craig's 21-Day Shape-up Program* [17] became a best seller, positively reflecting the middle-aged adult's preoccupation with the reshaping of sagging muscles. For those not inclined toward exercise, the body can be revamped by surgery. In addition to the classic face-lift, now available are thigh-lifts, arm-lifts and belly-lifts. Oversized breasts can be reduced and undersized ones can be augmented. Noses, ears, and chins can be reconstructed. A whole new science of "body contouring" has been developed by popular demand. It is even possible to have a fifteen-minute tuck (a skin-tightening "lift before lunch" that keeps sagging jowls taut between major face-lifts).[18]

Vivid descriptions of body sculpturing are given in a recent *Vogue*, featuring Brazilian Dr. Iro Pitanguy, an innovator in plastic surgery. Descriptions are given of a "riding breeches" lift, work on a severe breast hypertrophy, and a trochanteric lipodystrophy—an accumulation of adipose tissue on the external side of the thighs. The doctor is followed through a typical working day from 8 A.M. to 8:30 P.M.[19]

[16] Gisèle D'Assailly, *Ages of Elegance* (Paris: Librairie Hachette, 1968), p. 57.

[17] Marjorie Craig, *Miss Craig's 21-Day Shape-up Program* (New York: Random House, 1968).

[18] Gael Greene, "How the World's Great Beauties Stay Beautiful," *Ladies' Home Journal* (February, 1970), p. 69.

[19] Simona Morini, "Body Sculpturing," *Vogue* (October 1, 1969), pp. 190–193.

The Cost of Reshaping

What else does the middle-aged beauty do? To what lengths does she go?

She only eats on alternate Tuesdays. She sleeps 16 hours a day. She lives at her hairdresser's. She's had her face lifted nine times. She'd collapse without pep pills and hormone shots. She exists on wheat germ,

> yogurt, geriatric capsules, yeast and powdered raw liver. She never leaves the house before dark. She is photographed through layers of gauze.[20]

She keeps slim, smooth, and succinctly beautiful using sleep, silicones, surgery, and starvation. She uses pounds of vanity and tons of will power to accomplish her ends—to look and feel youthful.

Men also endure surgery, chemical peeling, and painful hair transplants to keep up their youthful appearance. Hair coloring products and hair pieces continue to gain popularity with middle-aged males. However, men need the proper imagery to entice them to purchase beauty aids. Masculine symbols are different: men do not use hair spray but "hair control," not bath oil but "sauna soak," not cleansing cream but "scrub wash," not facials but "face tone-up," and not make-up but "bronzer" or "after-shave tan." He needs to be reassured that he won't be considered lavender or "one of them," so he buys at a "Toiletrie Counter." [21] After all, "they" have been buying at women's cosmetic counters for years.

Clothing for late middle age is more difficult to find in a mass market geared to youth and sexual attractiveness. One must indeed spend more time in the search for the proper clothing—not too ridiculously youthful, but not so far behind the times to be labeled "old-fashioned." Quickly changing fashions and fads practically exclude the possibility of elegance, and one needs elegant symbols in the mature years. Here and there a cry for help is heard:

> We meet women in the suburbs—women well out of today's frantic mating-dating scene—who rarely buy anything new. They just keep in style by making modest adjustments at the hem. . . . We met a woman recently who hadn't bought a new dress in two years. . . . The fashion industry doesn't seem to be getting the word. It seems to be listening to a small group of designers, writers and junior jet-setters who live in a handful of urban watering places around the world. It is not listening to that vast army of consumers, both men and women, who aren't going to

[20] Greene, op. cit., p. 69.

[21] "The Great Male Exposé," *Town and Country* (February, 1970), p. 95.

> college, who are over 25, have tremendous quantities of money and taste—and aging wardrobes. This, in effect, is the largest single untapped market in the country. . . . So we wonder whether youth hasn't reigned too long.[22]

Gloria Guinness asks, "Where Has Glamor Gone?" She defines glamour in terms of make-believe, as sensations of beauty, romance, and magic, as a precious "superficial glass that makes anything and anyone seem more appealing and delightful to the eye." Her question really becomes meaningful when followed by her next question, "Where is the glamor in looking like a retarded school girl?"[23] This, indeed, is a valid inquiry for a mature woman in the world of the "youthquake."

Proponents of the midi look claim that it, too, is youthful and full of vitality. Here is *Harper's Bazaar*'s answer to "What makes the midi look young?"

> The *waist* fitted, hauled in or minimized by flaring skirts. The *dress,* in lean, racy versions. *Pleats,* releasing the legs for action. Shoes keeping the skirt in step with youth. . . . *Leather's* young voice demanding equal time with tweeds and woolens. The *neck,* up tight, lengthening the silhouette. . . . Unstructured *coats,* mobile, lightweight and young. *Capes,* flying and flashing along the Seine. The *body shirt,* tapered down along the rib cage. . . . *Gloves,* the suede gauntlet. . . . *Heels* higher, slimming the ankle.[24]

Now all the fashion copywriters have to do is to convince both the young and the middle-aged that the midi *is* young.

In a study comparing middle-aged women of comfortable means with college girls, Nancy Taylor found that college girls owned a greater variety of colors in their accessories, particularly shoes, handbags, and hose. These articles were generally in basic colors for the middle-aged women. While most women's shoes were in the pump style, girls' shoes included heavy heels with buckle, flat

[22] "The Forgotten Markets," *American Fabrics* (Spring, 1969), p. 86.

[23] Gloria Guinness, "Where Has Glamor Gone?", *Harper's Bazaar* (November, 1965), p. 200.

[24] *Harper's Bazaar* (October, 1970), p. 148.

with strap, brogans, slingbacks, loafers, and small heels. (Not one girl owned a pump-type shoe, compared with 63 per cent of the older women owning such a shoe.) Most girls decided to buy hose when they had a new dress so that the color and texture of the hose would complete their costume, while women bought hose in a flesh color when their old hose were worn out. Women were also more likely to buy handbags and shoes to go with a number of garments; girls carried handbags less often than women. Jewelry for girls usually consisted of rings and watches; women most often wore earrings. In general women were less concerned with style but rather chose their accessories to suit their personalities.[25]

Illustrations of Favorite Costumes

I. Young College Women
- Garment: Dark grey wool dress and coat; a scarf of grey black and red paisley
- Shoes: Black brogans
- Hose: Just a "hint" of grey
- Handbag: Black calf
- Bracelet: Silver with pearls
- Ring: Pearl

II. Young College Woman
- Garment: Black/brown tweed walking suit, beaver collar
- Shoes: Brown lizard
- Hose: Neutral tone
- Handbag: Brown lizard
- Bracelet: Gold
- Ring: Amethyst

I. Middle-Aged Woman
- Garment: Beige sheath type dress with hip length jacket
- Shoes: Brown alligator pump
- Hose: Neutral tone
- Handbag: Medium sized alligator
- Necklace: Pearls
- Ring: Diamond

[25] Nancy Taylor, "A Study of the Selection and Use of Dress Accessories," unpublished Master's thesis, University of Missouri, 1969, p. 100.

II. Middle-Aged Woman

Garment: Black silk ottoman suit
Shoes: Black silk pumps with bow
Hose: Black sheer
Handbag: Black silk
Pin: Diamond sunburst
Bracelet: Gold
Ring: Pearl and diamond [26]

It should be emphasized that these costumes are symbols of people with above-average incomes. The girls were students at Stephens College whose fathers were business or professional people earning more than $15,000 a year. The middle-aged women were chosen from a similar socioeconomic group. The study was designed to eliminate all differences except age.

Old Age

It is more important to consider our aging population now than in any other period of history. The following table shows some interesting comparisons of life expectancies, past and present:

LIFE EXPECTANCY

18	Bronze Age*
20	Ancient Greece*
27	India (today)**
31	Middle Ages (Europe)*
33	Bolivia (today)**
37	18th-century Europe*
30–40	Africa (today)**
40–50	Worldwide (today)**
50	United States, 1900*
over 70	United States (today)*
78	1964 U. S. Babies*

* J. C. Buckley, *The Retirement Handbook* (Evanston, Ill.: Harper & Row, 1962).

** Anne Simon, "The Vintage Mind," *McCall's* (January, 1968), p. 18.

[26] Ibid., p. 124.

Most discussions of old age have discouraging undertones. It is true that one's physical appearance is no longer an asset, but a liability. However, there are bright spots to be considered. With good nutritional practices, exercise, plenty of rest, and a special effort toward good posture, the body can be kept in reasonably good shape. In the entertainment world, where physical appearance is often directly related to earning power, scores of men and women over sixty have retained an attractive physique. Cary Grant, James Stewart, and John Wayne share the limelight with Marlene Dietrich, Ginger Rogers, and Katharine Hepburn. These people feel an obligation to themselves and to their public. Going beyond the sixties we find the Duchess of Windsor slim and vibrant at 73, Mae West co-starring in a movie at 75, and Rose Kennedy, "trim and lithe in turtleneck and slacks, carries her own golf clubs at 79." [27]

On an aesthetic plane, clothing can play at least three parts for the older person—it can accent or call attention to one's good points; it can camouflage poor ones; and it can give a psychological lift, just as can any other thing of beauty or work of art, loveliness is its own reward. Havighurst goes so far as to say that clothing is a rational defense against aging. "By dressing even more carefully than younger people, older people can make better use of their physical attractiveness." [28] In addition, E. L. Allen and H. E. Clow state that careless grooming shows feelings of disregard for others and that this attitude contributes to withdrawal and increased introspection. They further suggest that it is as important for the elderly to create a favorable impression through personal appearance as through behavior.[29]

Yet the pitfalls to creating a favorable impression by the elderly are many. Life is not a simple addition but a changing in form. Ingrid Brenninkmeyer feels that too many elderly people have a lack of feeling for form, thus have little harmony between themselves and their clothing. She

[27] Greene, op. cit., p. 69.

[28] Robert J. Havighurst, "Social and Psychological Needs of the Aging," CCLXXIX: *Social Contribution by the Aging* (Philadelphia: The Annals of the American Academy of Political and Social Science, January 1952), p. 16.

[29] Edward L. Allen, M.D., and Hollis E. Clow, M.D., "The Psychology of Retirement," *American Geriatrics Society Journal*, Vol. II (1954), p. 802.

says, "Youth is only a short period of life; there should be an appropriate way of behaving and of dressing in the years that follow youth, and a return to the idea of elegance and good taste."[30] G. Stanley Hall found that women not infrequently feel that as their personal charms decline they must "compensate by richness of attire, jewels, and perhaps lavish ornamentation, coiffure, etc."[31] In a rare article in *Vogue* (rare because the elderly are usually ignored in fashion magazines), a solution is proposed: that the mature woman wear clothes of richer and costlier fabrics than those worn by youth. These should be fashioned along simple lines in agreement with the remodeling of their lives along simpler lines in keeping with their years.[32]

Making the best of one's assets requires a thorough study not only of the face and body, but also of posture, of movements in sitting and walking. It also requires an honest look at the changes that have come through time, certainly changes in coloring, perhaps, added weight, or other changes in body proportion. Some older persons find that they can wear colors they never wore before, others may find that their favorites of youth look less well on them. Some garments actually look better on older people—a gracefully styled full-length coat of mink or Persian lamb usually needs the carriage of an older woman. Kenneth Jay Lane says, "I like the authority of age. A young man in a cape is a faggot, while an old man in a cape has style."[33]

Because elderly figures may have sagged at the bustline, increased size in the waistline and hipline, and added a dowager's hump or rounding shoulders, camouflage is necessary. Less extreme lines and styles and looser, graceful, longer dresses are generally pleasing. Wrinkles in the upper arms usually call for a sleeve rather than short or sleeveless dresses. The recent shift or sacklike unfitted garment style was easier to wear than one with a definite waistline. However, the A-line is probably better for most

[30] Ingrid Brenninkmeyer, *The Sociology of Fashion* (Paris: Librairie du Recueil Sirey, 1963), p. 170.

[31] G. Stanley Hall, *Senescence* (New York: Columbia University Press, 1947), p. 155.

[32] "I'm Glad I'm Sixty," *Vogue* (July, 1954), p. 154.

[33] Reported in *Women's Wear Daily* (October 31, 1969), p. 12.

elderly women than a tube or a full, gathered skirt. A softly draped scarf or cowl neckline often helps the appearance of a wrinkled neck. Sweaters, stoles, and jackets not only add warmth but also a covered-up dignity. The main emphasis is in hiding the less desirable features, thus putting emphasis on beautiful clothes rather than the body itself.

The use of camouflage for older people was never more dramatically presented than by Rudi Gernreich in January, 1970. "There will be the division of youth and age. The young with beautiful bodies will look as uncovered as possible and the old will look as covered as possible in burnoose-like garments." [34] These robelike garments have a stylish simplicity with bold patterns and stunning colors. This is indeed total camouflage.

Covered heads are also usually associated with the elderly, not only because the hair may be felt to be less attractive but because the head (as well as the rest of the body) may be more susceptible to heat and cold. Wigs and hair coloring are also making their way into the clothing and appearance habits of the elderly.

Clothing expenditure data have shown that older people spend less money on clothes and have fewer items in their wardrobes than younger people. This fact makes it all the more imperative that clothes are chosen with special care by and for the elderly.[35] Some of the reasons for fewer purchases are reduced income, fewer social contacts, being less active physically, and having less need for up-to-the-minute fashions.

Practicality also enters into the picture when we consider that older people's joints may be stiff and that the ease of putting on or taking off a garment is a very real consideration. Styles with front closings, very long zippers, or velcro fasteners, and wrap-around garments have been a boon to women, but designs for men's clothes and for underclothing for both sexes badly need a new and creative look.

Perhaps the cruelest blow of the Pop Decade was the idealization of the nymphet as the desirable creature in all phases of life. She was a heroine of novels and movies;

[34] Reported in *Women's Wear Daily* (January 5, 1970), p. 10.

[35] Sidney Goldstein, *Study of Consumer Expenditures—Income and Savings Consumption Patterns of the Aged* (Philadelphia: University of Pennsylvania, 1960), pp. 118–132.

Gernreich Cover-up for Elderly

she was personified by Twiggy and by young male rock singers. Bess Meyerson told a fashion show audience in 1966, "We used to dress like Jackie Kennedy; now we're dressing like Caroline." [36] For the older woman, the loss

[36] Reported in Bender, op. cit., p. 234.

of Mrs. Exeter, the chic and charming grandmother who gave inspiration from the pages of *Vogue,* was only symbolic of the loss of identity—with any symbol having the dignity of age. Only a Frenchwoman is still saying comforting words—elegance is "a privilege of age—a just compensation for loss of youth." [37] No wonder Madame Dariaux's books have been translated into seven languages!

CLOTHING RESEARCH

What have we learned about the clothing behavior of older people? Does clothing provide a meaningful symbol for them?

Older people are interested in their appearance and those who feel that their appearance is acceptable are more likely to participate socially and in general reflect a positive image. Older people also realize that they may have to spend more time and effort on their clothing and grooming in order to be attractive.[38] Older women are interested in fashion and in style changes, although studies have found that women over seventy-five had less interest than those sixty to seventy-four years of age.[39] Maloa Ebeling found that most of her sample window-shopped, and that design and fit of the garment were more important than price or ease of care. Although most women could find a dress in their size, they wished that stores would carry a wider variety. Many who sewed had difficulty finding a pattern to fit and wished that pattern companies would give them more choices of design. In addition, most women wished they had more money to spend on clothes and those with higher incomes more often received a psychological "lift" from buying something new.[40]

[37] Madame Genevieve Dariaux made this statement in an interview. See *Globe-Democrat,* St. Louis, Missouri, May 15, 1968.

[38] Ira M. Bader, "An Exploratory Study of Clothing Problems and Attitudes of a Group of Older Women in Iowa City," *Adding Life to Years,* Institute of Gerontology, State University of Iowa, Supplement No. 10, 1963, pp. 3–6.

[39] Maloa Ebeling and Mary Lou Rosencranz, "Social and Personal Aspects of Clothing for Older Women," *Journal of Home Economics,* Vol. 53, No. 6 (June, 1961), p. 464.

[40] Ibid., p. 465.

Suzanne Shipley found that the older women in her sample (seventy and over) preferred laced shoes with medium-height heels, half sizes, one-piece dresses, long sleeves, hats, and the color navy. She also found that department store buyers held a very conservative view of the older women and considered less than 27 per cent of stock suitable for the older woman. No advertising was directed toward this age group.[41]

Women were especially concerned with becomingness in design and color when selecting a garment to wear to church or social functions.[42] The fit of the garment was also an important consideration for "dressy" dresses. Women who belonged to fewer than three organizations seemed to refuse more invitations for lack of appropriate clothing than did those who attended three or more organizations. Those belonging to fewer organizations more often said that their clothing affected "feelings of ease" at a social gathering than did those who participated socially to a greater extent.[43]

There is also the fact that peoples with other cultural backgrounds are more likely to associate certain appearance symbols with age than pop-culture Americans do. A Clothing TAT given to Mexican-Americans and Anglo-Americans [44] brought out the greater number of age incongruities noted by Mexican-Americans (19 for Mexican-Americans compared with two for the Anglo-Americans).

Old age and even middle age is sometimes accompanied by impaired physical movements and physical handicaps. A compilation of theory, research, and good practical advice for the physically handicapped by May, Waggoner, and Boettke [45] has an informative chapter on self-help clothing for adults. Descriptions and illustrations for women include wrap-around coat dresses, women's slacks

[41] Suzanne Shipley and Mary Lou Rosencranz, "Older Women's Clothing Preferences," *Journal of Home Economics*, Vol. 54, No. 10 (December, 1962), p. 854.

[42] Lois Bartley and Jesse Warden, "Clothing Preferences of Women 65 and Older," *Journal of Home Economics*, Vol. 54, No. 8 (1962), pp. 716–717.

[43] Ebeling and Rosencranz, op. cit., p. 465.

[44] Carol Sanders Bathke, "Ethnic Responses to a Modified Clothing TAT," *Journal of Home Economics*, Vol. 60, No. 5 (May 1968), p. 354.

[45] Elizabeth E. May, Neva R. Waggoner, and Eleanor M. Boettke, *Homemaking for the Handicapped* (New York: Dodd, Mead & Co., 1966).

with full-length side-seam zippers on both legs, belts with attached pockets, wrap-around circular skirts fastened with Velcro, undergarments with front closings, and a combination cape and stadium rug for wheelchair use. None of these garments have an "institutional" look; all of them are both functional and fashionable.

For men, suggestions include trousers with full-length side zippers and trousers lined in the knee area to protect the pant leg from wear and tear caused by braces:

> Another "Functional Fashion" is the seat-length suit coat designed for comfort and appearance of men in wheelchairs. It eliminates having to sit on extra fabric that feels bulky and bunches up in wrinkles.
>
> Men who have difficulty with buttons will find Velcro a workable substitution. The buttons can remain on the shirt, but Velcro is positioned behind them, either in a strip or in patches. Some men prefer to put their dress shirts on over the head, with most of the buttons prefastened.[46]

[46] Ibid., p. 92.

15 Taste

Most students of taste shy away from a definition, preferring rather to describe some of the characteristics and elements that make up taste, usually referred to as "good" taste. Often these arbiters set up standards or limits and usually they compile or arrange certain symbols of taste. Sometimes one encounters a patterning according to a prescribed plan, and then again taste may be said to be found in an artistic arrangement without conscious attention given to any underlying principles. In a more passive context, taste is alluded to as an ability to appreciate fitness, beauty, and order.

Taste has limitations of time, place, and culture; thus it is not universal but is subject to continual change. Russell Lynes describes it ably:

> I do not know what *good* taste is. I do know that taste is not constant and that it is a creature of circumstance. I also know that one measure of a man's taste is what he will put up with. Furthermore, it seems apparent that not only is one generation's good taste very likely to be the next generation's bad taste, but one individual's ideas about what is good taste and bad taste change as he matures, moves to a different place or a different way of living, and acquires values for judging not only his surroundings but what

he wants out of life. It is not easy to pin a definition on anything so fluid or so elusive.[1]

The taste of a particular period generally is exemplified by a number of the creative arts. Fashion is only one of of the symbols of taste of an era. Paul Poiret's designs were similar to the feeling of interior decoration of the Art Nouveau decades; surrealism of the Salvador Dali school was expressed in the fashions of Elsa Schiaparelli; modern art's simplicity of the 1920's was interpreted by Coco Chanel.[2]

Many parallels can be drawn between clothes and architecture—the turban of Moslem dignitaries is shaped like a mosque, while a Siamese headdress is like a votive spire in that country.[3] A Gothic arch finds a repeat in a knight's helmet in the Middle Ages; the lady's hennin or high headdress is much like a Gothic pinnacle. The slashings on trunk hose resemble decorations on Elizabethan table legs, the Fontange headgear is like a William and Mary chair, crinolines echo the shape of the domes of the Crystal Palace exhibition hall of 1862, the straight lines in 1928 fashions look much like the Empire State Building in New York.[4]

In the decade of the 1960's the rectangular shifts mirrored modular building units; Paco Rabanne's plastic disks resembled architectural structures; slim trousers looked like slim furniture legs; Mrs. Kennedy's pill-box hat not only looked like a pill box but also resembled an oil storage tank; bell bottoms, puffed sleeves, and ruffles paralleled the relaxing of the straight lines used in décor of interiors and in textile prints, and, finally, actors wearing no clothes at all in recent Broadway plays reflect our free and easy attitudes toward sex.

Anspach defines fashion as public taste—"the result of many individual tastes simultaneously but separately selecting the same thing." [5] Lynes says that if anything can

[1] Russell Lynes, *The Taste-makers* (New York: Harper & Row, 1949), p. 340.

[2] Ingrid Brenninkmeyer, *The Sociology of Fashion* (Paris: Librairie du Recueil Sirey, 1963), p. 88.

[3] W. H. Webb, *The Heritage of Dress* (London: E. G. Richards, 1907), p. 50.

[4] James Laver, *Style and Costume* (London: Oxford University Press, 1949), p. 120.

[5] Karlyne Enspach, *The Why of Fashion* (Ames: Iowa State University Press, 1968), p. 243.

probe the mysteries of public taste, the fashion business takes the honors because it is a "ninety-five percent gamble in taste." [6] It is the best reflector of culture, without even trying. "The mood and morals and mores of a people are portrayed by their clothes even more readily than by their arts, because clothes are essentially ephemeral and respond easily and quickly to changes in the public temper." [7]

Thus, taste arbiters are among the fashion leaders and designers of any period. Sinclair notes that wives in the Victorian era were restricted to their homes by their husbands, yet they were given authority over spending and consumption and were elevated as superior in the "art of living." [8] Bender describes two kinds of "mother's" influence on the male designer who is providing the symbols to be consumed by public taste:

> The standard biography of the male homosexual designer contains a reference to a mother who had simply marvelous taste, far beyond the appreciation of the Philistines in the dreadful burg in which he grew up. . . . One designer will keep mother at his side and design dresses in the image of her heyday. That may be one reason for the constant revival of the twenties and thirties in current fashion. Another designer will put a continent between himself and the mother he refers to as a sot. His forte may be the tarty look.[9]

Of course, designers see their place very differently in cycles of taste. Gernreich has said that he sees his function as one who overstates and exaggerates, leaving "people who have taste" to adapt his creation to suit themselves.[10] Others see the designer and the artist as one who holds up a mirror for society to see things it might miss in passing. Hall believes that although the artist has a reputation for pace-setting and for creating new patterns,

[6] Lynes, op. cit., p. 305.
[7] Ibid.
[8] Andrew Sinclair, *The Better Half* (New York: Harper & Row, 1965), p. 357.
[9] Marylin Bender, *The Beautiful People* (New York: Coward McCann, Inc., 1967), p. 36.
[10] Alexander Weatherson, *Body Covering* (New York: Museum of Contemporary Crafts of American Craftsmen's Council, 1968), p. 22.

he reflects the overall pattern in which he participates. "Most artists know that what greatness they have lies in being able to make meaningful statements about what is going on around them. They say what others have tried to say, but say it more simply, more directly, and more accurately." [11]

Taste and Simplicity

Taste is often related to the concept of simplicity. Yet what is simplicity for one is not simplicity for another; personal taste defines what is plain, ornate, appropriate, or superfluous.

"You go beyond simplicity when you attempt to appropriate more than your wants, your aspirations demand —that is, to appropriate for show, for ostentation, more than your life can assimilate, can make thoroughly yours. . . . There is no merit in riches nor in poverty. There is merit in that simplicity of life which seeks to grasp no more than is necessary for the development and enjoyment of the individual." [12] Ernest Dichter likewise points to our adverse judgment of other people through their symbolic use of clothing. He particularly stresses the overdressed person who "not only shows poor taste but also reveals a frustrated personality. . . . It is as if such a person were attempting to secure the affection of others by psychological crutches." [13] These people don't trust their own abilities and perceptions so they overcompensate with clothes to gain recognition and affection.

Frank Barron draws up a list of traits relating to the simple person and the complex person. However, the sim-

[11] Hall, op. cit., p. 162.

[12] Charles Dudley Warner, "Simplicity in Fashion," *The Complete Writings of Charles Dudley Warner* (Hartford, Connecticut: The American Publishing Company, 1904), p. 86.

[13] Ernest Dichter, *Handbook of Consumer Motivation* (New York: McGraw-Hill, Inc., 1964), p. 87.

ple person is not synonymous with the idea of simplicity in the preceding paragraph but seemingly the very opposite:

The Complex Person

1. Is artistic.
2. Has unconventional friends, occasionally is visited by an impractical, not to say wild, idea, and would rather be creative and neurotic than normal and ordinary.
3. Is politically somewhat radical, and can be militantly opposed to racial prejudice.
4. Is aware of present imperfections, would welcome and has faith in future developments.

The Simple Person

1. Doesn't like modern art.
2. Particularly values kindness and generosity in a wife (as opposed to implied alternative values), and feels that the proper filial sentiments toward one's parents are love and gratitude.
3. Feels that a citizen should support his country, right or wrong, and that disobedience to the government is never justified. Somewhat allied to this, he prefers a team effort to individual competition.
4. Prefers symmetry to asymmetry, considers perfect balance the essence of good composition, and prefers straightforward reasoning to metaphors and the search for analogies.
5. Has clear plans for the the future, and considers that things seem simpler as you learn more about them.
6. Believes that a person with a problem or worry should not think about it and that inventions which take jobs away from people should be suppressed until new work can be found for them.[14]

It would seem that the person who appreciates simplicity in the abstract is not a simple person.

[14] Frank Barron, *Creativity and Psychological Health* (Princeton, N. J.: D. Van Nostrand Company, Inc., 1963), p. 196.

Social Class Levels of Taste

The well-known saying that describes someone with "champagne tastes on a beer salary" is indicative of the belief that there are socioeconomic levels of taste. Barber and Lobel describe the women at the top of the social class system as having taste that is more British than French, as being aloof and fairly independent of fashion, and as responding to advertising that stresses clothes that are "aristocratic," "well-bred," and "distinguished." Some of these upper-class people may even have "eccentric" taste in clothing.[15] Patrick O'Higgins calls such upper-class taste "Shabby Elegance." This is the quintessence of styles that mellow with age, an image of quality wardrobes allowed to mature at leisure. His examples include Amanda Burden's faded jeans of impeccable cut, the old Duke of Bedford, who always had his suits broken in a full year by his valet before wearing them himself, and Eleanora Sears, who walked from Boston to Newport (for exercise) in old white sneakers—with laces carefully pressed by her maid. However, the "locus classicus of shabby elegance is the late Queen Mary of England . . . [whose] majestic hats, artful monuments garnished with aigrettes and the pale glitter of seed pearls, were a signature of her indomitable character." [16] Her granddaughter, Princess Margaret, did not show elegance when attending a first night in "her unfortunate choice of stoles, open shoes, and beaded bags, but caught off balance, so to speak, trudging in the mud with a scarf over her head and tartan about her waist, occasionally projects a fleeting aura of the shabby elegance which Englishwomen . . . have enjoyed." [17]

The tastes of the high fashion leaders are reflected by the cosmopolitan "jet set" who patronize the Parisian designers. They value symbols of sophistication and chic and avoid obvious ostentation. That is, one must actually

[15] Bernard Barber and L. S. Lobel, "Fashion in Women's Clothes and the American Social System," *Social Forces*, Vol. 31 (1952), p. 127.

[16] Patrick O'Higgins, "Shabby Elegance," *Harper's Bazaar* (November 1967), p. 242.

[17] Ibid.

spend a great deal of money on clothes, but must not appear to have done so.[18]

The middle classes have tastes that emphasize the clean and respectable. Clothes can be "smart" if smart is what everyone else is wearing. There is a "distaste for high style." [19]

Lower class taste is frequently thought to be overdone and is exemplified by clothes that are overdecorated. Eve Merriam describes lower-class taste as including sweaters dripping with sequins (when the upper class was wearing plain ones), mules with pompoms (compared to black velvet flats), nylon panties with the days of the week embroidered on them (as opposed to cotton pants), and heavy musk-scented perfumes (when the upper class favored light floral scents). The lower classes speak of desired styles that are curvaceous and "cute." [20]

Russell Lynes has an impressive graphic presentation of taste in art during several decades, showing how the popularity of many paintings travels from the upper classes downward, during several decades.[21] Pictures like "Whistler's Mother" appeared in highbrow homes during the 1870's to 1890's; in middlebrow homes in the 1910's to 1920's; and in lowbrow homes during the 1940's to 1950's.[22] The highbrow [23] does not like to hang color reproductions and if he cannot afford real paintings, he will buy original drawings. The highbrow cares about taste and is a purist; the lowbrow "wants to be comfortable and enjoy himself without having to worry about whether he has good taste or not." [24] The upper middlebrow is unsure of his own tastes, but firm in his belief that taste is extremely important; the lower middlebrow ardently believes that he knows what he likes, and "yet his taste is constantly susceptible to the pressures that put him in knickerbockers one year and rust-colored slacks the next." [25]

Social science research reveals specific examples of differing aesthetic tastes of various social classes:

[18] Barber and Lobel, op. cit., p. 128.

[19] Ibid.

[20] Eve Merriam, *Figleaf* (Philadelphia: J. B. Lippincott Company, 1960), pp. 76–79.

[21] Lynes, op. cit., pp. 326–327.

[22] Ibid.

[23] Highbrow is not exactly parallel to upper-class. For Lynes' definitions, see Chapter XVII in *The Taste-makers.*

[24] Ibid., p. 319.

[25] Ibid., p. 331.

> People of low income prefer sweet chocolate, fabrics with a rubbery touch, and strong-smelling flowers; upper-class consumers favored what one might call more demanding sensory experiences: bitter-dry tastes, irregular weaves, and pungent fragrances. . . . One can give a more psychological explanation: the lower-class person is starved out for pleasant experiences; or a more sociological one: the upper-class individual exhibits his "sensual" wealth by conspicuous non-consumption of strong stimuli.[26]

Most authorities on taste believe that taste is a learned behavioral trait and that one is usually educated for such discrimination. Education can be formal or informal, but there must be an effort made on the part of the connoisseur. One of the joys of the tastemaker is that he can pass his ideas on to his followers, all the while staying ahead of the masses. Berelson and Steiner believe that the upper classes are interested in a wider range of life because of their better education. "By virtue of being upper (and better educated), they become arbiters of the proper use of money, physical appearance and dress, etiquette, language, and aesthetic taste." [27]

Contemporary Taste

One of the aspects of contemporary taste is functionalism. The true beauty of an object is in its appropriate use, according to the proponents of functionalism. In other words, it is functional (thus beautiful) to use nylon for stockings, woolens for sportswear, and silk for more dressy or formal clothing.

Another element in contemporary taste is related to multipurpose objects, housing, and clothing. McLuhan says it this way:

[26] Robert A. Dahl, Mason Haire, and Paul F. Lazarsfeld, *Social Science Research on Business: Product and Potential* (New York: Columbia University Press, 1959), pp. 108–109.

[27] Bernard Berelson and Gary Steiner, *Human Behavior,* An Inventory of Scientific Findings (New York: Harcourt, Brace and World, Inc., 1964), p. 488.

> Clothing and styling in the past decade have gone so tactile and sculptural that they present a sort of exaggerated evidence of the new qualities of the TV mosaic. . . . All this adds up to the compressional implosion—the return to nonspecialized forms of clothes and spaces, the seeking of multi-uses for rooms and things and objects.[28]

In clothing the "layered" look enabled one to be tastefully dressed by peeling off unnecessary layers of sports attire for more simple formal basics underneath.

One of the dangers with mass-produced design is that there is so little choice that it can be difficult to exercise discriminating taste. One answer to mass-produced design is a return to hand-made items. Hand-woven woolens, hand-embroidered blouses and dresses, patchwork-patterned and hand-quilted skirts and dresses all were designed to be unique and one of a kind. In addition, McLuhan reassures us that the electronic age will not bring uniformity.

> Nevertheless, the range of choice in design, stress, and goal within that total field of electromagnetic interprocess is very much greater than it ever could have been under mechanization. . . . Since electric energy is independent of the place or kind of work-operation, it creates patterns of decentralism and diversity. . . . Panic about automation as a threat of uniformity on a world scale is the projection into the future of mechanical standardization and specialism, which are now past.[29]

Lack of Taste

One of the rules of the game of taste is that the immediate past is generally despised. James Laver in *Taste and Fashion* says that "a costume is considered 'indecent' ten years before its time, 'shameless' five years before its

[28] Marshall McLuhan, *Understanding Media* (New York: Signet Books, 1966), p. 286.
[29] Ibid., p. 311.

time, 'smart' during its time, 'dowdy' five years after its time, 'hideous' ten years after its time, 'ridiculous' twenty years after, 'amusing' thirty years after, 'quaint' fifty years after, 'charming' one hundred years after and 'beautiful' one hundred and fifty years after." However, his time periods may have changed in our electronic era. We now consider clothes of the twenties and thirties quite wearable.

During the 1960's the author kept a running account of what students felt were "foolish" fashions—fashions that never should have been. Some two hundred students felt that these were indeed "foolish." Most of them were from the immediate past.

Foolish Fashions in Outer Garments

chemise
over-blouse with flared skirt
cut-offs
bikini
bermuda shorts
metallic evening dresses
extremely short or long skirts
sack dress
extreme necklines
tightly fitted suits with heavy shoulder pads
short shorts
sheer nylon blouse
thick shoulder pads
magenta-colored wardrobe pieces
knee-tickler skirts
full shifts
shift dresses
unproportioned look
floor-length skirts
strapless dress
suspenders
sleeveless dresses on some women
fleece coats
extreme dress silhouette
2-piece bathing suits [30]

Pop taste, like pop art, is a reaction against the immediate past—the taste of the "establishment." Some clothing examples of this would include Geoffrey Beene's designs with shock value in 1967: fashion copy described humorous long evening football sweaters with numerals in sequins sewn on chiffon and little evening dresses in men's tweeds shorter than ever. This the reporter concluded to be the exquisite expensive joke—put your tongue in your cheek and keep it there.[31]

[30] Compiled by students at the University of Missouri during 1964–1968.

[31] As reported in the *Kansas City Times* (Wednesday, April 17, 1967), p. 8A.

Lynes' lowbrows, of course, lack taste but they stay happy by not worrying about it. On the other hand, there are the pathetic women who search for taste and never seem to find it: "Women today tramp their whole lives through with limp little swatches clutched in their hot hands—trying to discover what they really like—if anything."[32]

There are those who aspire to a general improvement in the taste levels of people in general and Americans in particular. Yet it is not always easy to judge whether change is improvement or simply change. The author tends to agree with Russell Lynes' opinions concerning taste improvement.

> I can see no reason why we should want taste to improve. . . . We are fortunate in America that we have so many different ways of satisfying so many different kinds of tastes. . . . The point is that we have a tremendously diversified basis of morality, education, and sensibility and that the frictions among them generate the kind of heat that gives light. It is these conflicts of ideas and tastes that give the arts of our country vitality, and that make the museum and the corner movie houses equally important manifestations of our culture.
>
> Unless I completely misunderstand the real reason for having taste, it is to increase one's faculties for enjoyment. Taste in itself is nothing. It is only what taste leads to that makes any difference.[33]

Summary of Symbolic Use of Clothing

No better example of a "medium as the message" can be found than a person's use of clothing. In the past clothes were a convenient shorthand for identification; we knew at a glance how to tell the girls from the boys and

[32] Bernice Fitzgibbon, *Macy's Gimbels and Me* (New York: Simon & Schuster, 1967), p. 346.
[33] Lynes, op. cit., p. 341.

to whom to give deference because of age or social status. With closer inspection we usually could have identified various occupational groups: the fashion individualist, the conformist, the sex-pot, the sports enthusiast, the modest maiden, the nouveau riche, the underdressed snob, and the matinee idol. The obvious clothing symbols were and still are a language understood by most of us. Such symbols save us time in interpretation and spare us the embarrassment of mistaken identities.

Now that we are entering the electronic spheres of the space age we must learn new languages. All symbols are changing—clothing among many others.

In a critique of McLuhan's work called *McLuhan Hot and Cool,* Walter Ong says:

> The symbolism with which modern man has surrounded himself—the symbolism of his advertising, his clothes, comic strips, corpse literature, etiquette manuals, "greatbooks," cowboys and Hollywood dream walkers or "somnanbules," chum-tone news reporting, electric brains, picnics, Boy Scouting, mannequins—all this is a language which he both understands and does not understand.[34]

Needless to say, we need more research in order to understand the new language of clothing. How often do we now use clothing to make us feel our own worth and importance when so much of our computer age is reduced to numbers—to cold ciphers? As we seek to learn more about the universe with imaginative theories of stars and star clusters, of galaxies and clusters of galaxies, and even beyond into extragalactic space, what new meanings will clothing symbols have for us? Will uniforms and conformity give us comfort, or will we strike a blow for individuality?

With our expanding population problems, it makes economic sense to consider people in aggregates and in parameters of very large groupings. How can clothing help us feel less smothered by population pressure, less a look-alike, less bored with sameness? Won't we sometimes value fission versus fusion?

[34] Walter Ong, in *McLuhan: Hot and Cool,* edited by Gerald E. Stearn (New York: The Dial Press, Inc., 1967), p. 82.

We will undoubtedly come up against some very discouraging facts of life about our environment and about the nature of human beings in relationship to the environment and to each other. We are not going to have a more perfect world overnight; we will become discouraged and disillusioned. We need the language of *illusion* to soften the crush of the burden of reality. These remarks from *Human Behavior* say it so well:

> In his quest for satisfaction, man is not just a seeker of truth, but of deceptions, of himself as well as others. . . . For the truth is, apparently, that no matter how successful man becomes in dealing with his problems, he still finds it hard to live in the real world, undiluted: to see what one really is, to hear what others really think of one, to face the conflicts and threats really present. . . . Man maneuvers his world to suit himself. What makes him able to do this, largely, is his symbolic capacity and the language that goes with it. . . . If this means that the scientist has found what the artist has always known about the place of illusions in life, so much the better for both—and for the continuity between them.[35]

Let us hope that the silent language of clothing will make life not only more endurable, but more enjoyable for everyone. Yes, we probably need to retain some of the old symbolism of experimentation and excitement for the young and of grace and dignity for the old, but we also need to develop new symbols of a sense of worth and well-being for all of us on global earth and whatever worlds beyond we may inhabit.

[35] Berelson and Steiner, op. cit., p. 665.

16 Measures of Symbols

Clothing TAT[1]

Much of the thematic content of the Clothing TAT is related to the recognition of clothing symbols. Informants relied heavily upon the clothing of the various characters for clues concerning age of the character, occupation, sex, and the occasion for which the character was dressed. A list of themes used in order of frequency by female respondents for the various cards appears on p. 238.

Other symbols mentioned were clothes of another culture; clothes out of style; clothes of a newcomer; new clothes; Western clothes; urban clothes; clothes of a prisoner, a radical, or a sissy. Women from white-collar groups were more likely to notice symbol incongruities (characters dressing differently from other characters), characters dressed to go out, and the suitability of characters' clothes to the occasion than were women from the blue-collar group. Women with high incomes used themes of age, attracting attention, dressing differently, social

[1] See pages 70–76 for TAT pictures.

class, and being well dressed more often than did those with low incomes. Women with higher education tended to note age, sexual attraction, clothes of another culture,

Theme or symbolic meaning of clothing	*Cards*							
	I	*II*	*III*	*IV*	*V*	*VI*	*VII*	*Total*
Age	6	27	32	23	16	17	0	121
Occupation	0	10	1	23	4	51	26	115
Sex	0	0	0	0	30	0	84	114
Poorly dressed	3	4	57	0	0	11	5	80
Occasion	57	3	0	1	11	7	0	79
Well dressed	28	6	0	18	23	1	3	79
Economic status	0	3	0	10	15	21	5	54
Visitor	0	0	0	35	7	0	0	42
Social class	5	0	5	0	0	23	0	33
Immodest clothes	11	0	14	0	0	0	0	25

and suitability for occasion more often than women with less education. Young women used themes of attracting attention, clothes conflicting with background of picture, different dress of characters, and occasion more frequently than older women did. It was apparent that the clothing of female characters was noted more frequently than the clothing of male characters.

Symbolism of Masculinity and Femininity

A number of words are listed in the table that follows.* Will you please read these, one by one, and write beside

* G. A. DeWit, *Symbolism of Masculinity and Femininity* (New York: Springer Publishing Co., Inc., 1963), p. 34.

each word the first word that comes to your mind immediately after reading the word.

Don't think or reason about it, just put down the first word that comes to your mind, whatever it is.

rose	ship	sausage	square	six	key
three	eagle	deer	circle	broom	gun
stick	bracelet	balloon	pocketbook	saber	earth
flower	dustpan	mouth	umbrella	dog	bee
necktie	room	chapel	suitcase	door	moon
peacock	hammer	serpent	pocket	cat	foot
eight	machine	shoe	slipper	one	dishwasher
pin	hand	banana	butterfly	jewel case	
apple	house	sun			

As reported earlier (page 168), some words are associated with females most frequently while others are usually associated with males. The words producing female images are rose, flower, bracelet, dustpan, butterfly, jewel case; words with masculine connotations are stick, necktie, pocket, eagle, gun, saber, hammer, and machine.

Analysis of Stories— Situational Analysis

In order to probe general attitudes toward the use of clothing on the job, five stories were designed to reflect problems or issues concerning clothing. These are reported in Michigan Technical Bulletin No. 247, *The Social Significance of Clothing in Occupational Life.* Two stories are reprinted below—one involving a deviation from established clothing norms, the other a relationship to clothing and occupational mobility.

The first story involves a violation of clothing expectation of a client on the part of a lawyer.

Situation I

Tom needed a lawyer's advice for the first time in his life. He asked his neighbor to recommend somebody. The neighbor advised him to see Mr. Drake, a competent lawyer who had handled several legal matters in town with great success. After making an appointment with Drake, Tom arrived at the lawyer's office and was surprised to find him casually dressed in a faded sport shirt that hung out over an unpressed pair of slacks.[2]

In answer to the question, "If you were Tom and needed a lawyer's advice, what would you have done?" see Table 3.[3]

TABLE 3 Responses of Vansburg Men Confronted with a Decision to Use the Services of a Lawyer Who Is Inappropriately Dressed

Reactions	*Number*	*Percentage*
Rejection of the situation because of lawyer's inappropriate dress	18	17
Actor attempts a more thoroughgoing definition of the situation in view of lawyer's clothes	15	14
Lawyer's dress prompts actor to impose conditions before hiring him; e.g., if he had a good reputation	12	11
Actor evaluates lawyer's clothing negatively, but continues with act	14	13
Actor evaluates lawyer's clothes as irrelevant and continues with act	21	20
Actor does not evaluate clothes and continues with act	14	13
Actor evaluates lawyer's clothes positively	3	3
Actor mentions that a successful person doesn't have to wear good clothes	9	9
Indeterminate	5	5
Totals*	111	105

* Totals equal more than 100 per cent because some respondents gave more than one answer.

Two thirds of the Vansburg men disapproved of Mr. Drake's clothing. Confronted with the situation, roughly

[2] Form and Stone, "The Social Significance of Clothing in Occupational Life," Michigan Agricultural Experiment Station Technical Bulletin, No. 247 (1955), p. 42.
[3] Ibid., p. 43.

equal proportions (about one seventh each) would refuse to use Mr. Drake's services; try to learn more about him; make certain reservations before deciding to employ him; or employ him despite the poor impression he makes. Thus it appears that although two thirds evaluate his *dress* negatively, two fifths approve of *him* sufficiently to consider using his services.

The man's established reputation minimized his use of nontraditional clothing. Some informants were willing to allow comfort or personal choice to be the guide to the lawyer's dress in his own office.

Situation II

> *Elsie got a job working as a typist in an office.* At first, she got along well with the other girls. She liked to wear good, new clothes to the office. As a result, she spent most of her salary on clothes and was the best dressed girl in the office. After a short time, Elsie was promoted to the job of receptionist, a job that some of the older girls wanted. They complained to the office manager. He told them that Elsie was given the job because she was always so well-dressed, and that it was important to have someone at that job who would make a good impression on the public.

If you had worked in the office and seen Elsie promoted above you, how would you have felt? [4]

About half of the Vansburg men approved of Elsie's promotion, while 33 per cent disapproved. Some blamed the managers for the promotion, others blamed the other workers, and only nine per cent actually blamed Elsie.

> The reasons they gave for supporting his behavior in order of frequency were: (1) that good appearance (which they often equated with desirable personality) is as much part of the job as ability; (2) that a person of good appearance is needed to meet the public; (3) that an attractive receptionist is good for the company's sales and prestige; and (4) that people with good appearance usually have other good character traits, such as ability, perseverance, and work capacity.[5]

[4] Ibid., p. 44.
[5] Ibid., p. 46.

The following story involves economic mobility:

Situation III

Mrs. Jones inherited a large sum of money from a distant relative. For years she had lived in Mapleville on the small income her husband made as an office clerk and had always purchased her own clothing in a large chainstore because of its low prices. After inheriting the money, Mrs. Jones changed clothing stores and began to patronize a small, exclusive shop in a nearby city. She dressed as she always had when she shopped in the chainstore at home, but she noticed that the clerks in the shop did not give her nearly as much personal attention as they gave the other customers. One day she tried to engage another customer in conversation. The other customer snubbed her and cut her short. Embarrassed by this, she no longer patronized that store.[6]

Informants were asked what they thought of Mrs. Jones' actions and that of the other customers. They were evenly divided in relation to Mrs. Jones' behavior, but they disapproved of the behavior of the other customers in a ratio of five to one. Approximately 60 per cent of the women in the upper-income groups approved of Mrs. Jones, while only 30 per cent of those in the lower-income group approved of her behavior. In this study, women in the upper-income levels were more indulgent to changing patterns of store patronage as a result of economic mobility. When data were analyzed according to other social class variables, approval of Mrs. Jones' behavior was found at the extremes of the social class scales, while disapproval was greatest among the middle class.

The above situations are recorded as examples of attempts to measure clothing symbols in an imperical fashion along with possible interpretations. Those responding were limited by time (1950's), place (Midwest) and sex (the first two were asked of males, while the third situation was given to females). Answers to these same situations

[6] Stone and Form, "The Local Community Clothing Market," Agricultural Experiment Station, Bulletin No. 262, Michigan State University (1957), p. 55.

would undoubtedly be different given under conditions of changing time and place. The importance of the situations is their *method*—the semiprojective approach to measuring symbolic clothing usages.

A Semantic Differential

Three pictures of male attire were chosen to represent (1) a beatnik, (2) a dressy lace-shirted model and (3) a conventional business suit. Respondents were asked to rate the three pictures on the following scale: [7]

Females tended to rate the beatnik as warm, low-status, powerless, and unromantic. Males rated the beatnik as rebellious, reasonable, impulsive, and sensitive. The man in the dressy outfit was seen as excessive, extravagant,

[7] Data recorded in Elaine Lindgren, "First Impressions—A Semantic Differential to Measure Clothing Responses," unpublished paper, University of Missouri, 1967. The scale used here was developed by Mrs. Lindgren.

	1	*2*	*3*	*4*	*5*	*6*	*7*	
excessive								reasonable
extravagant								frugal
feminine								masculine
flexible								rigid
cheat								honest
cold								warm
competent								incompetent
conforming								rebellious
desirable								undesirable
dull								exciting
high status								low status
hypocritical								straightforward
idealistic								realistic
imaginative								unimaginative
impulsive								methodical
informed								uninformed
optimistic								pessimistic
powerful								powerless
romantic								unromantic
sensitive								insensitive

high-status, imaginative, informed, and romantic by females; males also perceived the dressy lace shirt as extravagant, imaginative, and excessive. The man in conventional clothes was rated as reasonable, masculine, honest, realistic, and straightforward by females; and in addition to these qualities, males also saw the conventional attire as methodical, conforming, and competent. Males and females, at least in the year 1968, were more likely to view the beatnik differently.

A Measure of Modesty

In various clothing classes the author has used a list of ten "states of dress" and had them ranked from one to ten with number one being the most modest and number ten being the least modest. In practically all classes the extremes are identical, but there are many differing views regarding what is modest and what is not, depending upon sex and age of the informants. This technique usually proves the point that our ideas of modesty are not identical.

Rank the following list according to your ideas of what is modest. Use the number one to designate the most modest.

________ **A.** Backless dress; backless to waist
________ **B.** Bare midriff exposing eight inches of skin
________ **C.** Décolleté showing cleavage
________ **D.** Going barefoot
________ **E.** Going without stockings
________ **F.** Topless bathing suit
________ **G.** Skirt slashed on side to point ten inches above knee
________ **H.** Miniskirt, six inches above knee
________ **I.** Shorts with bra top
________ **J.** Sleeveless dress [8]

[8] The Modesty Test was developed by the author.

Test for Taste

An example of a test for contemporary taste in accordance with fashion etiquette:

How Do You Rate As "Best Dressed"? [9]
By Elizabeth Post
of The Emily Post Institute

Woman's fashions change from year to year and it would be ridiculous to try to make rules about styles.

If you answer eight or more of the following questions correctly, you will be considered well-dressed in any circumstances.

1. Is it still considered incorrect to wear a fur stole before 5 p.m.? Yes ______ No ______
2. Do women keep on the hats they wear to a church wedding when they arrive at the reception? Yes ______ No ______
3. May a mink stole be worn with a cocktail suit? Yes ______ No ______
4. Must one wear long gloves with an evening gown? Yes ______ No ______
5. Must pins or corsages always be placed on the left shoulder? Yes ______ No ______
6. Does a lady remove her glove to shake hands? Yes ______ No ______
7. May one wear gold jewelry in the evening? Yes ______ No ______
8. May a hostess wear "hostess slacks" at an informal party even though her guests do not? Yes ______ No ______
9. Is it incorrect to wear patent leather shoes in the winter? Yes ______ No ______
10. May a guest at a wedding wear black? Yes ______ No ______

For correct answers, see next page.

[9] Appeared in *St. Louis Globe-Democrat* (Wednesday, March 13, 1968), Section C, p. 6.

Answers to How Do You Rate As "Best Dressed"?

1. No. It is permissible to wear a stole to any "dressy" affair—a tea, a luncheon, the theater, etc.
2. Yes, unless they feel uncomfortable in a hat, in which case they may remove it.
3. Yes, although if it is a bulky wool suit it will look "heavy."
4. No. They look lovely with a sleeveless gown but it is not required.
5. No. They may be placed wherever they look best.
6. No. In fact, in receiving lines, she should definitely keep them on.
7. Yes. With a long evening gown, gems are most appropriate, but gold is perfectly acceptable with cocktail and dinner dresses.
8. Yes. She may also suggest that her guests wear evening slacks.
9. No. I am delighted that it has been accepted as stylish wear this winter.
10. No. Wedding guests should choose gay and pretty colors—befitting the occasion—rather than try for a "chic" effect.

Beauty Is in the I.Q. of the Beholder
What Matters About Taste

Vogue printed an interesting quiz to gauge contemporary taste. Questions are recorded below:

1. Which of these words relate to taste: small ________ medium ________ large ________?
2. Would you say that taste is: holy ________ funny ________?
3. Popular ________ unpopular ________: which words ring a taste bell?
4. Which is the greatest compliment to a woman's appearance: Impeccable ________ chic ________ charming ________ impressive ________?
5. Match "provincial" with the appropriate places: New York ________ Billings, Montana ________ London ________ Paris ________ Rome ________
6. Check the one that seems to you to come closest to describing taste: furious self-possession ________ beautiful manners ________ neither ________

7. Do you consider that contemporary dressing is: art ________ decoration ________?
8. Which has the greatest bearing on taste: money ________ time ________ spirit ________?
9. Is taste evident: always ________ sometimes ________ never ________?
10. Which décor indicates the surest sense of taste: Regency ________ eighteenth-century English ________ contemporary ________ French provincial ________?

The Answers

1. Small and large are both right answers. Taste has to be one thing or another: good, bad, but not indifferent. It's a definite choice. In fashion, for instance, a pin as small as a ladybug or as large as a butter plate is infinitely more effective taste than one that's middle-sized, middle-of-the-road, middle-aged looking.
2. Funny. No one need bend the knee to taste, to accepted, holy taste in particular. There is no need, if you like a china bowl, to turn it over and see if it bears the Meissen markings, or look for a label *before* you like a dress. Fashion can be funny, sometimes a little wild, a little off-centre, maybe even a little ridiculous (the Stanford-Binet test includes a test for this), and things can often be so terrible they're wonderful. A very tasty man around town has just lately uncovered in a thrift shop what seems to him a marvellous object—a china bust of Shakespeare with a doll's face—a doll's round blue eyes, rose-petal skin, cupid-bow mouth. And the books Mr. Shakespeare rests on are the same colour as his jacket. Well . . . anyway, this man thinks it's funny.
3. Unpopular. It's pretty well accepted that the higher the I.Q., the less popular the taste . . . few intellectuals rush to read down the best-seller list, wait in line at the Music Hall, take up the In painter; they are most apt to seek out the un-popular, the un-everywhere, the un-in. And in fashion, intellectuals shun the too-in-fashion messages, the too lavish furs, the colour on everyone's back. A good place to see taste taking its out-of-the-way course is Fifth Avenue right now. At the Metropolitan Museum, gigantic crowds streamed suddenly in to see the Rembrandt that cost so much money, while down the street at the Frick, a small but steady trickle of regular viewers continued to touch base to visit their Rembrandt, the small, perfect "Polish Rider." And none of them knew what it cost.

4. Charming. Because it implies that this woman has an outgoing aura of attraction that doesn't let you know exactly what it is. She has secrets. The impression *she* makes is of fastidiousness-as-a-matter-of-course, not as an end in itself, of having arrived at a look by her own mysterious methods. She *may* have just come from the hairdresser, spent an hour on her make-up, weeks constructing the whole effect, but you'd never guess. There's no sense of inhuman perfection here—she's a plan with the pencil lines wiped out.

5. All five places. Provincialism is not purely for the provinces but a universal taste fault popping up as readily in a great metropolis as in a hamlet. Provincialism can be applied to taste in decoration, cooking, architecture, fashion. As a way of dressing, it can turn up as relentlessly safe clothes—as irrelevant selection ("I bought it because I liked the buttons")—as a collection of ideas instead of a central plan.

6. Beautiful manners. There can be such a thing as rude taste, and this applies to clothes particularly. Taste is never: clothes for ostentation, clothes for status-seeking, clothes for one-up-manship (the furiously self-possessed); but it can be clothes that communicate an idea, outward signs of an inward grace.

7. Art. Once there was an era—when Schiaparelli was using door-hinges for suit-fastenings—when fashion was a sort of surrealist decoration. Now—in an age of no one-look—there is a clear feeling of fashion as an art form, dependent on line and colour and the additions each woman gives to it as a matter of personal commitment.

8. Spirit. There's a very deep attachment to the idea that taste and money go hand in hand. And they quite often do—as Dr. Johnson once said, "Poverty makes the practice of all virtues hard and some impossible." It *is* harder to indulge taste or display it without money, but it's far from impossible, and if you were to say, "Beauty is in the bank account of the beholder," wouldn't that be nonsense? Time, too, is helpful to have, but not essential. If you listen carefully to "I haven't the time . . ." doesn't it sound like an excuse? It is. The exercise of Taste does require a certain energy—moving that muscle in the mind, perhaps—and then, it's a free spirit.

9. Always. There isn't such a thing as a really mute object. Each inanimate thing, even if scrupulously picked for anonymity, will have its say. A vase, a glass, a sweater, a pair of gloves, if chosen by you, will talk about you. And the dreariest coat in the world has just as insistent a little voice as a zebra jacket's.

10. Contemporary—which means managing the present with a great deal of ease and *not* that any of the furniture was necessarily designed the day before yesterday. The most contemporary room imaginable could be pure Sheraton without the intrusion of a single stick from another era. A magical ability with flowers, a trick of lighting, or a juxtaposition of pieces that wasn't heard of in the eighteenth century could be the immediacy here. The reason there is something faintly wrong with "we've left it just as it was during the Civil War" is that taste never lives in the past, although the past may be all about it, but gives, above everything else, a sense of the moment.

Scoring

Score one point for each right answer. 10 right answers—you must have looked. Any count from 6 to 10—your taste is in good shape; 4 to 6—you lack conviction; 3 or lower—maybe you weren't interested.[10]

[10] Reprinted from *Vogue*. Copyright © 1962 by the Condé Nast Publications Inc. (February 15, 1962), pp. 100–101.

Part Three

ROLE

Role is regarded as a key concept in social psychological theory. In its broadest terms it involves interdisciplinary elements and research variables "drawn from studies of culture, society and personality." [1] In some societies role performance is structured so that there is little variation from performer to performer; in other more complex societies roles are more ambiguous, yet contain generalized standards expected from role performers. Usual standards of behavior or *norms* enable us to organize action even in complex situations; through a process of sanctioning and social pressure norms tend to enforce patterns of conformity for particular situations. Role, as it is most often used, refers to the set of *all norms* or expectations held for particular positions or acts. Many of these norms relate to clothing and appearance features of the actors in given social situations.

Another important aspect of role centers around the identity of the performer. Before social action or meaningful communication in a social transaction transpires, identities must be established. One needs to be aware of who the performer is and what he is likely to do. Here the *awareness of clothing symbols* becomes very important in locating or identifying persons in social terms. "Identity stands at the base of role. When inappropriate identities are established or appropriate identities are lost, role performance is impossible." [2]

Thus, in order to play a role one has an awareness of his own identity, and of the self he is presenting, as well as the identity of others involved in the social transaction. Reciprocal awareness of clothing and appearance symbols is an invaluable aid in the ensuing role performance:

> To establish *what* he is in social terms, each person assembles a set of apparent symbols which he carries about as he moves from transaction to transaction. Such symbols include the shaping of the hair, painting of the face, clothing, cards of identity, other contents

[1] Theodore R. Sarbin, "Role Theory," *Handbook of Social Psychology*, edited by Gardner Lindzey (Cambridge, Mass.: Addison Wesley Publishing Company, Inc., 1954), p. 223.

[2] Edward Gross and Gregory P. Stone, "Embarrassment and the Analysis of Role Requirements," *American Journal of Sociology*, Vol. LXX, No. 1 (July, 1964), p. 3.

of wallets and purses, and sundry additional marks and ornaments.[3]

Further conditions for the ensuing role performance are imposed on the clothing and appearance symbols. That is, the items used should be congruent and should complete the expected visual image. Incongruent symbols are in fact the main cause for mistaken identity or embarassment, which in turn hinders or disrupts the social action. A case in point is illustrated by difficulties of communication between college administrators and college students in "hippie" garb. Where the traditional administrator's expectation of a college student had been a clean, neat, well-groomed appearance, confrontation with a dirty, bearded, long-haired youth in frayed or torn clothing uttering four-letter words is a classic example of noncommunication and of role performance ending abruptly.

Attempts to assess the importance of clothing incongruities were made in the original Clothing TAT and in the TAT-MA (the TAT for Mexican-Americans and Anglo-Americans).

Try as we may to the contrary, it is a fact that we are rarely if ever totally prepared for roles except for very ritualized occasions. Even such formalized events as weddings and religious ceremonials can go awry, although prescribed clothing and appearance norms are usually well known and accepted by the role performers. Unusual attire for weddings such as miniskirts, pants-suits, or the nearly nude look attract widespread attention and appraisal by the more conservative and traditional members of society, who, with reason, wonder if these actors wearing unconventional symbols are serious in the performance of their roles.

As a guard against embarrassing situations, two performance norms are noted by Gross and Stone. First, "the standards of role performance almost always allow for flexibility and tolerance," and second, the other fellow is often given the "benefit of the doubt." [4] However, ignorance of conventional performance norms is quite likely when so many role performances are "carried on in thickly peopled and complexly imaged contexts." [5]

3 Ibid., p. 4.

4 Gross and Stone, op. cit., pp. 12–13.

5 Anselm L. Strauss, *Mirrors and Masks* (New York: The Free Press, 1959), p. 57.

In the chapters that follow, attention will be directed toward the use of clothing in role preparation, changing roles, multiple roles, and in selected specific role situations. We will, in fact, examine the statement that clothing "makes real the role one plays." [6]

[6] Gardner Murphy, *Personality* (New York: Harper & Row, 1947), p. 495.

Preparation for Roles

As Mead, Cooley, and Dewey have observed, the "self" is central to all social acts. One behaves in terms of the kind of person he wants to be and usually prepares himself for such behavior. The self reflects patterns of meaningful relations with individuals and groups. "The dynamics for the support or modification of the self and therefore the dynamics for the organization and redirection of action lie in one's group relationships. As a new individual is inducted into the group, he takes on its objects, whose attributes derive from the group's communicative categories." [1] Artifacts that are meaningful to the group and its role relationships are delineated as distinctive to the group itself, frequently making use of such non-verbal symbols as clothing. Thus one learns to manipulate these symbols in role playing, through the process of socialization.

Examples of the socialization processes that function as role preparation include most types of education, both formal and informal. Particularly noteworthy are "preparatory" schools that equip upper-class boys and girls for roles they will later play. Stephen Birmingham labels the conglomerate of eastern preparatory schools for boys "St.

[1] Manford H. Kuhn, "The Reference Group Reconsidered," Jerome G. Manis and Bernard N. Meltzer, editors, *Symbolic Interaction* (Boston: Allyn and Bacon Inc., 1967), p. 178.

Prep School Boy

Grottlesex."[2] Although rules for clothing to be worn may not be specifically stated, "prep-school" boys look very much as if they were turned out from a mold. The "old school tie" has symbolic meanings of many dimensions, including an appearance vector. Military schools in the South and Midwest accomplish much the same purpose for future role performance, but in this instance, the uniform is used to strengthen likeness in role behavior. The wearing of the uniform reinforces the characteristics of neatness, cleanliness, polish, crispness, uprightness, and a military bearing.

William De Rham's dancing school in New York tutored two generations of the Four Hundred in various dancing classes. Cleveland Amory says that De Rham might address a typical class in this way:

> Dammit, you're a gentleman, not a hoodlum. I want your hair brushed and your trousers creased and I don't want to see a single shirt that was put on yesterday doing business today. I want dark neckties and dark socks and, if you can't keep your socks up any other way, I want garters. In the old days gentlemen carried little bags with their pumps in them. I don't ask you to do that but I want your shoes polished sometime between your last football game and here. I want your hands out of your pockets and nothing in them except a clean white folded handkerchief in your handkerchief pocket. I don't want any sprawling. The first thing you are going to learn to do is sit. You sit still and you sit straight and you sit up. . . . I want you to choose a girl, offer her your right arm and march into the ballroom and stop with your heels together. . . . You bow from the waist. You shake hands with Mrs. De Rham and you give your whole name—your Christian name and your surname. . . . Then you take your girl to her seat and, if there is a seat, you sit beside her. And you don't leave her until she gets another partner or gets married.[3]

Girls of the upper class also prepare for their roles in "finishing schools," dancing schools, and through the

[2] Stephen Birmingham, *The Right People* (New York: Dell Publishing Company, Inc., 1969), p. 46. St. Grottlesex is a term coined to describe Groton, Middlesex, St. Paul's, St. Mark's, and St. George's.

[3] Cleveland Amory, *Who Killed Society?* (New York: Harper & Row, 1960), p. 538.

process of the debut. The tradition of "coming out" goes back to the eighteenth century "when the fifteen or sixteen-year-old daughters of prosperous families were given parties, ostensibly to introduce them to polite society people of all ages."[4] Actually, attention was being called to the fact that they were available for marriage. Tradition changed somewhat after the Civil War, for girls married a little later (around eighteen years of age) and parties began to be more elaborate. The season in New York began in November and ended with Lent. Wardrobes were as elaborate as trousseaux. However, modern debutantes appear more often in group affairs, playing down as much as possible the ostentation of debuts of former decades. Even the $100,000 debutante party given for Charlotte Ford in 1959, which included one thousand two hundred guests varying from Lord Charles Spencer-Churchill to the Gary Coopers, and sported a Middle Ages décor, was not as elaborate as many balls of earlier years. Cleveland Amory declares that compared to the good old days of debuts "the Ford party was scarcely more than a cook-out."[5]

All this points to the fact that the role of today's debutante has changed. She often spends many hours as a volunteer worker and does not spend all her time in pleasure for pleasure's sake. Her coming-out no longer emphasizes the stereotyped role of the idle rich.

Middle-class children prepare for future roles during their public-school years. In a mixed and mobile mass society teenagers do much experimentation to find their ideal self. Murray Wax believes that while adolescents, particularly girls, search for self-images, they are preoccupied with experimentation with appearance.[6] Dewey and Humber also note that adolescence involves continued socialization and searching for identity in preparation for adult roles.[7] Yet adolescents who have like opinions and aspirations tend to group together.

[4] Mary Cable, *American Manners and Morals* (New York: American Heritage Publishing Company, Inc., 1969), pp. 283–284.

[5] Amory, op. cit., p. 519.

[6] Murray Wax, "Themes in Cosmetics and Grooming," *American Journal of Sociology*, Vol. 62 (May 1957), p. 591.

[7] Richard Dewey and W. J. Humber, *The Development of Human Behavior* (New York: The Macmillan Company, 1951), p. 297.

A longitudinal study by Hendricks, Kelley, and Eicher made during four years of schooling (ninth, tenth, eleventh, and twelfth grades) for girls, supported the hypothesis that "the extent to which members of individual reciprocal friendship structures have similar opinions regarding clothing, appearance, and group acceptance is positively related to the cohesion of the group." [8] Another hypothesis was true 50 per cent of the time: "The similar opinions of members of individual reciprocal friendship structures regarding clothing, appearance, and group acceptance differ from the opinions of nongroup members." [9] Thus those students who were searching for their identity and experimenting with similar kinds of roles tended to group together with other girls of similar life styles.

On any college campus, near the end of the senior year, it is often noticeable that the clothing behavior of these students undergoes change. Girls, besides wearing the usual sweater and skirt outfit, have newly purchased suits and dresses, surely bought in preparation for the adult work role. A few decades ago, when bobby sox were the thing for school, wearing stockings signaled the approach of a change in work status. Boys, in similar preparation, often wear more conservative colors and the more formal-looking suit, rather than sweaters and casual pants. In this decade of long hair and dirty clothes one director of student placement comments: "They're paying more attention to their demeanor and their appearance. They're reading up on the companies' literature before they go in to see a recruiter. They're cutting off their long hair, even their mustaches, and they're putting on a suit and tie." [10]

The factor of newness is frequently associated with preparation for a role. New outfits are often purchased when a new and important phase of life begins. "For the soldier returning to civilian life, this buying of a complete new outfit is a very important and significant factor. It is

[8] Suzanne H. Hendricks, Eleanor A. Kelley, and Joanne B. Eicher, "Senior Girls' Appearance and Social Acceptance," *Journal of Home Economics*, Vol. 60, No. 3 (March, 1968), p. 171.

[9] Ibid.

[10] David Smothers, "1970 Graduates Face Cutback in Campus Recruiting," reported in *Columbia Missourian* (March 8, 1970), p. 7.

an indication of his general desire to start his life anew."[11] When people change jobs, change from being a student to being a worker, or get married, they tend to buy new clothes.

[11] Dichter, *Handbook of Consumer Motivation* (New York: McGraw-Hill, Inc., 1964), p. 83.

18 Symbols of Changing Roles

Some historical and cultural examples of changing roles may be recalled at this point. Immediately after the French Revolution, roles and the clothes symbolic of them went through great changes. Because extravagant apparel was associated with the decadent life of the aristocracy under Louis XVI, one's life might depend upon his clothes. Simplicity was the new order—elaborate silken costumes were replaced with simple muslin dresses gathered at the waist. The towering hairdresses were replaced by bonnets. Men changed from brocades, embroidery, ruffles, cuffs, purses, swords, and tight-fitting hose to baggy breeches, plain coats, and neckties. Ominously, men wore a hair style called the guillotine; women wore an upturned hairdo called the victim in memory of the Revolution. Five years later wigs for women were less grim, having such playful names as "fiddle-de-dee," "young-lover-gone" and "roll-me-over." [1]

When Rasputin gained favor with the Russian royal family he changed his whole appearance. Robert Massie writes this memorable description in *Nicholas and Alexandra:*

[1] Gisèle D'Assailly, *Ages of Elegance* (Paris: Librairie Hachette, 1968), p. 152.

> Success at Tsarskoë Selo ensured Rasputin's success in society. As his social position improved, his wardrobe became more elegant. The rough linen shirts were exchanged for silk blouses of pale blue, brilliant red, violet and light yellow, some of them made and embroidered with flowers by the Empress herself. Black velvet trousers and soft kid leather boots replaced the mud-spattered garb of the peasant. The plain leather thong belted around his waist gave way to silken cords of sky blue or raspberry with big, soft, dangling tassels. On a chain around his neck, Rasputin wore a handsome gold cross. It too was a gift from Alexandra. . . . In his new trappings, Rasputin strode confidently into crowded parlors and became the immediate center of attention. His rich clothes were in contrast to his rude, open, peasant's face with its unkempt hair, matted beard, broad pockmarked nose and wrinkled, weatherbeaten skin.[2]

Among the Amish, changes in attire accompany changes in role and status. His hat not only distinguishes the Amish man from the outsider, but also symbolizes his role within the social structure:

> When the two-year-old boy discards a dress and begins wearing trousers for the first time, he also receives a stiff jet-black hat with three or more inches of brim. Hat manufacturers produce at least twenty-eight different sizes and a dozen different styles of Amish hats. The bridegroom in Pennsylvania gets a telescopic hat that is worn during the early married years. The hat is distinguished by a permanent crease around the top of the crown. Grandfather's hat has a four-inch crown and a four-inch brim. The bishop's hat has a four-and-one-half-inch crown, slightly rounded, and a wide seam around the brim. A hat which has a flatter crown is worn by the rank and file of Amish fathers. The outsider may never notice these differences, or if he does he may regard them as accidental. But to the Amish these symbols indicate whether people are fulfilling the expectations of the group. A young man who wears a brim that is too narrow is liable for sanction.[3]

[2] Robert K. Massie, *Nicholas and Alexandra* (New York: Dell Publishing Co., Inc., 1969), p. 205.

[3] John A. Hostetler, *Amish Society* (Baltimore: Johns Hopkins Press, 1963), p. 135.

A change in role can be a once-in-a-lifetime affair. An amusing example of this is recounted by Lucius Beebe. When Mrs. Hamilton McKown Twombly wanted to attend the wedding of her grandson in Hollywood in 1935 she was forbidden to fly so she took a dim view of trenching through the hostile Great Plains. Her solution was ingenious: "For 3000 miles going west and an equal distance coming back, the last grandchild of Commodore Cornelius Vanderbilt, dressed as her personal maid, rode in the front seat next to the chauffeur in one of the Twombly Rolls-Royces while for an equal time and distance Mrs. Twombly's maid, dressed as Mrs. Twombly, rode in lonely state in the back seat." [4]

The shedding of historical and traditional accouterments by Roman Catholic sisters signifies in some cases a new way of life through the wearing of new clothes. Sister Francetta, a former president of St. Louis' Webster College, was the first nun hired by the Women's Job Corps in Washington, D. C. To work in this antipoverty agency she ventured forth for the first time in street clothes. On the job she visited Israeli kibbutzim and most of the existing Job Corps centers in the United States. Dressed in her recently adopted street clothes, she commented, "The important thing is the individual. I'd rather have one personal confrontation than have a thousand people saying 'hello, Sister' because of a habit." [5]

Suzy Knickerbocker reported on a symbol change underwritten by fashion for a marriage ceremony. "D. D. Ryan got married in a peasant's babushka. Orange blossoms? They're for peasants!" [6] More serious consideration was given by several students at the University of Missouri to an "ideal trousseau" to be worn following a May wedding:

For a Trip to the West Coast

1 peignoir set; 2 other nightgowns; robe
4 bra's; 4 pair of nylons; 2 girdles
2 whole slips; 2 half slips; 6 pair panties
Dressy dress for evening; purse; jewelry

[4] Lucius Beebe, *The Big Spenders* (New York: Pocket Books, 1967), p. 210.

[5] Judith Coburn, "New Clothes and a New Way of Life," *St. Louis Globe-Democrat* (May 13, 1966), p. 1, Section B.

[6] Described in *Look* (August 11, 1964), p. 60.

2 skirt and blouse outfits
Shirtwaist dress
2 cotton dresses
2 pair heels; 2 pair flats; 1 pair tennis shoes; thongs
1 swimming suit; cap; beach coat
2 pair bermuda shorts
1 pair cotton slacks; 1 pair wool slacks
Several blouses and sweaters
1 spring coat
1 trench coat (raincoat)
1 scarf; 2 pair gloves

For a Trip to the East Coast

4 sets of colored underwear (white, beige, black, green) bra, girdle, slip, pants (extra pants)
2 peignoir sets—nylon tricot
1 pair fancy slippers
1 bathing suit and robe
1 pair slacks, 2 T-shirts, and 1 jacket
1 pair of loafers and small clutch purse
3 suits
  2—3-piece knits (navy and white, gold)
  1—3-piece linen (beige)
2 pair heels and 2 purses, 2 pair of gloves, 1 hat
3 day dresses
Stack heels and tote bag
2 cocktail dresses—black crepe and green silk (black crepe with removable bolero top) shoes, gloves, and clutch bags
1 linen dress and jacket
1 beige raw silk coat
2 casual dresses (pair of flats to go with both)
1 all-weather coat
8 pair of nylons [7]

Wass and Eicher found in studying ideal clothing choices that footwear selections were what changed most from role to role. The girls reported that they would wear certain types of footwear for church only and others only at home or in school. Thus clothing regarded as appropriate in one social situation was not thought of as proper in another role. Discrepancies between ideal and actual attire were apt to be related to high fashion items. "For

[7] These lists were compiled in 1967.

example, current-fashion items chosen first as ideal wear for school and basketball games were coats with raccoon collars, car coats and pleated skirts; the garments worn most often were plain colored coats and straight skirts." [8] In their responses the teenage girls revealed that certain roles demanded clothing so specific that if they did not have the appropriate dress they did not take part in that role.[9]

Avoiding a role because of lack of the proper clothes can be associated with any age group. The following is a vivid example.

> In a certain nursery school the children were dressed in overalls over their playsuits for out-of-door play. Judy's mother neglected to purchase overalls, and for the first four or five weeks Judy was not dressed like the others. During those weeks Judy held back and did not join the group play. Then one day the overalls came. The change was illuminating. That very day Judy joined the group and she played with the other children from then on. Her feelings of being like everyone else made her feel secure within her group and her attitude toward play was different.[10]

[8] Betty M. Wass and Joanne B. Eicher, "Clothing as Related to Role Behavior of Teen-age Girls," *Quarterly Bulletin*, Michigan Agricultural Experiment Station, Vol. 47, No. 2 (November, 1964), p. 210.

[9] Ibid., p. 213.

[10] Rebekah Shury, Elizabeth Woods, and Esther Young, *Learning About Children* (Philadelphia: J. B. Lippincott Company, 1958), pp. 201–202.

19 Multiple Roles

Personality can be defined as an individual's typical behavior or the roles he most frequently assumes. In the foregoing sections discussion centered upon preparation for major roles and those role changes that were associated with more or less permanent life styles. However, variations in the roles we play depend upon the social situation. Mary Ryan paraphrases James's statement, "A man has as many social selves as there are individuals who recognize him," [1] by saying that "a man plays as many roles as he has different types of costume." [2]

Gross and Stone advise us that social transactions require the manipulation of equipment, but that clothing and props stay the same during a transaction. Clothing, they feel, is changed between social transactions. "Taking off a necktie signals a change in the situation. The special case of the strip-tease dancer is no exception, for her act transforms clothes into equipment" [3] rather than clothes. They further contend that one always brings to social situations more identities than roles necessary for role per-

[1] William James, *Principles of Psychology* (New York: Holt, Rinehart and Winston, 1890), p. 294.

[2] Mary Shaw Ryan, *Clothing: A Study in Human Behavior* (New York: Holt, Rinehart and Winston, 1966), p. 133.

[3] Edward Gross and Gregory P. Stone, "Embarrassment and the Analysis of Role Requirements," *American Journal of Sociology*, Vol. LXX, No. 1 (July, 1964), p. 9.

Appeal to Multiple Senses

formance. Thus, two or more roles are often performed at once by each participant. Ordinarily, symbols of reserve identities are concealed, "as when a court judge wears his golfing clothes beneath his robes." [4]

Our roles change many times during the day, and we feel best when our clothes relate to the needs and appearances of what we do and with whom we interact. "The

[4] Ibid., p. 5.

Body Bubble—Designed in 1968 by Robert Malone. When all sections are inflated the body can roll, bounce, and float.

chance of seeing someone in different guises, in different facets, the kind of cubistic self, gives a richer knowledge of the person we confront."[5] Alwin Nikolais believes that we have not taken full advantage of all sources for stimulating and imaginative costuming. He notes that the young people in particular desire experiences in an environment "of beating sound, shifting lights, colors and shapes. We no longer trust any of our senses in isolation; we want as animals to combine all our senses to verify experience."[6]

When we join with all this it will reflect in our dress. A "Body Bubble" designed by Robert Malone proposes an inflatable garment which becomes, when all sections are inflated, a large rubber sphere in which the wearer can roll, bounce, and float. A garment-structure by Les Levine made of extremely light-gauge nylon mylar laminate would cover the body completely, surrounding the wearer with a pocket of air; being equipped with vibrating devices, it would not only be able to exercise the body, but would

[5] Alwin Nikolais, "Clothing and Environment," in Alexander Weatherson, *Body Covering* (New York: Museum of Contemporary Crafts of the American Craftsmen's Council, 1968), p. 42.

[6] Ibid.

also help the wearer to remain in a tension-free state by means of a miniature computer, which would at the same time warn him against people or things that might upset him and allow him to avoid their presence.[7]

Lest the above description seems to dwell too much on fantasy, it should be mentioned that we play such roles and observe others in their play of fantasy roles more often than we suspect. As Goffman says:

> Take clothing. Female dress is designed to be "attractive," which must mean in some sense or other that the interest of unspecified males is to be aroused. And with this arousal the basis is laid for one type of action. But the probability of this action occurring is very often very low. Fantasies are thus invigorated, but reality is not. A clearer version of the same vicarious tease is the wide current sale to horseless cowboys of Stetson hats, high-heeled boots, Levi's and tattoos. Delinquents who carry knives and own a piece similarly exhibit a heightened orientation to action, but here perhaps appearances have a better chance of intruding on reality.[8]

Goffman believes that action and vicarious experience are closely allied though seemingly different on the surface. Vicarious experience reinforces values and often emerges as a part of our identity for current roles; one of the heroes in the movie *Midnight Cowboy* is an excellent example of fantasy influencing clothing and role behavior.

Historical examples of escape or fantasy roles are almost infinite. Queen Marie Antoinette shed her elaborate court costumes to play at being a milkmaid at the Petit Trianon. Lord Cornbury, a seventeenth-century governor of New York strutted around in petticoats and dresses on the front porch of the governor's mansion, claiming that he was impersonating his royal relative, Queen Anne.[9]

Masked and costume balls are the height of fantasy roles. Perhaps one of the most famous was the Bradley Martin Ball held in New York in February, 1897, which

[7] Ibid., p. 40–41.

[8] Irving Goffman, *Interaction Ritual* (Garden City, N. Y.: Doubleday & Company, Anchor Books, 1967), p. 269.

[9] Mary Cable, *American Manners and Morals* (New York: American Heritage Publishing Company, Inc., 1969), p. 50.

represented the hosts' attempt to give the most lavish ball in New York history. It was!

> The Waldorf Hotel ballroom was decorated with some five thousand orchids arranged in clusters to conceal electric lights and around five mirrors as well as over the chandeliers. Roses trailed from a balcony, and there was not an empty space that had not been festooned with . . . roses, or lilies-of-the-valley or orchids. . . . The Bradley Martins hired four hundred carriages for the convenience of guests who did not want to keep their own coachmen up all night. As for the costumes, Mrs. Bradley Martin appeared as Mary, Queen of Scots, in black velvet and cerise satin over a white satin petticoat, topped off with a ruby necklace formerly owned by another beheaded queen, Marie Antoinette, a cluster of diamond grapes, once the property of Louis XIV, and a fabulously jeweled stomacher. . . . There were several Louis XVs at the ball, including Mr. Bradley Martin. Anne Morgan was Pocahontas and James Lawrence Breese, of Tuxedo Park, was resplendent as Henry VIII in white satin, seed pearls and a fascinating leer. August Belmont wore a full suit of armor inlaid with gold, reputed to have cost ten thousand dollars.[10]

The ball, however, gave the Martins a bad name instead of a good one, and in the wake of the criticism that rained from the pulpit, press, and public the indignant couple moved permanently to England.

An earlier ball given by the Vanderbilts for 1,000 people in 1883 received no real criticism as "society at play." Here there were such colorful costumes as Hungarian Hussar (Mr. John Lawrence), Electricity (Mrs. Cornelius Vanderbilt), Dresden Figurine (Mr. Francis Appleton), Gypsy Queen (Mrs. Cornelius Lee) and a Matador (Mr. Frederick Beach).[11] Lest it be thought costume balls are past, we should recall Truman Capote's Black and White Masked Ball in November, 1966, and the Scorpio Birthday Party given by Princess Grace of Monaco in the fall of 1969.

The mask has been used historically to hide a performer, to aid him in assuming a new role, or to allow him to imi-

[10] Ibid., p. 279.
[11] Ibid., pp. 308–309.

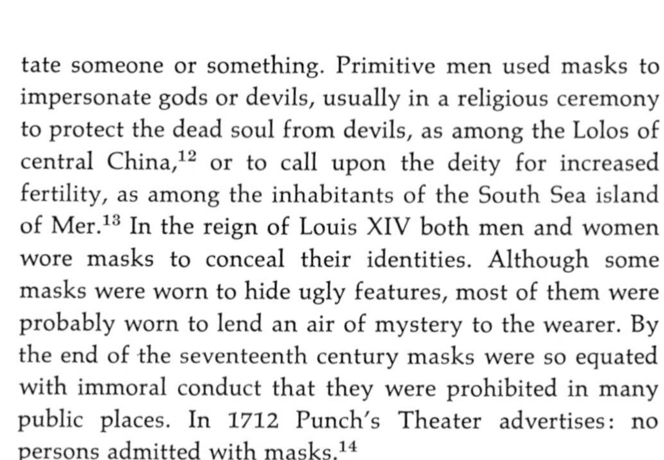

Masks—1966

tate someone or something. Primitive men used masks to impersonate gods or devils, usually in a religious ceremony to protect the dead soul from devils, as among the Lolos of central China,[12] or to call upon the deity for increased fertility, as among the inhabitants of the South Sea island of Mer.[13] In the reign of Louis XIV both men and women wore masks to conceal their identities. Although some masks were worn to hide ugly features, most of them were probably worn to lend an air of mystery to the wearer. By the end of the seventeenth century masks were so equated with immoral conduct that they were prohibited in many public places. In 1712 Punch's Theater advertises: no persons admitted with masks.[14]

Contemporary youth really believes in multiple roles and in the appropriate attire for such roles. It would seem that having many identities is an indispensable survival kit. Examples appear in a *Life* article entitled "Male Plumage," which would have been considered bizarre only a few years ago. A Japanese designer (male) wears a beaded choker, an appliquéd T-shirt and a snakeskin suit; an American musician wears a leather Captain America suit decorated with two feet of fringe and appliquéd leather

[12] Edward Weyer, Jr., *Primitive Peoples Today* (Garden City, N.Y.: Doubleday & Company, 1959), p. 234.
[13] Ibid., p. 250.
[14] "False Faces Through the Ages," *Life* (October 25, 1963).

stars; a French novelist wears a purple velvet suit; Italian men are pictured in leopard-printed nylon and pants so tight that keys and money are carried in purses; an American Negro (male) wears an Afro hairdo, a hooded African dashiki, and a necklace from Kenya made of seed pods and animal teeth; and a French photographer poses in an eighteenth-century Afghanistan wedding tunic with several necklaces, pendants, and an ornate Greek belt.[15] It is indeed a global theater where everyone does his thing by playing his very specialized role of the moment before changing to another role with similarly elaborate trappings.

Charles Reich, however, notes the use of nonspecialized clothes by the present generation of young people, particularly those who have the kind of humanitarian concern that he labels Consciousness III.

> The freedom of the new clothes expresses a second principle as well: a wholeness of self. . . . There is not one set of clothes for the office, another for social life, a third for play. The same clothes can be used for every imaginable activity, and so they say that it is the same person doing all these things—not a set of different masks or dolls but one many-sided *whole* individual. At the same time, these clothes say that an individual may do many different things in the course of a day. He is not limited to a single role, or to a role-plus recreation, each individual is truly protean, with unlimited possibilities, including the possibility of whatever new and spontaneous thing may come along.[16]

Reich seems to contradict himself when he suggests that costume—a feather, a cowboy hat, a Mexican shawl, a to achieve expressions of a state of mind one adds to the phantom-of-the-opera cloak, boots, a gangster suit, and so on. These changes would certainly appear to be changing clothes to fit a change in role.

[15] "Male Plumage," *Life* (September 25, 1970), pp. 42–49.

[16] Charles A. Reich, *The Greening of America* (New York: Random House, 1970), p. 235.

20 Role Variation and Role Conflict

During the daytime hours occupational or business roles are the norm for most adult Americans, whether male or female. At home, however, a businessman usually replaces his business suit and tie with more comfortable and casual wear, perhaps slacks and a sweater. He is ready to play a more relaxed and informal role than he played in the industrial "jungle." If he is an active sports enthusiast, he may dress like a ski pro on winter weekends and a fisherman or hunter as the other seasons progress. The clothes for sporting activities are practical as protection from the snow, water, or sun, but they are more than that. Appropriate dress enhances enjoyment of the activity. This does not mean wearing the latest and most fashionable sports attire, but rather clothes that the individual and his social group feel to be appropriate for the role.

The career girl or the working wife may appear to be efficient and competent wearing the feminine counterpart of the business suit at her desk or office. Later in the day she may change roles along with her clothes to become a seductive date in lace, an elegant theatergoer in brocade, a volunteer scout leader in uniform, a lodge member in white, a "cleaning lady" in jeans, or an understanding mother in a Japanese kimono. Indeed, it would be a rare day that she would play but two roles; on her way to work she might be a chauffeur dropping off husband and children, or a concerned consumer discussing high prices with fellow passengers on the commuter train; during the noon hour she might be an organization woman, presiding at luncheon in hat and gloves, or a frustrated shopper deciding upon a mini, midi, or maxi length for a new addition to her wardrobe.

Jim Bishop gives us a run-down on the "roles and robes" of the American housewife of the mid-1960's.

> Most mothers do not dress at all unless they are going to be taken out. They wear night clothes and robes all morning. The postman and the milkman wouldn't recognize them in clothes. In the afternoon the women step into slacks "in case the bell rings," and they pat a little makeup on faces which need more care than that.
>
> They parade through supermarkets in pants and curlers, the hair looking like something designed to kill the sex instinct in men. At night, they dress and dress and dress for whatever the occasion might be, and when they make an entrance, they appear to be back in the night gowns again. The dress starts six inches above the waist, displaying a few yards of powdered flab, and it dies somewhere around the ankles.
>
> The eyelids are blue, the lashes are the legs of a black widow, the lips are moist wounds. The deft touch of perfume smells as though it has been put on with a soup spoon. The coiffure, for the moment, is precise. Do not—repeat—do not open a window in the car.[1]

William Goode proposes a theory of "role strain" at times when the individual is faced with a wide array of role obligations. If one cannot meet all his demands to the satisfaction of all individuals who make up his total role network, "role strain—difficulty in meeting given role demands—is therefore normal. In general, the individual's total role obligations are overdemanding." [2] Goode's sug-

[1] Jim Bishop, "A Critical Look at American Dress," *St. Louis Post-Dispatch* (March 31, 1965), p. 3D.

[2] William J. Goode, "A Theory of Role Strain," in Edward E. Sampson, editor, *Approaches, Contexts, and Problems of Social Psychology* (Englewood Cliffs, N. J.: Prentice-Hall, Inc., 1964), p. 441.

gested solution to the dilemma is that the individual must try to make his whole role system manageable and allocate energies and skills to "reduce role strain to a bearable proportion." [3]

Role conflict or role strain has important implications for clothing behavior. If there are several possible unrelated roles to be played at once, an individual makes a choice according to some hierarchy of values—the role most important to him is the one that is adopted. In the late 1960's the miniskirt might have met with objections from a girl's parents, and been outlawed by regulations and dress codes at school, but a girl would still wear a mini if the social roles she played in her peer group demanded such behavior.

The adult woman may experience role conflict and role strain in not knowing what type she really wants to emphasize. Does she want to be Sexpot Sally in a tight miniskirt, or Velma the Clinging Vine in a draped harem skirt, or Beach-Party Betty in a bikini, or Heidi the Housewife in a gingham dress? Her closest friends *will* tell her; all she needs to do is ask them, and they may have more influence than does her husband.

Our involvement in military conflict and conflict over the military-industrial complex brings out many symbols of role conflict, even in so rigid a structure as the U.S. Army. When in history could one find a soldier wearing a peace symbol, some religious medals, and a bandolier of bullets around his neck—all at the same time? Because the traditional GI haircuts were at odds with the preferred appearance symbols of today's young men, wig merchants were doing fantastic business in women's wigs (before men's wigs were available in quantity) near Army posts. Soldiers gave a variety of reasons for wearing wigs—to wear among their civilian contemporaries; to play in bands as musicians; and to wear while dating so that local girls won't know they are GI's. The soldiers kept their wigs in their foot lockers and officers conducting inspections "never touch them because they're a personal item." [4] In civilian life a stock broker in New York wore a short-haired wig during daytime hours because "in dealing with

[3] Ibid.

[4] Reported in the *Hartford Courant* (Saturday, January 31, 1970), p. 23.

mutual funds the straight image is of utmost importance."[5] In off hours his hair was long.[6]

Role conflicts sometimes produce what appears to be deviant behavior to society at large. The Beatles, the singing phenomenon of the second half of the twentieth century have performed a variety of roles in the course of time. First, they were struggling entertainers, sporting typical clothes and haircuts for young English popular musicians; when they became successful, they wore more extreme garb, very long shaggy hair, mustaches, large glasses; next they became philosophers, voices of the young, and in this stage they adopted a mixture of Oriental and Indian garb, all the while collecting Oriental retainers and lovers, including Yoko Ono, who has since married John Lennon. During this phase of vacillation between the roles of entertainers and philosophers, the general public over age thirty considered them to be deviants. Now that they appear to be back in business separately as entertainers, at least some of them are wearing less extreme attire.

Other examples of role conflict from the entertainment world are Mia Farrow and Vanessa Redgrave. Mia spun from actress to wife, to student of Oriental philosophy, to actress again, to mistress, and to mother. She shed the role of ingenue actress with her hair; she was equally dramatic in her Oriental phase, wearing flowing robes above her ornamented bare feet. Her conflict between being a professional and a woman is echoed in Vanessa Redgrave's role performances. Vanessa's seemingly deviant behavior and clothes may have been inspired by her movie role of Isadora Duncan, but she has added her own unique touches. Vanessa's peasant-type clothes symbolize rejection of her aristocratic background, her appearance at the Academy Awards in granny glasses displays rejection of the glamorous movie star role, and the rather shabby wardrobe she wears while living with Franco Nero mocks the role of the elegant mistress of history.

Most professional women have role conflicts, but seldom do they go to the extremes or get the publicity that Mia and Vanessa have.

[5] "The Kindest Uncut of All," *Life* (March 20, 1970), p. 35.

[6] As long hair for men gained more public acceptance, both the U.S. Army and the business world have somewhat relaxed their sanctions against wearing long hair.

Cultural Variation in Roles

What is a male role, a female role, an occupational role, an adult role, or a religious role? The answers may be quite different, depending upon time, place, and culture. Ruth Benedict, a functional anthropologist, describes the roles most valued by four tribal groups of North American Indians. Her theme in *Patterns of Culture*[7] centers on role diversity among and within several Indian tribes. In her book on Japan, *The Chrysanthemum and the Sword*,[8] Benedict examines roles related to aggression and guilt within a single culture.

As noted earlier, Margaret Mead has documented the range of behavioral patterns that would ring true for males and females in many cultural settings. Mead has also explored the interaction patterns of age and sex roles among a variety of peoples.[9] However, behavioral patterns for males and females differ even in so-called Western societies:

> In much of Latin America it was long thought that a man could not possibly suppress the strong urges that took possession of him every time he was alone with a woman. Women, of course, were considered unable to resist a man. The result was that the patterns of association contained safeguards and protective measures. Americans who were going to Latin America had to be cautioned that if they let themselves get into a situation with a member of the opposite sex where something could have happened, it would be no use to tell people that it had not. The Latin response would be "After all, you're a man, aren't you? She's a woman, isn't she?" The point the Americans couldn't get through their heads was that these people really considered that men and women were constituted differently from the way the American views them. In Latin America both sexes expect

[7] (Boston: Houghton Mifflin Company, 1934).
[8] (Boston: Houghton Mifflin Company, 1946).
[9] Margaret Mead, *From the South Seas* (New York: William Morrow and Company, 1939).

> their will power to be provided by other people rather than by personal inhibition.[10]

Hall also describes the reversal of sex roles in Iran—that is, a reversal from our ideas of behavior associated with males and females:

> Men are expected to show their emotions—take Mossadegh's tantrums. If they don't, Iranians suspect they are lacking a vital human trait and are not dependable. Iranian men read poetry; they are sensitive and have well-developed intuition and in many cases are not expected to be too logical. They are often seen embracing and holding hands. Women, on the other hand, are considered to be coldly practical. They exhibit many of the characteristics we associate with men in the United States. A very perceptive Foreign Service officer who had spent a number of years in Iran once observed, "If you will think of the emotional and intellectual sex roles as reversed from ours, you will do much better out here." [11]

[10] Edward Hall, op. cit., pp. 66–67.
[11] Ibid., p. 67.

21 Role-Types

The use of clothing symbols to establish role-types depends upon the awareness of the performer as well as the awareness of casual observers and those predisposed to interact with the performer. The recognition of a role-type depends upon the commitment of the performer and his ability to get his message across to the significant others around him. In addition, role-types vary with time and place; indeed, roles are subject to the pressures and whims of fashion. As Herbert Blumer says, "Fashion operates in many diverse areas of human group life. It may be observed in the arts, medicine, industry, literature, history, politics, and science as well as in costume and adornment." [1] Selected role-types of the past and present will be reviewed. With the vicissitudes of fashion, neglected role-types may again emerge as social media.

[1] Herbert Blumer, "Fashion from Class Differentiation to Collective Selection," *Sociological Quarterly*, Vol. 10, No. 3 (Summer, 1969), p. 275.

The Role of the Gentleman

The gentleman was as much an ideal as an actuality, but for several centuries it was an important role which the male population of Western Europe directed their efforts toward playing. Castiglione's book, *The Courtier,* may have inspired that role, for Castiglione directed men to seek learning, social graces, and connoisseurship, "not as ends in themselves, but in order to enable them to act—and, above all, fight—more effectively." [2] In England men like Raleigh and Sir Philip Sidney were known for their literary achievements as well as for their reputations as courtiers and soldiers. The tradition of the gentleman—"an accomplished amateur, literate, dashing, and always cool under fire, was derived directly" [3] from *The Courtier.*

The role of the gentleman continued to be a demanding one. In mid-nineteenth-century England an unidentified countess cites these prescriptions for a gentleman:

> He was expected to know how to fence, box, ride, shoot, swim, play billiards, dance, walk and to carry himself. Furthermore, . . . the power to deliver a good scientific blow may be of inestimable value under certain extreme circumstances. . . . While no gentleman would willingly resort to so strong a measure, he may be attacked by a garroter or need to rescue a woman from a ruffian and in such cases a blow settles the matter . . . but there is a way of doing it gracefully.[4]

Thorstein Veblen remarked that the gentleman must spend his time in conspicuous leisure and must at all costs abstain from labor. In Veblen's view, however, leisure does not mean indolence but rather nonproductive consumption of time.

[2] Lacey Baldwin Smith, *The Horizon Book of the Elizabethan World* (New York: American Heritage Publishing Company, Inc., 1967), p. 37.

[3] Ibid.

[4] *Vogue's Book of Etiquette and Good Manners* (New York: Condé Nast Publications, Inc., 1969), p. 40.

> But the whole of the life of the gentleman of leisure is not spent before the eyes of the spectators who are to be impressed with that spectacle of honorific leisure which in the ideal scheme makes up his life. For some part of the time his life is perforce withdrawn from the public eye, and of this portion which is spent in private the gentleman of leisure should, for the sake of his own good name, be able to give a convincing account. He should find some means of putting in evidence the leisure that is not spent in the sight of spectators. This can be done only indirectly, through the exhibition of some tangible, lasting results of leisure so spent. . . . The criteria of a past performance of leisure therefore commonly take the form of "immaterial" goods. Such immaterial evidences of past leisure are quasi-scholarly or quasi-artistic accomplishments and a knowledge of processes and incidents which do not conduce directly to the furtherance of human life. So, for instance, in our time there is the knowledge of the dead languages and the occult sciences; of correct spelling; of syntax and prosody; of the various forms of domestic music and other household art; of the latest proprieties of dress, furniture, and equipage; of games, sports, and fancy-bred animals, such as dogs and race-horses.[5]

So, the gentleman was accomplished and learned in non-productive arts and skills. He was also fastidious about his appearance. He was abreast of the details of fashion and enjoyed the pomp and ceremony of dress occasions. We are told that when Beau Brummell, the arbiter of men's fashions in early ninteenth-century England (also cited as a fashion individualist in Chapter 8) sat down to make his toilet prior to a ball or recption at Bath, "three hair-dressers were in attendance, one concentrating on the back of his head, one on the front, and a third consolidating the work of the other two. So meticulous was the Beau about the making of his gloves that the thumbs were entrusted to one glovemaker, the fingers to another." [6]

The gentleman probably rose to the top of his pedestal during the Victorian era. He was personified by Prince Albert and by others of the English nobility. Yet even the

[5] Thorstein Veblen, *The Theory of the Leisure Class* (New York: Modern Library, 1934), pp. 44–45.
[6] Francis R. McCabe, "Modesty in Clothes," *Harper's Weekly* (August 30, 1913), p. 29.

Victorian gentleman had several roles, with several states of formality of attire. John Taylor makes these observations:

> It is typical of the Victorian philosophical confusions that formality was only regarded as essential if ladies were present. Thus it must have been regarded not as something having merit for its own sake but as a kind of reminder of the necessity to behave yourself when there were women about. Men at evening functions would inevitably be dressed in full evening kit, tails and white gloves, but at their clubs or during a bachelor evening they relaxed into the relative informality of the smoking jacket.[7]

The gentleman's role revolved around seasons and occasions. His wardrobe was extensive, with specific clothes intended for specific purposes. In the 1890's a gentleman would own a wardrobe much like the following, with a minimum of fourteen coats:

> A fur-lined top coat for the opera; an Inverness fur-lined, without the fur showing; a Chesterfield, in black or dark gray, or a Newmarket, to be worn over dress clothes ordinarily; a long loose sack overcoat, silk faced for Spring and early Autumn; a double-breasted Newmarket, a single-breasted Prince Henry coat, a Strand coat, which is double-breasted with tails; rain and steamer coats, yachting suits, a double-breasted ulster, made of homespun; golf costumes and a short covert coat for between seasons. . . . Driving and automobile coats, of course, vary with the season. For four-in-hand driving, the Newmarket coat must disport a flaring skirt.[8]

The rightness of dress for the occasion is carried to the ultimate in Lucius Beebe's account of the sinking of the *Titanic.* Such pedigreed notables as Sir Cosmo and Lady Duff Gordon, the Countess of Rothes, and Colonel and Mrs. John Jacob Astor were on the sailing list. Because it was Sunday evening not all of the passengers had dressed for dinner in their usual fastidious style. "Unwilling to

[7] John Taylor, *It's a Small, Medium and Outsize World* (Cleveland, Ohio: The World Publishing Co., 1966), p. 101.

[8] Mary Cable, *American Manners and Morals* (New York: American Heritage Publishing Company, Inc., 1969), p. 283.

make an exit on this note of informality, the aged Benjamin Guggenheim summoned his valet and retired to his stateroom, presently to reappear in full evening dress with tails and his best pearl studs. 'Now we are dressed like gentlemen,' he said, 'and ready to go.' No nobler sentiments are on record anywhere."[9]

Gentlemen of the nobility dressed like fashion plates and were copied by the masses as well as by other gentlemen. The Duke of Windsor credits his grandfather, Edward VII, with an imposing list of innovations:

first bringing the Homburg hat to Britain,
first applying double-breasted lapels to a single-breasted jacket,
first creasing trousers down the front and back of the leg,
first formalising the double-breasted jacket,
first wearing a white waistcoat and stiff dickey shirt for evening wear, and,
first popularising the bowler hat for wear in town.[10]

The Duke of Windsor reserves credit to himself for the following:

popularising turn-ups on trousers,
popularising the wide spread shirt collar and the Windsor tie knot,
popularising the Fair Isle sweater,
popularising the 'midnight blue' dinner jacket, and,
giving the accolade of Royal approval to suede shoes.[11]

Cleveland Amory says that the obituary of the word *gentleman* took place in 1930.[12] We are inclined to agree, for very few men either look or act the part today. Jim Bishop bemoans the fact that men are not only poor dressers but they are downright slovenly. Casual wear has invaded the professions to such an extent that the man "who wears a tie must be prepared to defend himself."[13]

[9] Lucius Beebe, *The Big Spenders* (New York: Pocket Books, Inc., 1967), p. 270.

[10] Quoted in Taylor, op. cit., p. 118.

[11] Ibid.

[12] Reported in Cable, op. cit., p. 357.

[13] Jim Bishop, "A Critical Look at American Dress," *St. Louis Post-Dispatch* (March 31, 1965), p. 3D.

> Some well-dressed businessmen don't feel comfortable unless their socks are falling down. The man affects loafers, often with crepe soles. His belt is cinched tight, and he feels relaxed if his belly hangs out over the top. He may not like to wear a wrinkled suit, but he is too lazy to have it otherwise. Some have no respect for a good tie and will not unknot it at night; just loosen the loop and lift over the head.[14]

Thus, from the age of the Renaissance through the early twentieth century the gentleman was a connoisseur—accomplished, learned, and skilled in the arts of conspicuous leisure; adept in the social graces; and always wearing distinctive apparel, fashionable for his role in his time. Somewhere during the mid-twentieth century he has faded from view.

The Role of the Lady

Another dying role is that of the lady, for she played a reciprocal part to the gentleman. In a description of the gentry of London during the Elizabethan era, ladies were observed to be "fond of taking it easy. . . . They sit before their doors, decked out in fine clothes in order to see and be seen. . . . They employ their time visiting their friends and making merry."[15]

In all decades the lady had an ideal to follow. Marie Antoinette played the role of the queen and fashion ideal to the hilt; she spent several hours with her dressmaker, Rose Bertin, every morning concocting apparel that reached the ultimate in exaggeration. New language had to be invented to describe these spectacles. She or one of the ladies of the court might wear "a dress of *stifled sighs* covered with *superfluous regrets;* in the middle was a *spot of perfect candour,* ornated with *indiscotte moans* and ribbons of *marked attention.*"[16] Shoes might be the color of

[14] Ibid.
[15] Smith, op. cit., p. 271.
[16] Gisèle D'Assailly, *Ages of Elegance* (Paris: Librairie Hachette, 1968), p. 139.

the "*Queen's hair* . . . embroidered with diamonds, *treacherous blows* and *come-and-see* buckles made of emeralds; on her head she wore a *sure success* bonnet decorated with *fickle feathers* and streamers of *woebegone eyes.* Over her shoulders she had a shawl of *newcome beggars* color, a *Medici* mounted *in seemliness* and she carried a muff of *momentary agitation.*" [17] The queen and her ladies spent much of their day with hairdressers, who had created three thousand ways of arranging the hair. Elaborate scaffoldings were constructed to hold sarcophagi, frigates, miniature coaches, and flower gardens atop the head.

Ladies of Colonial America looked to the continent of Europe for their inspiration in roles and clothing. Until the American Revolution, nearly every business letter included orders for bolts of cloth, worsted stockings and silver shoe buckles, kid gloves, aigrettes, masks, and mittens. "George and Martha Washington were among the most lavish buyers of silk and velvet gowns, greatcoats and riding outfits. From France Benjamin Franklin sent his daughter Deborah, white cloaks and plumes, satin cardinals and paste shoebuckles." [18]

Veblen reminds us that the general rule for women of the late nineteenth century was that they should consume only for the benefit of their masters—that wives and daughters became ceremonial consumers of goods he (the master) produced. Ladies could work in make-believe only; "as for instance in social duties and in quasi-artistic or quasi-scholarly accomplishments in the care and decoration of the house, in sewing-circle activity or dress reform, in proficiency in dress, cards, yachting, golf and various sports." [19]

When Henry James revisited New York in 1904 he was struck by the emptiness of ritual practiced by the upper classes. After attending a dinner party he wrote: "The scene of our feast was a palace and the perfection of setting and service absolute; the ladies, beautiful, gracious and glittering with gems, were in tiaras and a semblance of Court-trains." [20] He continues by saying that the occa-

[17] Ibid., pp. 139–140.

[18] Ishbel Ross, *Taste in America* (New York: Thomas Y. Crowell Co., 1967), p. 171.

[19] Veblen, op. cit., p. 94.

[20] Reported in Cable, op. cit., p. 276.

sion did not demand a tiara and all the glitter, for there was nothing to do after eleven o'clock. "There was nothing as in London or Paris to go on to." [21] In any case, James did not think that the husbands were up to it, for as in many wealthy families husbands of the so-called leisure class were too tired at night to engage in social ceremonials.

In 1922 Mrs. Emily Post published *Etiquette: The Blue Book of Social Usage.* This book sold out its first printing of 10,000 copies practically overnight, for etiquette to the ladies and gentlemen of the day was thought to be the "science of living; it is everything." [22] Some thought its popularity was due to the need for a social code in a period of bewildering flux in social conventions and social roles; others were enjoying vicarious snobbery with Mrs. Post.

Patrick O'Higgins describes some of the eccentricities of ladies in his article, "Shabby Elegance."

> Another original lady, Yankee to the bone, was the late Mrs. Cornelius Vanderbilt. Her clothes, too, in the course of a long life made no concession to fashion. Waistlines, adventurously looped by Doucet, reached to well below the level of her hips, and when she ventured out on a shopping spree, a footman would hurl a carpet from the front door of her house on Fifth Avenue across the pavement, filled with leaping pedestrians, to her waiting car. This vintage maroon Packard, with polished brass headlamps, matched to perfection her cloche hat, pink fox, and the sensible shoes safely anchored with large snaps.
>
> At night Mrs. Vanderbilt's forehead was always resplendent in a "bandeau" (matching her dress), from which a mass of tinted curls, finer than spun silk, rose in a gyrating pyramid. When summering at Newport or wintering in New York, Mrs. Vanderbilt changed her clothes four times a day and knew every dress hanging in her extensive, mirrored wardrobe. These were carefully classified and numbered with matching accessories.[23]

Although Amory believes that the gentleman vanished in 1930, fashion reporters and arbiters of etiquette would

[21] Ibid.

[22] Ibid., p. 346.

[23] Patrick O'Higgins, "Shabby Elegance," Harper's Bazaar (November, 1967), p. 242

have us believe that a few real ladies still exist. In 1955, *Vogue* followed Madame Philippe Hengel, the wife of a French music publisher, in her daily routine. Madame Hengel starts her day with the mail, the paper and the telephone (in pink dressing gown from Dessés Bazaar); next, a visit with the children, twins of two and a half and a baby of one year; and midmorning at the Paris market shopping for flowers, butter, and meat, and a delicacy shop for parmesan cheese. (For this round of errands, she wears a sweater, skirt, and turquoise corduroy jacket from Lanvin's Boutique.) The Hengels lunch at home with a guest who plays the piano for them after lunch. (Madame wears a dress of pale beige alpaca from the Griffe Boutique.) Then "Madame Hengel writes a quick note before setting out for the afternoon in a Givenchy suit of periwrinkle-blue corduroy." She stops off in the gardens to see the children, then goes antiquing for bibelots. At home again, she tries on a new Dior ball gown, then goes to cocktails at the studio of an artist friend. (Madame Hengel wears a satin-bound black cable-stitch wool suit from Givenchy.) On her way to dinner she says goodnight to the twins, then dines with her husband in a restaurant near their apartment. They are on their way to a première for which Madame is wearing a short evening dress of green and gold brocade from Dior. Madame Hengel has made six changes for her various roles during her busy day.[24]

Eugenia Sheppard describes a lady of the seventies and compliments her for the way she plays her international role:

> I have a valentine for Gloria Guinness. Not because she is the wealthy Mrs. Loel Guinness, always described, between commas, as a perennial on the best-dressed list, but also because she has never fallen in love with her own publicity. Through the years, Gloria Guinness has had enough admiration for her face, her black hair, her fine bones, her posture and the clothes she chooses to spoil most women rotten. She has always managed, though, not to take all the hoop-la seriously and even to regard her fame as a passing fancy. She is always trying to do more, be more, not to impress the world but to satisfy herself.

[24] Described and pictured in "Paris: A Day in the Life of Mme. Hengel," *Vogue* (March 15, 1955), pp. 112–115.

> Gloria's valentine will be simple and direct with few words of decoration. Gloria, herself, is like that. Discipline and ruthless editing are the essence of her successful life style. In her dressing Gloria throws away all the details and fantasies dear to most women. Her houses are romantic, built without any sentimental clutter. Like an arrow, the message comes through.[25]

No, there aren't many who play the role of the lady in contemporary society. Only a few have the artistic finesse, time, money, and patience to "keep their cool" in our world of shifting, kaleidoscopic patterns and roles.

The Courtesan and Related Roles

Another role that flourished for many centuries, but now has almost disappeared is that of the courtesan. Her greatest asset was usually her physical beauty, for which she showed great concern and which was enhanced by cosmetics, clothes, and ornaments. A rich courtesan of Corinth living around the fourth century B.C. is described:

> Her slaves massaged her from head to foot before placing her in a scented bath; she was then caressed with swan's feathers so as to dry the parts of her body which were still damp. Then, she was rubbed with perfumed oils brought from the Orient. A depilatory was then carefully applied. Her hair was washed, perfumed and pomaded before being plaited. Her coiffure was completed with filigree braid, gold and silver lamé ribbons. A black coating touched up her eyebrows and the edges of her eyelids were touched with a brush dipped in incense black. Her eyes were widened with lines of kohl.[26]

Further information about the Corinthian courtesan reveals that she touched up her cheeks with purpurissium obtained

[25] Eugenia Sheppard, "I Have a Valentine," *Harper's Bazaar* (February, 1970), p. 142.
[26] D'Assailly, op. cit., p. 24.

from a root found in Syria; she kept a fragrant liquor in her mouth to perfume her breath, and cleaned her teeth with aromatic powder. Her hair might be dyed blonde or powdered gold, silver-white, or red. If her hair was blonde, she used a potassium solution followed by brushing with a pomade of yellow flowers.[27]

Actually the word *courtesan* means court mistress, so it is most aptly applied to the mistresses of kings. Agnes Sorel became the leader of fashion when she became the mistress of the French King Charles VII in the fifteenth century. Although she was criticized for her boldness (having bared her shoulders and bosom to the middle of her breast), she was envied and copied by other ladies of the court. Agnes is credited with the invention of the hennin (towering headdress), and the introduction of the widened skirt fastened with a cord at the waist, and hemmed with a band of velvet or fur. Rank was signified by the length of the train and the width of the hem.[28]

The courtesan is not always young—to play her role well calls for both practice and experience. James Laver reminds us that in ages of prostitution fashion is "dictated by the Grande Cocotte" and tends to favor the older woman. In ages of promiscuity fashion tends to favor the younger woman, "the school girl just escaped from her leading strings." [29]

Lucius Beebe laments that fashions in jewelry have changed, but that the most radical change has applied to the status of the recipients of jewels. According to his interpretion of the "Dow Jones Index of bracelets and earrings," [30] the courtesan is in decline, for the best-dressed bosoms, throats, wrists, and hairdos belong today to married women of irreproachable moral façade.

> The period when Liane de Pougy and La Belle Otero making an entrance at Maxim's in Paris on the arms of King Leopold of Belgium or Prince Orloff of Russia were so covered with emeralds, rubies, and diamonds that they were followed by personal maids carrying the overflow on velvet cushions never had any precise equivalent in the United States, although

[27] Ibid.
[28] Ibid., p. 61.
[29] James Laver, *Taste and Fashion* (London: George G. Harrap and Company, 1937), p. 55.
[30] Beebe, op. cit., p. 296.

Diamond Jim Brady is certified in the record as having bestowed no less than $1,500,000 in gems on lady friends in the course of an animated life time.[31]

In fact, the woman today often pays for a love affair herself. This reversal of roles may be caused by the fact that women now outnumber men and thus men must be sought after, or stem from the new "equality" in role relationships. Perhaps Maria Callas is one of the last of a vanishing breed.

Suzy has written a tongue-in-cheek article called the "Cost of Conducting an Affair." She suggests that there is no point in starting an affair unless it's done with panache; to bring it off "with brio" and in the proper scene she lists these pared-to-the-bone necessities:

1 dozen nighties (short and see through) at $100 each (I may never wear one, but they look pretty tossed on the floor)	$1,200
4 devastating negligees at $195 each	$780
6 pairs of pretty slippers at $25 each	$150
2 ounces of Fleurs de Rocaille at $27.50 an ounce	$55
1 dozen lace and satin baby pillows at $20 each (I mustn't forget a heart-shaped one. Sentiment is important.)	$240
6 sets of Porthault linen sheets at $290 a set (Blue—to match his eyes)	$1,740
12 Porthault linen pillow cases at $32 a case (To match the sheets—and his eyes)	$384

She continues with some twenty-five more items, then ends with:

A pink baby spot concealed in the bed canopy	$30
21 days shaping up with Miss Craig	$252
The hairdresser every day	$350
1 month's supply of The Pill (If love doesn't last that long—well, they keep.)	$2.75

Now let's see—that comes to $8,746.23. Eight thousand, seven hundred forty-six dollars and twenty-three cents! In one month! Never! I'll be wiped out. If we're going to do it, we'll do it at *his* place or forget it! After all, I don't want to marry him.[32]

[31] Ibid.
[32] Suzy, *Vogue* (February 15, 1970), pp. 70–71.

The male homosexual playing the role of the female is not new, but the role seemingly gets more public attention and may even be reported to an international audience. Christine Jorgenson changed from male to female with all the clothing and appearance symbols any attractive female could want. The fictionalized Myra Breckenridge is depicted as a superwoman, but somehow the buxom and beautiful (by her own account) Myra, clad in garter belt and one dress shield [33] is very far removed from the Corinthian courtesan. Perhaps, too far!

The Role of a Religious

We will examine some of the symbols that relate to the role played by the nun as an example of a religious way of life. Until very recent times the garb of the nun had remained unchanged through as many as ten centuries.

The *Rule of St. Benet,* written about the year 516, was quite specific in regard to clothing. Along with the general recommendations for the habits to be worn in very cold climates, he stated that the clothing was to be plain and cheap, made of fabrics that could be readily obtained in that country, and that the number of garments be limited to those that were absolutely essential. A description of the habit is found in the ritual which he wrote for the ordination or profession of nuns. This ritual states that after a special Mass, the novice's next of kin offer her to the high altar, and after the priest blesses her habit, she shall leave the chapel and exchange her secular clothing for the habit and veil. It states that she receives a habit, mantle, wimple, veil, and girdle or cincture. Upon returning to the chapel she pronounces her vows and receives the ring which signifies final profession.[34]

Tertullian distinguishes between those virgins who took the veil publicly in the assembly of the faithful, and others

[33] Gore Vidal, *Myra Breckenridge* (Boston: Little, Brown and Company, 1968), p. 1.

[34] Ernest A. Kock, editor, *Rule of St. Benet* (London: Kegan, Paul, Trench, Truber and Co., 1902).

known to God alone; the veil seems to have been simply that of married women and from the earliest times these consecrated virgins were called the spouses of Christ. Virgins vowed to the service of God at first continued to live with their families, but as early as the end of the third century there were community houses. One who put on the religious habit and veil, and lived for some time among the professed, was herself considered as professed.[35]

One of the letters of St. Jerome, written in the latter part of the fourth century, tells of the decision made by a young woman to enter religious life in spite of the opposition of her family. He writes:

> Having wrought herself up with these and many more incentives to action, she cast from her the ornaments of her person and her secular dress, as if they were encumbrances to her resolve. Costly necklaces, precious pearls, brilliant jewels, she replaces in their cabinet; she puts on a common tunic, and over it a more common cloak; and without giving any notice, suddenly throws herself at her grandmother's knees, showing who she was only by weeping and lamentation. Aghast was that holy and venerable lady, seeing the altered dress of her grandchild; while her mother stood astounded. . . .[36]

The Daughters of Charity, founded by St. Vincent de Paul, adopted the garb of the peasant girl of 1633; once so inconspicuous on the streets of Paris, the blue gown and white cornette so broad and starched that it appears to hinder the wearer are now easily recognized. The spiritual symbolism and role of the wearer was explained thus:

> Others might be called to a life of silence and contemplation, of kneeling and adoring, but this was not her vocation. Vincent did not ask it of her. He expected her to be active, to talk, to laugh, to sing songs rather than canticles, and to be found everywhere that life was busiest. So absorbing must her work be to body and soul, that he took from her the time for

[35] A. Vermeersch, "Nuns," in *Catholic Encyclopedia* (1913), p. 164.

[36] A. Vermeersch, *Any Saint to Any Nun* (New York: P. J. Kenedy and Sons, 1946), p. 3.

piety, as though it were a penance, . . . that her habit is of blue and white, in order to honor the Mother of God, that he crowned her with coif of purest linen, with great wings on either side to make her journey easier; that she wore no veil—that is for the cloistered religious—but that her eyes would be protected from the world by two white walls meeting in a point straight ahead of her line of vision, so that she cannot lift her eyes without directing them toward heaven, that everything leads her in that direction. . . .[37]

The first general congress of nuns in Christianity's two thousand years was called in Rome in 1952. Among other subjects, such as decisions about the education of sisters and new types of work, "the feminine question of the nun's habits, those picturesque, inconvenient, hot, trailing robes and troublesome starched coifs—a costume specifically cited by the Vatican as calling for change," [38] was debated.

Now even congregations who trace their heritage to the seventh, thirteenth, or seventeenth centuries have been modifying their habits. Most communities founded within the past fifty years wear habits very similar to secular dress. However, some symbol, a large crucifix or perhaps a headdress, usually denotes the nun and calls attention to her religious role.

Among the very religious of the Hasidic Jews, clothing serves as a barrier against assimilation with non-Jews and as a shield against sin. As one member of the Hasidic community says, "With my appearance I cannot attend a theater or a movie or any other places where a religious Jew is not supposed to go. Thus, my beard and my sidelocks and my Hasidic clothing serve as a guard and shield from sin and obscenity." [39]

Persons who wear extremely Hasidic garments play the role of the most intensely religious members of the group. Besides the *bord and payes*, the beard and sidelocks, Class I males or *Rebbes* also wear a large-rimmed beaver hat, a *kapote* or long overcoat worn as a jacket; a *bekecher*, or

[37] Joseph B. Code, *Great American Foundresses* (New York: The Macmillan Company, 1929), p. 100.

[38] "Letter from Rome," *New York* (October 4, 1952), p. 123.

[39] Solomon Poll, *The Hasidic Community of Williamsburg* (New York: The Free Press, 1962), p. 60.

long silk coat, "*shich* and *zocken*." The latter are slipper-like shoes and white knee socks into which breeches are folded.

Women have their hair cut off upon marriage and never display any of their own hair in public. Since her head is covered at all times, a truly modest Hasidic woman wears a wig (*sheitel*) that gives the appearance of her own hair; the most zealous in their religious roles wear a turban that does not even give the appearance of hair.

Solomon Poll states that religion, as exemplified by the external clothing and appearance symbols, is the major criterion for social stratification. "These external status symbols and the frequency and intensity of religious behavior must be parallel and consistent with each other." [40] Only the most religious, and consequently those holding high status, wear all of the clothing items listed above; other members of the community may wear only one or two identifying garments. It is assumed that wearing a garment symbolizing higher status will create a chain reaction of more and more intensified religious observance.

The Role of the Mourner

Another role with changing symbols is that of the mourner. D'Assailly believes that the wearing of black for mourning was first observed in France during the reign of Philip the Fair and that it probably was copied from the Spanish. Yet, at this time (the fourteenth century), mourners in other countries wore color: "In Egypt it was yellow as in withered leaves; in Ethiopia, grey for ashes; for women in Rome white (purity) turned to violet (mixing red for royalty and blue for sorrow); men of Rome wore black as a sign of immortality." [41]

In 1303 Mahant of Artois, while mourning for her husband, not only wore black on her person, but also had

[40] Ibid., p. 67.
[41] D'Assailly, op. cit., p. 46.

her bed and the walls of her house hung in the same color.[42]

Mourning was more strictly enforced for women than for men; it is reported that a fifteenth-century queen of France had to remain a whole year in her bedroom draped with black—"princesses were to stay in their room for six weeks and lie all the while on a white sheet upon the death of their fathers; wives of knights stayed only nine days on their beds for a father's death, but must sit before the bed on a black sheet for many weeks more." [43]

Ross reports that during the nineteenth century widows hid themselves from head to toe in bombazine and crepe. "Their faces were screened with heavy veiling flowing from tiny crepe bonnets. Their handkerchiefs and gloves sustained the funeral note." [44] After six months dull ornaments might be worn, but nothing that glittered until a full year had passed. By degrees a woman could turn to half-mourning by wearing white, lavender, and gray.

Geoffrey Gorer recounts his vivid memories of the death of King Edward VII of England in 1910. Gorer, who had just turned five, recalls:

> On the Sunday morning after his death, our nanny took my brother Peter (two years my junior) and me for our customary walk on Hampstead Heath. It was a fine morning and the Heath was crowded. As we came out of Heath Street to the White Stone Pond we could see a mass of people out to enjoy the sun; and practically every woman was dressed in full mourning, in black from top to toe. Nearly all the men were in dark suits too, but that was customary for "Sunday best." This mass of black-garbed humanity struck me as a most depressing sight.
>
> We used to have Sunday lunch with our parents; and there was Mother, too, dressed in black. I grizzled and nagged at Mother to get out of those horrid clothes, and finally she agreed to wear "half-mourning"—grey or purple—in the house; but, she explained to me, she *had* to wear black when she went out. King Edward was a good king, we were very sorry that he had gone, and wearing black was a sign

[42] Ibid.
[43] Ibid.
[44] Ross, op. cit., p. 172.

that we respected and missed him and shared the grief of his family.[45]

Although in 1965 Gorer reported that most English women had abandoned the wearing of mourning, a minority still do wear mourning for three months after the funeral. These he identifies as being over forty-five, from the unskilled working classes, and concentrated in larger towns in the North-West of England. It is the husbands they mourn more frequently than any other relative. "The customs of the mourning dress, which were general when I was a boy, are now predominantly maintained by the old, the poor, and the unskilled." [46]

Gorer also uses the term *mummification* in a metaphorical sense to depict the type of mourner who preserves grief for the lost husband or wife by keeping the house, and everything in it, exactly as he or she had left it, as though it were a shrine that might be reanimated at any moment. The most striking example of mummification in recent times was that of Queen Victoria, "who preserved every object as Prince Albert had arranged them, but continued the daily ritual of having his clothes laid out and his shaving water brought." [47]

But for Americans, most of the mourning symbols have faded away. During the funeral the immediate family may show the appropriate symbols, then return to their usual wear the next day.

Academic Roles

The history of academic attire goes back at least to the fourteenth century. A statute in 1321 decreed that all "Doctors, Licentiates and Bachelors" of the University of Coimbra wear gowns.[48] In the second half of the fourteenth century, certain colleges in England warned against

[45] Geoffrey Gorer, *Death, Grief, and Mourning* (Garden City, N. Y.: Doubleday & Company, 1965), p. xv.
[46] Ibid., p. 42.
[47] Ibid., p. 86.
[48] *An Academic Code and Costume Guide,* 8th edition (Washington, D.C.: American Council of Education, 1960).

any excess in apparel and prescribed the wearing of a long gown. A practical reason for long robes was certainly related to the unheated buildings of medieval times, just as hoods kept the tonsured head warm. European institutions today are diversified in their requirements for academic dress, but many prescribe its wear for daily use.

American universities adopted a systemic code for academic apparel following a conference at Columbia University in 1895.[49] The code was revised in 1932 and again in 1959. American professors and other officials usually wear robes on prescribed ceremonial occasions such as commencement exercises, baccalaureate services, and inauguration exercises. A detailed description of one item of the academic costume is recorded below:

Hoods

Pattern: As usually followed by the colleges and universities of this country, but with observation of the following specifications:

Material: The same as that of the gown in all cases.

Color: Black in all cases.

Length: The length of the hood worn for the bachelor's degree to be three feet, for the master's degree three and one-half feet, and for the doctor's degree four feet; while that worn for the doctor's degree only shall have panels at the sides.

Linings: The hoods to be lined with the official color or colors of the college or university conferring the degree; more than one color is shown by division of the field color in a variety of ways, such as chevron or chevrons, equal division, etc. The various academic costume companies have in their files complete data on the approved colors for various institutions.

Trimmings: The binding or edging of the hood to be of velvet or velveteen, in width two inches, three inches, and five inches for the bachelor's, master's and doctor's degrees respectively; while the color should be distinctive of the subject to which the degree pertains:

Agriculture	Maize
Arts, Letters, Humanities	White
Commerce, Accountancy, Business	Drab

[49] Ibid., p. 1133.

Dentistry	Lilac
Economics	Copper
Education	Light Blue
Engineering	Orange
Fine Arts, including Architecture	Brown
Forestry	Russet
Journalism	Crimson
Law	Purple
Library Science	Lemon
Medicine	Green
Music	Pink
Nursing	Apricot
Oratory (Speech)	Silver Gray
Pharmacy	Olive Green
Philosophy	Dark Blue
Physical Education	Sage Green
Public Administration, including Foreign Service	Peacock Blue
Public Health	Salmon Pink
Science	Golden Yellow
Social Work	Citron
Theology	Scarlet
Veterinary Science	Gray [50]

During the period of student unrest and student strikes in the spring of 1970, some graduation exercises were performed under unusual circumstances and in unusual costume. Academic robes were changed by the addition of new symbols. Tradition was shattered by placing peace signs on mortarboards; peace doves, clenched fists, or flags on the backs of robes; the wearing of hippie jewelry over the robes, white armbands on the arms, and the foreswearing of caps and gowns altogether at some institutions. Self-styled changes included an ultra-conservative hard hat ornamented with tassel at Brown and with doves at the University of Massachusetts [51] to the wearing of exotic hippie clothes at Yale and street clothes at Oberlin (where money that would have spent on traditional garb went for welfare).[52]

[50] Ibid., p. 1134.
[51] *Life* (June 19), 1970), p. 22.
[52] *U.S. News & World Report* (June 22, 1970), p. 34.

Academic Robes—1970

The Role of the Reformer

Many colorful reformers are associated with the field of dress reform. During a reform movement some issue is brought to public attention through discussion, proclamation, or example in the hope of gaining support. All too often the public is indifferent or disinterested; at other times reformers are ridiculed and scorned as impractical and visionary. Only when dress reformers were connected with the Church or heads of state did their causes gain favor and actually bring about change in fashion.

The latter half of the nineteenth century and the early years of the twentieth century saw efforts to improve the health, safety, and moral nature of clothing. In 1848 a medical pioneer, Dr. William D. Purple, detailed the symptoms that could be attributed to the then-fashionable hourglass figure: hectic flush, palpitation, empty feeling in the stomach, torpid bowels, hemorrhoids, prolapse, edema of legs, and back pain. Dr. Purple reproached the gullible public:

Bloomer Costume—1851

It is our duty to expose the folly of fashion. In reply to their complaints we should endeavor to convince them that medicine will have little or no effect unless the cause is removed. We should cry aloud and spare not until the galling bonds of fashion cease to drag our ladies in the dust.[53]

The first woman to gain notoriety for wearing trousers was Mrs. Amelia Bloomer. As a member of the Women's Rights Movement, she wrote about dress reform in a periodical called the *Lily*. Although the introduction of the bifurcated garment that later bore her name is generally associated with Mrs. Bloomer, she disclaims the honor in this statement:

In March, 1851, Elizabeth Smith Miller, daughter of Hon. Gerrit Smith of Peterboro, N.Y., visited her cousin, Elizabeth Cady Stanton, at Seneca Falls, N.Y., which was then my home, and where I was publishing the *Lily*, and where Mrs. Stanton also resided. Mrs. Miller came to us in a short skirt and full Turkish trousers, a style of dress she had been wearing some two months. The matter of woman's dress having just been previously discussed in the *Lily*, Mrs. Miller's appearance led Mrs. Stanton to at once adopt a style, and I very soon followed, Mrs. Stanton introducing it to Seneca Falls public two or three days in advance of me.[54]

In spite of the incomplete and contradictory accounts regarding this mode of dress, a fairly faithful picture can be formulated on the basis of pictures and sketches of Mrs. Bloomer to be found in various historic costume books. Her favorite garment in this mode was of red and black silk, and consisted of a jacket with close-fitting sleeves, a skirt falling a little below the knee, and a pair of Turkish trousers.[55] This type of garment was worn by Mrs. Bloomer for seven consecutive years, and it should be noted that the then-obligatory five to ten petticoats were entirely omitted.[56]

[53] Reported in "Fashion and Medicine," *M.D.*, Vol. 2, No. 9 (September, 1958), p. 72.

[54] Bernard Rudofsky, *Are Clothes Modern?* (Chicago: Paul Theobold, 1947), p. 183.

[55] Herbert Norris, *Costume and Fashion* (London: Dent, 1925), p. 11.

[56] Rudofsky, op. cit., p. 183.

Mrs. Bloomer's followers tried to pursuade the English public to adopt the "bloomer" costume. Lectures were given throughout England with the speakers wearing trousers. After many disappointments Mrs. Bloomer inquired in *The London Daily News:*

> Sir,
>
> May I be allowed in your columns to ask why the British public is so horrified at the idea of women dressing in trousers, seeing that they have for many years tolerated a number of men from the North of the Tweed in wearing petti-coats, and shockingly short petti-coats too?
>
> Amelia Bloomer.[57]

Some objections were raised concerning the aesthetics of the costume:

> The disadvantages of the dress are its novelty—for we seldom like a fashion to which we are entirely unaccustomed—and the exposure which it involves of the foot, the shape of which in this country is so frequently distorted by wearing tight shoes of a different shape from the other foot. The short dress is objectionable from another point of view, because, as short petticoats diminish the apparent height of the person, none but those who possess tall and elegant figures will look well in this costume: and appearance is generally suffered to prevail over utility in consequence. If to the Bloomer costume had been added the long-under-dress of the Greek women, and had the trousers been as full as those worn by the Turkish and East India women, the general effect of the dress would have been much more elegant although perhaps less useful.[58]

However, the end was on its way when waitresses and vaudeville performers adopted the garment. Women of "respectable" middle and upper classes would not in any case dress as those in the lower class. Perhaps the main reason for failure was the distrust of the men of the period for the Women's Reform Movement in general.

[57] Julius Mendes Price, *Dame Fashion* (London: Sampson Low, Marston & Co. Ltd., 1913), p. 103.

[58] Ibid., p. 104.

When masculine pride objected to the new role proposed by these women, no wonder the costume was also vigorously opposed.

Various health reforms were suggested for both male and female costumes. Both Oscar Wilde and his wife advocated that hygienic and aesthetic principles be applied to clothing and subsequently formed the Rational Dress Society. Possessing a genius for publicity, Wilde soon had made the word *aesthete* a familiar one.[59] The typical aesthetic dress for women was a kind of mixture of the Empire style, with its straight flowing lines and loose drapery, and that of the 1830's, with large sleeves. This was not a conscious imitation but rather a mixture in the minds of the wearers of the dress of the medieval heroine and that of the heroine of the Renaissance. The aesthetic lady wore a loose robe embroidered with large sunflowers, flat shoes, no corsets, and brushed her hair down over her eyes.[60] On the proper figure, this mode of dress was becoming.

The Aesthetic Movement did not gain the support it might have in part because of the peculiarities of its adherents. Although Oscar Wilde suffered setbacks in public esteem in later years, he had abandoned his regulation aesthetic garments much earlier, thus giving the movement a catastrophic blow.

Turning to modern-day reformers, we have several women's groups that are agitating for women to be treated as human beings instead of second-class citizens. The right to vote is no longer at issue. "Women today are imprisoned more by a style of life than by social oppression. They're rebelling against the nuclear family in a suburban setting," [61] says Margaret Mead. She also feels that women aren't free enough to dress as they please, but they would like to be. "There's not enough freedom in fashion . . . there's a multiplicity of fashion dictators, not just one." [62]

How do these new feminists dress for their role? They don't have a style, in fact, they are rather nondescript. They do know what they don't want to look like. They

[59] Carrie A. Hall, *From Hoopskirts to Nudity* (Caldwell, Idaho: The Caxton Printers Ltd., 1938), p. 63.

[60] Ibid.

[61] Margaret Mead, quoted in *Women's Wear Daily* (February 11, 1970), p. 14.

[62] Ibid.

do *not* emphasize their sexual attractiveness—they are not sex goddesses; they do *not* dress like men—although some of them may wear trousers, they are not copying male attire because it's male. Actually, they need a "look" to identify them as they evolve their new role. Sally Kempton says:

> The very notion of women gathering in groups is somehow anti-sexual, anti-male, just as the purposely all-male group is anti-female. There is often a sense of genuine cultural rebellion in the atmosphere of a Woman's Liberation meeting. Women sit with their legs apart, carelessly dressed, barely made-up, exhibiting their feelings or the holes at the knees of their jeans with an unprovocative candor which is hardly seen at all in the outside world. Of course, they are demonstrating by their postures that they are in effect off duty, absolved from the compulsion to make themselves attractive, and yet, as the world measures these things, such demonstrations could in themselves be seen as evidence of neurosis: we have all been brought up to believe that a woman who was "whole" would appear feminine even on the barricades.[63]

Of course, with a proposed radical fashion change, there are reformers or at least abstainers from the midi. Mrs. Juli Hunter, a leggy, long-haired wife of a Los Angeles banker, formed an organization called POOFF (Preservation of our Femininity and Finances) to squash the midi. She and her cohorts have set up POOFF booths to get women to sign pledges not to buy or wear a midi, no matter what.[64] Also proposed are bumper stickers in shocking pink and shocking language: UP YOUR MIDI.[65] Men, too, are getting in the act with their own organization, called POOFF (Professional Oglers of Female Figures). Founder Neil Kneitel bemoans that "there isn't anything but smog and beer cans around here, and when we get out of the boardrooms . . . we want to see all those lovely mini-skirted girls." [66] Ah well, there are some who can remember an organization formed in 1947—it was called

[63] Sally Kempton, "Cutting Loose," *Esquire* (July, 1970), p. 53.

[64] "Battle of the Hemline," *Newsweek* (March 16, 1970), p. 71.

[65] "Modern Living," *Time* (March 23, 1970), p. 42.

[66] Ibid.

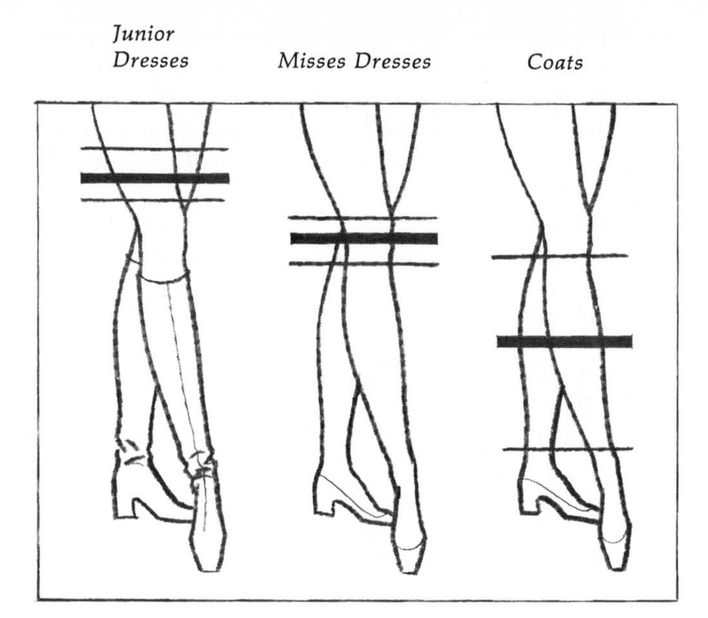

Average Worn Fall 1970
Variations from Average

Mini vs. Midi

"The Little Below the Knee Club." The New Look was adopted anyway.

The Social Butterfly and the Bon Vivant

The roles of social leaders today are changing as are all other roles. The Social Register has a narrowed field—now only eleven cities print the sacred blue book as opposed to twenty-one cities in 1925.[67]

John Fairchild tagged the group he believes now controls society "Les Locomotives"—these are people under forty who "live the big life . . . they are European minded, gay, intellectually hungry, outwardly casual, but

[67] Ross, op. cit., p. 265.

inwardly nervous."[68] They are daring, set trends, have dash and style, and they sample the riskiest of sports.

Lucius Beebe sees a difference between males and females in this jet set. With women, being best-dressed is a career; most of the women who make these lists are little known for anything else. They may spend more than $100,000 a year (and be dressed by name designers) if they have any international aspirations of recognition. Another requirement is that they be in the news, often by virtue of their husbands:

> Mrs. Jacqueline Kennedy, while no frump, would probably never have attracted attention in the realm of fashion if her husband had lost the election.[69]

According to Beebe, males who are considered best-dressed men are as different from women as the words *amateurs* and *professionals.* Even though a man might spend considerable time, money, and effort on his appearance, it seldom is a way of life but only one aspect of his personality. He feels that even such well-dressed men as the Duke of Windsor, Berry Wall, or Grover Whalen "never allowed their attire to dominate their overall image or to become a pre-occupation."[70]

Marylin Bender describes Mr. Joseph Tankoos, Jr., an international real estate investor and a regular on the Best-Dressed Men's List. He usually wears pink or green in Palm Beach or Monte Carlo. In London he chooses grays and blues.

> I like to go out a lot and I'm very busy . . . I often don't have time to go home to change from a gray check to a dark suit. So I start out in the morning ready for anything that turns up.[71]

This is made possible, he goes on to explain, by wearing tasseled loafers with everything and by keeping an electric razor in his office. Thus his midnight-blue Chesterfield coat and light gray homburg go beautifully with his blue and silver Rolls-Royce.[72]

[68] Ibid.
[69] Beebe, op. cit., p. 288.
[70] Ibid., p. 289.
[71] Marylin Bender, *The Beautiful People* (New York: Coward McCann, Inc., 1967), p. 286.
[72] Ibid.

John Taylor complains that there is so little that is romantic or even respectable in men's fashion language today. In the eighteenth and nineteenth centuries there were interestingly descriptive names for dandies. Among them were "Swells, Knuts, Blades, Toffs, Bucks, Corinthians, Johnnies, even Beaux; but post World War II days found no fond or even pleasant identification for its male monde." [73] The only terms in wide usage ring with anti-social connotations, such as Spiv, Teddy Boy, Rocker, and Flash Harry. On the other hand, the real perpetrators of crime have changed from flashily dressed gangster types to men in ordinary business suits. The gray fedoras, black shirts with white ties, spear-pointed collars, and two-toned shoes have been replaced. "The Cosa Nostra and the Mafia do not want to use clothing to identify their roles!" [74]

The Role of the Career Girl

For most men there is no choice about whether to work or not. But a woman has several kinds of choices before her: she can decide whether to work, and what part of her life to devote to her work. However, for men work choices are wide, while for women the range of choice is restricted. "This restriction is only secondarily the result of employment discrimination against women. Primarily it results from the attitudes that surround a woman's behavior in her family role, for it is the expectation of society and of women themselves that no matter what else they may do, they will also, ideally, have a family." [75]

This idea of the family persists despite the sexual revolution of the 1920's, when short-skirted cloche-wearing girls became what F. Lewis Allen calls "men's casual and

[73] Taylor, op. cit., p. 31.
[74] Ibid.
[75] Lotte Bailyn, "Psychology of Professional Women," in Robert Lifton, editor, *The Woman in America* (Boston: Beacon Press, 1964), p. 238.

lighthearted companions; not broad-hipped mothers of the race but irresponsible playmates." [76]

Married women who want to work also have problems with lack of geographical mobility and cannot follow the best opportunities; if working part-time, a woman is impeded in her professional advancement and seldom is allowed to rise to her level of ability. Exceptions occur in fields that might be called feminine areas—those devoted to the same concerns of women that she faces in her private life—social work, home economics, pediatrics, or fashion. This is only because the distance between the two roles is less and her role conflicts are fewer.

Alice Rossi likewise points to the fact that, for the majority of women, their occupational roles are subordinate to those of men who are their social equals.[77] Another problem may be occupational competition between husband and wife, but unless the male is totally oriented toward "male breadwinner dominance" this could lend some social spice and stimulation in a marriage of equals. Rossi emphasizes that new social roles and social goals exact a price.[78] So the career woman has many challenges thrown her way.

Ofttimes the other role looks better. Wayne Healy says that one of the most "interesting dialogues in the world goes on between the beat, free housewife and the lively, slave secretary. Each knows the other has got it made." [79]

Clothing worn by women for work roles varies, of course, with the job. Usually, a woman should avoid the extreme and the avant-garde. Heavy make-up, micromini's, and tight sweaters have all been the subject of a "proclamation against their use" in one firm or another. On the other hand, those who take no pride in their appearance may suffer by being overlooked. Adele Starbird cites an example of an exception to this rule:

> I knew a woman who ignored all the rules, and who reached the pinnacle of her profession just the same. I shall call her Lucy Lockwood. She had a plain,

[76] Cable, op. cit., p. 347.

[77] Alice S. Rossi, "Equality Between the Sexes" in *The Women in America*, p. 118.

[78] Ibid.

[79] Wayne Healy, *You're Better Off Naked* (New York: Avon Book Division, The Hearst Corporation, 1962), p. 93.

pleasant face untouched by any cosmetic; she twisted her sandy hair into a tight little knot squarely on top of her head when everybody else was wearing short hair and pin-curls; her feet were comfortable in oxfords. I can't remember her dresses except that they were dark. . . . In her case it seemed unimportant. Her eyes twinkled and her speech was humorous, dry and pungent. She never uttered a dull word. I think that she was the only woman in her exalted position who was not a target for criticism.

A few years later Miss Lockwood retired and at the same time married a distinguished scholar who, it seemed, had been waiting in the wings for a number of years.

Not long after her marriage I saw her again, once more on a platform, and it was a real jolt. From head to foot she looked as if she had been turned out by a great designer. Her suit of tie silk was beautifully tailored, her brimmed hat of grey-blue straw was tilted at exactly the right angle; low-heeled pumps had replaced the oxfords.

Then she spoke, and once more what she wore was unimportant. That she was attractive and smartly dressed faded into the background.

Had I misled the students in telling them that while appearance was only packaging, as such it was worthy of attention? No, because usually that is true. I could honestly say, "If you have the personality and character of a Lucy Lockwood, you won't need glamour. Since, however, few women in the world are so endowed, you had better do what you can to improve your package." [80]

Women workers who traditionally wear uniforms used to have no problem with suitable clothing. Yet the world of uniforms, too, is changing. Styles for nurses or dental assistants could be numbered on one hand twenty years ago, now perhaps the limit might be nearer fifty than five. Even the color white is changing for some nurses. Psychiatric nurses in Park Ridge, Illinois, now wear red, green, or even plaid. "The starched uniforms of medical personnel do not provide adequate comfort to mental patients because you don't deal with germs in psychiatry, you deal

[80] Adele Starbird, "The Package Didn't Matter," *St. Louis Post-Dispatch* (July 5, 1966), p. 23.

with problems."[81] The real role of a psychiatric nurse is better filled without a uniform—she no longer wishes to seem to be a figure of authority. The nurse out of uniform relates better to the patients.

A guide for American officials called *Social Usage Abroad* has these suggestions for female officers:

> A basic minimum wardrobe should include: a formal evening dress; a dinner dress; a cocktail dress; an afternoon dress; a suit or dress with jacket, with of course the accompanying accessories. . . . Every lady's wardrobe should include a black dress and hat as occasions may arise when they are needed, such as funerals or official mourning.[82]

Full evening dress is described as a floor-length evening gown, no sleeves, no hat, long white gloves, and appropriate jewelry. The dinner dress suggested is long or short, décolleté, and sleeveless. Gloves are advised for all social occasions—luncheons, teas, and receptions—although they should be removed for eating or drinking.

> When the occasion calls for white tie, long white gloves are worn above the elbow. These should not be removed when standing in or going through a receiving line, or during the course of an evening, except when eating or drinking at a table. At this time, either the hands are slipped from the gloves and the hands tucked in at the wrists, or the gloves are removed entirely."[83]

The Role of the Contemporary Kid

In the 1970's the "contemporary kid" is of college age, whether or not he is in college, and about to enter the

[81] "Psychiatric Nurses Have New Look," *Hartford Courant* (Thursday, August 7, 1969), p. 20.

[82] *Social Usage Abroad,* A Guide for American Officials and Their Families, Department of State Publication No.: 8219, Government Printing Office, Washington, D.C. (Revised 1967), pp. 21–22.

[83] Ibid., p. 22.

labor force. He (or she) is unlike generations before him, having the appropriate symbols—a language, a set of values, a look of his own. He is not a hippie, for the hippie has "copped out" by rejecting the human race; he is a new breed seeking his own solutions to his present-day problems. He is against being "a smooth coin, negotiable in any market." [84] He is trying to get out of the established trap so aply described by John W. Gardner:

> The individual is fixed in a network of abstractions. Instead of working for a known boss, he is employed by a corporation. Instead of coping with a rival across the street, he copes with the forces of the market. Instead of fashioning a product with his own hands, he shuffles papers, juggles figures, or pushes buttons. He receives orders from people he has never met and makes recommendations without knowing those who will be affected by them. A well-known government official offered a poignant vignette of modern organizational life when he said: "What we sign we haven't written and what we write someone else signs." [85]

The contemporary kid wants to be inside, involved, "with it." He is the exact opposite of the detached observer of the Renaissance era with its vanishing-point perspective. As McLuhan interprets the message: "The viewer of Renaissance art is systematically placed outside the frame of experience. . . . [now] The instantaneous world of electric informational media involves all of us, all at once. No detachment or frame is possible." [86] The contemporary kid knows this—that the time to be involved is now and that real living is living in depth. "The young today reject goals. They want roles—ROLES. That is, total involvement. They do not want fragmented, specialized goals or jobs." [87]

Nor does the contemporary kid want to be culture-bound. He seeks the involvement of all peoples—an understanding of universals. There is danger in being tied to only one culture, in understanding only one set of values. Edward Hall's analysis of Clarence Darrow is to the point:

[84] John W. Gardner, *Self-Renewal* (New York: Harper & Row, 1965), p. 58.
[85] Ibid.
[86] Marshall McLuhan and Quentin Fiore, *The Medium is the Massage* (New York: Bantam Books, 1967).
[87] Ibid.

> Darrow dressed in an old sloppy suit. He appealed to the common man—people could identify with him. He was their type, the country bumpkin who outsmarts the city slicker. Now it is obvious that in addition to knowing his law well he also knew his culture. He realized that most people do not understand the law but will stand up for their own formal systems and even weep over them when they see them outraged. This was Darrow's strength, and the only time he really failed to capitalize on it was when he was called to Honolulu for the Massie case in 1932. There he faced a jury made up of members who had different formal systems. The Chinese jurors weren't a bit moved by his culture-rooted strategies.[88]

If clothes are part of the environment, then they are not passive wrappings. Clothing symbols have an effect in the role the contemporary kid is trying to play. Sometimes he may be mistaken for the hippie because he dresses too much like one. Even in the United States there are those (over thirty) who measure degree of radical views by length of hair or beard. The use and abuse of drugs are at times attributed to unwashed hippies. In Europe during the summer of 1969 the problem became acute. Many countries, including France, Holland, Austria, Italy, and Germany, considered hippie-type individuals to be undesirable. France has been particularly careful since the student uprisings of 1968 and as a result hippie-looking people are often stopped on the street by police and asked for identification papers. Long hairs, considered to be trouble makers and riffraff, have been run out of villages in the Alpine regions and have been jailed elsewhere.

> Last summer two square but long-locked and blue-jeaned high school students from Manhattan were pulled off a train at the Dutch-German border along with other hippie-looking youth and held in jail overnight on a drug possession charge. "They insist it was guilt by association." [89]

Only in Scandinavia do the long hairs seem to be unmolested, where practically all youth wear long hair and

[88] Edward Hall, *The Silent Language* (Garden City, N. Y.: Doubleday & Company, 1959), p. 98.
[89] "Longhaired Youth Get Short Shrift Abroad," *The New York Times* (March 1, 1970), Section 10, p. 1.

beards; it is almost impossible to tell the imported hippie from a domestic square.

Nor does the contemporary kid want to be confused with the revolutionary, who wants to destroy society as it exists today.

The Manson Family, accused of killing a dozen persons in cold blood, acted in a bizarre and grizzly fashion. Their clothes were only a little more extreme than those of the average hippie. The Weathermen, the most radical group of the SDS, paraded in open defiance in Chicago wearing helmets and carrying sticks. Without helmets, they, too, look fairly harmless, so the added symbol was necessary to proclaim their role. Those involved in the rash of bombings in early 1970 state that they want to destroy the Establishment, so that a just society can be built on human values instead of commercial values.[90] Having declared guerrilla warfare, no doubt they will have to camouflage their extreme appearance, so as to look like the contemporary kid next door.

Some contemporary kids go to unusual lengths to be individuals. Andy Warhol's underground movie queen, Ultra Violet, has hair that hangs in black strings like yesterday's shoe-laces, eyes made up in purple and orange, and clothes that look as if "they were ordered out of a mail order catalogue from the moon." [91]

Others dress up like American Indians, wearing ponchos, headbands, beads, and feathers. Some are dyeing their own psychedelic garments using the ancient method of tie-dyeing. As no two pieces ever come out alike, here is real individuality. In addition, for those who dye their own clothes, it's a creative yet inexpensive adventure. "It can turn a thirty-two cent T-shirt into strawberry fields forever, or an old pair of jeans into a tiptoe through the tulips." [92] Yet some of them also look to Europe for inspiration; when they do, it's England for birds (girls) and Paris for dancing dandies (boys).

It is possible that we are entering a period of the new Renaissance man, who will have a wide range of interests and values. Perhaps the man of the future needs to

[90] "A Real Bomber's Chilling Reasons," *Life* (March 27, 1970), p. 30.

[91] "Underground Films Star Ultra Violet," *Columbia Missourian* (July 10, 1969), p. 12.

[92] "Modern Living," *Time* (January 26, 1970), p. 36.

Contemporary Kid

be part hunter, part adventurer, and part researcher. McLuhan says he cannot be the narrow-gauge male of the industrial age who operated inside "boxes of fragmented civilization." [93] The new man needs to develop all of his senses to solve the world's problems. For the new role, he needs to be highly creative:

> Highly creative people are more likely than others to view authority as conventional rather than abso-

[93] Marshall McLuhan and George B. Leonard, "The Future of Sex," *Look* (July 25, 1967), p. 57.

Women Today Reflect Men of Yesterday

lute; to make fewer black-and-white distinctions; to have a less dogmatic and more relativistic view of life; to show more independence to judgment and less conventionality and conformity, both intellectual and social; to be more willing to entertain, and sometimes express, their own "irrational" impulses; to place a greater value on humor and in fact to have a better sense of humor; in short, to be somewhat freer and less rigidly controlled.[94]

[94] Bernard Berelson and Gary Steiner, *Human Behavior, An Inventory of Scientific Findings* (New York: Harcourt, Brace and World, Inc., 1964), p. 230.

The lines between masculinity and femininity are also being less sharply drawn in this new role. As this topic was discussed at length in the section on Symbols, we only mention it as a new element in role behavior. Havelock Ellis pointed to the falseness of the distinction between the two sexes, while Freud urged the recognition of the difference of the two sexes featuring the importance of male dominance.

> Freud won the argument, because most Americans still thought in Victorian and family terms. This meant different roles of sexes and separate spheres of women, where women were more conscious of being women than of being human beings.[95]

The last third of the twentieth century is seeing the rejection of the Freudian view; freedom of the sexes is expressed not only in clothing, but at some times and places in the absence of clothing. Perhaps in order to change our roles we need a period of nudity in which to shed roles along with clothing. Or we might embrace an entirely new concept in the use of "plural dress." A design by James Lee Byars[96] has four persons, two male and two female, draped in a single piece of black silk. Here the self is extended beyond the boundaries of male and female and black and white to form the closest of all possible role relationships with clothing.

[95] Andrew Sinclair, *The Better Half* (New York: Harper & Row, Inc., 1965), p. 361.
[96] *Body Covering*, op. cit., p. 6.

22 Measures of Role as Related to Appearance

There have been several questionnaire-type research methods employed to ascertain clothing roles; most of these, however, center on the adolescent age group.[1] Some questionnaire research on the elderly could be classified as having role-related dimensions.[2]

Nevertheless, to measure the more elusive aspects of role, methods other than or in addition to questionnaires must be employed. The sociogram technique was used by Hendricks, Kelley, and Eicher to code answers to choices of best friend. A sociogram was constructed by using circles for each person and connecting lines for choice of friends that were reciprocal. Three distinct types of social acceptance were noted in this study:

Isolate: an individual who had no reciprocal choices.
Mutual pair: a reciprocated choice of only two members.

[1] Two examples are: Betty M. Wass, and Joanne B. Eicher, "Clothing as Related to Role Behavior of Teen-age Girls," *Quarterly Bulletin*, Michigan Agricultural Experiment Station, Vol. 47, No. 2 (November 1964); Janice Hamilton and Jesse Warden, "The Student's Role in a High School Community and His Clothing Behavior," *Journal of Home Economics*, Vol. 58, No. 10 (December, 1966), pp. 789–791.

[2] Ebeling and Rosencranz, op. cit.; Shipley and Rosencranz, op. cit.

Reciprocal friendship structures: three or more individuals with at least one reciprocated choice each who form a cluster or group.[3]

Each pattern was analyzed to see if opinions coincided. Hypotheses are stated and statistical measures are used.

Norma Compton developed the Compton Fabric Preference Test,[4] which she and her associates have used along with measures of personality including the dimensions of sociability and self-acceptance. In a study of personality correlates of dress conformity, four instruments were used including the Aiken Clothing Opinionaire, the Compton Fabric Preference Test, the Bass Orientation Inventory and the Allport-Vernon-Lindzey Study of Values. Five null hypotheses were formulated and tested statistically. Two important findings were that conformity in dress related to interaction-orientation and that conformity in dress correlated negatively with the aesthetic value.[5]

A classic study by Form and Stone shows that occupational roles and clothing behavior have significant relationships.[6] This study has also been described under methods for studying clothing symbols. The two studies using Clothing TAT's also have given new approaches to occupational roles and to social and cultural aspects of role.[7]

In answer to the question, "How do you see dressing for your role as different from or similar to someone else?" the author tried an experimental approach. Subjects were asked to list five fashions suitable for their own social situation and five fashions suitable for someone else. Here are examples from two subjects for the spring of 1963, using Mrs. Jacqueline Kennedy as the "someone else."

[3] Suzanne H. Hendricks, Eleanor A. Kelley, and Joanne B. Eicher, "Senior Girls' Appearance and Social Acceptance," *Journal of Home Economics,* Vol. 60, No. 3 (March 1968), p. 168.

[4] Norma H. Compton, *Compton Fabric Preference Test Manual,* Special Report 19, Utah State University Agricultural Experiment Station (August, 1965).

[5] Lucy C. Taylor and Norma H. Compton, "Personality Correlates of Dress Conformity," *Journal of Home Economics,* Vol. 60, No. 8 (October 1968).

[6] William H. Form and Gregory P. Stone, "The Social Significance of Clothing in Occupational Life," Agricultural Experiment Station Bulletin, No. 247, Michigan State University (1955).

[7] Mary Lou Rosencranz, "Clothing Symbolism," *Journal of Home Economics,* Vol. 54, No. 1 (January, 1962), pp. 18–22; and Carol Sanders Bathke, "Ethnic Responses to a Modified TAT, *Journal of Home Economics,* Vol. 60, No. 5 (May, 1968).

Subject One

Me

1. Shift dresses
2. Knit suits
3. Bell-bottom trousers
4. Sweater suits, also called open-air suits
5. Floral printed lingerie

Mrs. Kennedy

1. High-waisted bustline seaming
2. Long hair worn elaborately piled up on the head using a false hair piece
3. Three-piece costume suits
4. Natural dresses
5. Norell's dinner dresses that are shorter in front, longer in back

Subject Two

Me

1. Pale pink
2. Skinny coats
3. Informal sweater-top suits
4. Spongy mohair
5. Comfortable stack-heels

Mrs. Kennedy

1. Fedora hats
2. Floor-length lounging skirts
3. Large handbags
4. The new shades of brown
5. Important little details in styling

In both cases Mrs. Kennedy was seen with more variety of styles ranging from formal to informal, none of the subjects included high fashion or extremely formal clothes for themselves.

Two Suggested Projective Techniques

Another type of technique could be used to focus on self-concept as compared with an evaluation of how we think others see us.

1. Draw yourself as others see you.
2. Draw yourself as you really are.

Underlying the drawing technique is the basic assumption that "personality develops not in a vacuum, but through the movement, feeling and thinking of a specific body." [8] Woven into the drawing of a person is the concept of body-image and the self-image, usually extended and modified by grooming and clothing. Since nude figures are rarely drawn,[9] clothing has been used by psychologists to represent the surface layer of personality. It is *not* suggested that the researcher become an instant psychologist, but that differences between the self-image of the subject and the image he feels that others have of him should be analyzed by researcher and subject jointly, in order to get at the meanings intended by the subject. This awareness of self-image could be thought of as the keystone in the building of role relationships.

A second technique could involve a series of stick figures in different postures [10] and a series of types of garments and ornaments to use with the figure. Instructions could simply be:

1. Select a figure.
2. Select a costume for the figure for a work role.
3. Select a costume for the figure for a leisure role.

Although many social-psychological methods could be adapted for the study of clothing, very few have really been tried. We have not scratched the surface of the methods available, nor have we been very creative in the development of new methods. There is much to be done!

The publication *National Goals and Guidelines for Research in Home Economics* [11] contains many fruitful ideas for research. A partial listing of suggestions for research on clothing and role appears below:

[8] Karen Machover, "Drawing of The Human Figure. A Method of Personality Investigation," in Harold H. Anderson and Gladys L. Anderson, editors, *An Introduction to Projective Techniques* (Englewood Cliffs, N. J.: Prentice-Hall, Inc., 1951), p. 358.

[9] Ibid., p. 358.

[10] Idea based on drawings in Theodore R. Sarbin, "Role Theory" in *Handbook of Social Psychology*, edited by Gardner Lindzey (Cambridge, Mass.: Addison Wesley Publishing Company, Inc., 1954), p. 231.

[11] Jean Davis Schlater, *National Goals and Guidelines for Research in Home Economics.* Information Services, Box 231, Michigan State University, October, 1970.

1. Effects of merging traditional male-female roles upon behavior and interpersonal relationships.
2. Peer influence on role development and behavior.
3. Use of clothing in role identification, self-concept development, image projection and social acceptance.
4. Use of increased leisure: clothing as an expression of personal creativity.
5. Role of clothing in establishing identity through individuality or conformity.
6. Role of clothing in fulfillment of human needs and aspirations.
7. Clothing as a function of beliefs, sentiments, religion, ritual and ceremony.
8. Functions of dress in various cultural and social situations.
9. Potential role of clothing and fashion as a tool in psychotherapy.
10. Social-psychological effects of clothing deprivation on man (and his role behavior).

Conclusion

Although we have shown the importance of some of the dimensions of clothing awareness, we have probably raised as many questions as we have answered. Is an awareness of body and clothes more important than ever in a mass society? Is fashion an imperative of the *gesellschaft,* contractual society rather than of an intimate tribal social group? Do fashion and fashion change run counter to the uniqueness of the individual?

Our reliance on clothing symbols is very real, but here, too, are unanswered questions. Clothing symbols change with time, yet how often are we one step behind the change in meaning? Is fashion always an expression of public opinion and public taste? Can we retard fashion change and if we could, would we want to? Do lower classes dress for a generalized "other" while upper classes dress for specialized audiences? Does unisex mean that men and women want to be exactly alike or is it only symbolic of certain common values?

We have said that clothing makes real the roles we play. What about changing and emerging roles? Does the role of the reformer ever have an immediate pay-off? Is the hippie ahead of his time or is he out of step? Or is he the new barbarian erasing what he was, staying loose, in a holding pattern? Does his drab, gray garb and shaggy hair keep him from relevant roles or does it allow him to experiment with many roles? Is his role at odds with the total environment or is he only reacting against the Establishment with its nineteenth-century values? Will the "new" Renaissance man and woman emerge from it all?

Change is inevitable. The sewing needle may give way to the mold; garments fashioned in modular units may be added or subtracted as desired; inflatable clothing and sleeping cushions may merge; combinations of permanent and temporary clothes may become a reality. Thus, the person who tries to understand clothing behavior from awareness through symbol manipulation to role performance must have the cognition of the social-psychologist, appreciate the know-how of the technologist, and have the perception of the artist. It has been said that the artist is engaged in writing a history of the future because he is the only person aware of the nature of the present. Catching hold of that same shaft of light, we see that clothing awareness, symbol, and role merge as surely as do past, present, and future. "Thus in this one pregnant subject of Clothes, rightly understood, is included all that men have thought, dreamed, done and been. . . ." [1]

[1] Thomas Carlyle, *Sartor Resartus* (New York: Charles Scribner's Sons, 1921), p. 63.

Author Index

Subject Index